Relics for the Present:
Contemporary Reflections on the Talmud
Berakhot II

Levi Cooper

RELICS
FOR THE
PRESENT

CONTEMPORARY REFLECTIONS
ON THE TALMUD

Berakhot II

Maggid Books

Relics for the Present:
Contemporary Reflections on the Talmud

Berakhot II

First Edition, 2015

Maggid Books
An imprint of Koren Publishers Jerusalem Ltd.

POB 8531, New Milford, CT 06776-8531, USA
& POB 4044, Jerusalem 91040, Israel
www.korenpub.com

ISBN 978-1-59264-442-1, *hardcover*

A CIP catalogue record for this title is
available from the British Library.

Printed and bound in the United States

CONTENTS

Contents

BERAKHOT: CHAPTER EIGHT

BERAKHOT: CHAPTER NINE

Contents

THIS VOLUME OFFERS contemporary readings of passages from the Talmud, specifically from *Berakhot*, chapters 6–9. Following the publication of the first volume of *Relics for the Present* in 2012, readers expressed surprise at the unorthodox title. I think it is appropriate, therefore, to reiterate one of the reasons I selected it.

A relic is an object surviving from an earlier time that has often been conscientiously, painstakingly, and lovingly preserved. It is a hallowed object of historical interest, of sentimental value, of unquestionable worth. The Talmud is such a relic. This work strives to explore the Talmud and commentators, search for meaning, and offer readings that are relevant to our generation. In this sense, my goal is to bring these talmudic relics into our present day: *Relics for the Present*.

In the preface to the first volume, I recounted the birth of this work. As a way of expressing my thanks and appreciation for those who had a hand in this volume, allow me to recap some of the waystations of this work. The initial impetus for the project was provided by Amanda Borschel-Dan, then of *The Jerusalem Post*, who in 2005 believed that there should be a weekly column on Talmud in Israel's oldest and largest English daily newspaper. Amanda had studied at the Pardes Institute of Jewish Studies in Jerusalem and had participated in my Talmud class. The task of coming up with new weekly content was both exciting and challenging, and the National Library of Israel provided the perfect environment for my mission.

I was able to complete this second volume while I was a postdoctoral fellow – first in Bar-Ilan University's Faculty of Law (2012–2014) and then in Tel Aviv University's Buchmann Faculty of Law (2014– 2015). Since 2013, I have been a research fellow with *Da'at Hamakom*: Center for the Study of Cultures of Place in the Modern Jewish World, established by the I-CORE (Israel Centers of Research Excellence) Program of the

Planning and Budgeting Committee and the Israel Science Foundation. I am deeply grateful for these opportunities.

From the earliest stages of the journey to this book, I have been fortunate to benefit from encouragement and support from Joel Wolowelsky. The editorial contributions of Yehudah Ber Zirkind, Yocheved Engelberg Cohen, and Nechama Unterman have greatly improved this work. I am also grateful to Eli Witkin and Jeremy Borovitz, who offered their thoughts on the manuscript while studying at Pardes in 2013/14.

This work is jointly published by Pardes and by Maggid Books, a division of Koren Publishers Jerusalem. Since 1998, I have been privileged to teach at Pardes and to be part of a great team dedicated to Torah and the future of the Jewish people. I am grateful to Matthew Miller and all the Koren/Maggid team who have been professional and gracious.

Despite her busy schedule, my wife, Sarah, read and vetted each passage in this book. Without her unwavering support, these reflections would never have seen light. Our parents and grandparents have provided encouragement for all my endeavours.

I am happy to express my sincere gratitude to all those who have a portion in this work. I am humbled by the faith you have shown in me; I aspire to live up to it.

The goal of the book is to make classic Jewish texts accessible. I hope that readers will embrace the opportunity to contemplate the wisdom and relevance of the texts of our tradition. My dream is that this volume will provide an additional window into the wealth, depth, and contemporary significance of the Talmud. In particular, I hope that my students and our children – Itai, Yedidya, Choni, Neta, Aviya, and Adi – can find meaning in these relics.

With gratitude to God,
Levi Cooper, Zur Hadassa

B. = *Talmud Bavli,* Babylonian Talmud
M. = *Mishna*
T. = *Tosefta,* addition to the *Mishna*
Y. = *Talmud Yerushalmi,* Jerusalem Talmud, Palestinian Talmud, or
    Talmud of the Land of Israel
A full list of cited sources can be found at the back of the volume.

Berakhot
Chapter Six

Is there a blessing over manna?

O UR LIVES ARE saturated with blessings. Before almost any act and in almost every situation, there is an appropriate benediction. This is most certainly the case when we put food into our mouths. Our sages set out the rules for blessings to be recited before eating (*M. Berakhot* 6:1–3).

On fruits – that is, crops that grow on trees which produce fruit annually without withering away in the winter – we recite: "Blessed are You, O God, our Lord, King of the universe, Creator of the fruit of the tree." Wine, despite its similarity to fruit, has its own unique benediction in recognition of its importance. The opening words are the same, and we conclude by saying: "Creator of the fruit of the vine." The benediction over certain other fruits such as bananas, and over vegetables, ends: "Creator of the fruit of the ground." There is a dissenting opinion, not reflected in normative practice, which maintains that the blessing over vegetables is "Creator of various species of herbs."

A special blessing is mandated for the all-important staple – bread. This blessing concludes: "the One Who brings forth bread from the earth." The Mishna does not describe a benediction for non-bread grain products – such as pasta, cake, and porridge – but the Talmud does so. It mandates the blessing: "Creator of various kinds of food" (*B. Berakhot* 35a–b).

Further in the Mishna a general blessing is coined: "for everything exists by His word." This blessing is recited over food that is not grown in the ground, such as meat and milk. This blessing is universal and comprehensive. It is effective if it is recited before eating any food, even if that substance has its own blessing.

After explaining all of this, the Talmud rules that it is forbidden for a person to benefit from this world – that is, to eat anything – without first reciting a blessing. The Talmud goes further, explaining that eating without a blessing is akin to embezzling Temple property; that is, items that have been set aside for a holy purpose.

A further talmudic condemnation of eating without the preceding benediction does not evoke Temple imagery. Rather it states that benefiting from this world without reciting a blessing is akin to robbing the Almighty and the Congregation of Israel. One Hasidic master – the Gerrer Rebbe, Rabbi Avraham Mordekhai Alter of Góra Kalwaria (1866–1948) – once quipped that since eating without reciting the appropriate blessing is akin to stealing, this obligation is not primarily religious in nature and hence should be incumbent on Jew and gentile alike.

Rabbi Menaḥem Azarya da Fano (1548–1620), the famed Italian kabbalist and halakhic authority, describes the grand feast that will celebrate the End of Days (see *B. Bava Batra* 74b–75a). The main course will be the Leviathan, a gargantuan sea creature that will satisfy all. The tent where the righteous will gather will be made from the hide of this creature of mythical proportions. A real meal should be accompanied by bread, yet our sources are surprisingly silent on whether bread will be served at this banquet. The Rema of Fano – as he is known – offers a novel suggestion. According to a midrash, a jar of magical manna was preserved from the desert-wandering days. As the threat of the destruction of the First Temple loomed, this jar was spirited away to a safe hiding place. According to the Rema of Fano, for the Leviathan feast this jar will be recovered and served as the bread of the meal.

What blessing should be recited on the manna? We can hardly say "the One Who brings forth bread from the earth," since manna did not come from the ground. Following the pattern of our sages, the Rema of Fano suggests that before eating the manna we will make the novel blessing: "the One Who brings forth bread from heaven."

Years later, the Hasidic master Rabbi Zvi Elimelekh Shapira of Dynów (1783–1841) recounted a discussion he had at the table of his teacher and relative by marriage, Rabbi Zvi Hirsch of Żydaczów

(1763–1831). His teacher wondered aloud what blessing would be recited on the manna. Rabbi Zvi Elimelekh suggested the approach of the Rema of Fano: "the One Who brings forth bread from heaven." Those present were unconvinced and continued to debate the possibilities.

Finally one student impishly suggested that no blessing would be recited on the manna. Those present were shocked at the thought: eating the Almighty's holy manna with no blessing? Absurd! But the student was not deterred, and he explained his reasoning to those sitting around the table. Every object in this world contains sparks of godliness, for there is no reality in this world devoid of the Divine. Without godly sparks, no physical matter would exist. When a blessing is recited before eating, it targets the Divine sparks hidden inside the food and releases them from the physical bonds of this world. In this way the recital of a blessing elevates a mundane physical food from the plane of the material to the realm of the spiritual. The benediction changes the culinary experience from a routine satisfaction of bodily needs to a sacred act with mystical significance.

Thus far with regard to normal foods. The manna, however, was an otherworldly substance, a Divine food. It was so infused with godliness that it had no fully physical manifestation. As such, its consumption was not a physical act that required spiritual elevation and hence no blessing was called for.

Hearing this explanation, Rabbi Zvi Elimelekh was so impressed that he wondered how the holy Rema of Fano had said that a blessing would be recited on manna in the End of Days. Indeed, a close reading of our talmudic passage seems to support the student's approach: "It is forbidden to benefit from *this world* without a blessing." The manna was not of this world, and hence required no blessing.

Until we are fortunate enough to taste the manna, when we derive benefit from this world it is appropriate to acknowledge the hand of the Almighty by reciting a blessing. In this way we reveal the Divine even in the mundane.

Let the Torah not depart from our mouths

A s Joshua is about to lead the Jewish people into the Promised Land, the Almighty instructs him that Torah should never depart from his mouth. He should immerse himself in Torah study day and night. This directive is understood not only as a private command for Joshua, but as a dictate for the entire Jewish people, who are charged with being constantly involved in the pursuit of Torah.

This edict alone might suggest that there is no room for any other venture; our time should be dedicated solely to the study of Torah. In response, Rabbi Yishmael opines that the biblical verse *And you will gather your grain* (Deuteronomy 11:14) balances the all-encompassing requirement to study Torah (*B. Berakhot* 35b).

Rabbi Shimon ben Yoḥai, however, feels differently: "If a person ploughs at the time of ploughing, sows at the time of sowing, harvests at the time of harvesting, threshes at the time of threshing, and winnows at the time when the wind blows – what will become of Torah?" Saying "I will just take care of this, and then I will begin study Torah" is a trap – declares Rabbi Shimon ben Yoḥai – for at every stage there is always some task that will prevent Torah study.

Rabbi Shimon ben Yoḥai therefore suggests a different formula: "When the people of Israel do the will of God, their work is done for them by others; then indeed Torah need not depart from their mouths." The prophetic verse *And strangers will arise and shepherd your flocks* (Isaiah 61:5) describes this reality. Rabbi Shimon ben Yoḥai continues detailing the flip side: "When the people of Israel do not do the will of the Almighty, they must do their work themselves." This is the situation described by the verse *You will gather your grain, your wine, and your oil.* Moreover, the people of Israel will be forced to do the work of others, as per the biblically described punishment *And you will serve your enemies* (Deuteronomy 28:48).

Rabbi Shimon ben Yoḥai himself put this outlook into practice during the years that he and his son hid in a cave from the Roman authorities (*B. Shabbat* 33b). Buried up to their necks in sand and involved solely in plumbing the depths of Torah, Rabbi Shimon and his son Rabbi Elazar subsisted on water and carobs that were miraculously provided.

Elsewhere in the Talmud, Rabbi Shimon ben Yoḥai sends a very different message, perhaps reflecting his view later in life (*B. Menaḥot* 99b). The Talmud first suggests that studying a single chapter of Torah during the day and a single chapter of Torah at night is a fulfilment of the directive that Torah should never depart from our mouths. The Talmud immediately cites a tradition in the name of Rabbi Shimon ben Yoḥai that further lessens the minimum requirement. Even if a person only reads *Shema* in the morning and in the evening, that person has fulfilled the requirement encapsulated in the verse: *This book of the Torah shall not depart from your mouth* (Joshua 1:8).

The question arises whether this minimum requirement should be publicised. Rabbi Shimon ben Yoḥai declares that it is forbidden to disseminate this teaching, for such a simple road would be too seductive for the unlearned. Seeking the easiest and least taxing way to fulfil the obligation, the masses would go no further than the twice-daily *Shema*. Sadly, earnest Torah study would be the lot of scholars alone.

The Talmud cites a later sage who suggested the opposite: it is a *mitzva* to cite this rule before the unlearned, for it opens a door to Torah for the uninitiated.

On the practical level, one commentator recommends scheduling a daily time slot for Torah study (*Ben Ish Ḥai*). It should not be cancelled, even if an important business opportunity suddenly arises. The logic for this suggestion is twofold.

First, even though in this scenario Torah study is occupying only two or three hours of someone's day while the rest of the time is spent earning a living, it is as if the entire day is dedicated to learning Torah. This surprising claim is creatively based on a legal principle concerning presumptions. We generally assume – for instance in matters of *kashrut* – that a single item removed from a group of items belongs to the category of the majority of the group. However, if one item alone lies before us, we no longer consider it as having departed from the majority. In this case we say that the particular item has an even chance of coming from either the majority or the minority. This item has the status of *kavua*, being set, and therefore is not considered as having the status of the majority. So too, if one's Torah study is *kavua*, that is, set at certain times of the day, we do not look at what is being done during most of one's daylight hours. The *kavua* nature of the study session means that we have no recourse to majority/minority calculations. A few hours dedicated to learning can affect how we view the entire day.

The second advantage of the practical suggestion that set times be established for Torah study is based on a psychological observation, not a legal maxim. Those who put aside all money-making opportunities, even for a few hours, and commit this time to Torah instead are making a strong statement about the relative worth of the two endeavours. People who do not cancel a study session for the sake of a business deal are expressing their faith in the Almighty, Who provides a livelihood for each person. The money that could have been earned will come through other avenues. In the meantime, the person has clearly prioritised Torah study.

To this analysis we can add an insight gleaned from a comparison to ritual law. One who eats on Yom Kippur is liable to the severe punishment of excision. However, in order to be liable for this, one must eat an amount greater than a plump date. Eating less than this proscribed measurement – a *ḥatzi shiur* (literally, half measurement) – is forbidden as well, but it is not an infraction of the same magnitude and does not carry the same punishment. When it comes to many positive commandments, there is no concept of *ḥatzi shiur*. For example, a four-cornered garment needs *tzitzit* on each corner to render it wearable. There is no value in tying such fringes on only two of the four corners. While the obligation to study Torah is a positive commandment, its fulfilment is not defined by a minimum measurement. As Torah study is a requirement at every moment, whenever we study Torah we fully fulfil the obligation at that time. A small effort, therefore, is never wasted. This is why even reciting *Shema* fulfils the Torah requirement of that moment. The number of hours spent with Torah is less important than one's relationship to those hours.

If Torah time takes place only when there is nothing else to do, Rabbi Shimon ben Yoḥai's lament is appropriate: "What will become of Torah?" In contrast, if the hours spent in Torah study are consecrated for this purpose, the result is that they illuminate the entire day, express the relative importance of Torah, and fulfil the requirement that the Torah should not depart from our mouths.

BERAKHOT 35B

Torah and labour

O UR SAGES SEEK to define the relationship between the grand enterprise of Torah study and the necessity of earning a livelihood. They begin by questioning the message of the verse (Deuteronomy 11:14): *And you will gather your grain, your wine, and your oil* (*B. Berakhot* 35b). One of the commentators explains the question (*Tzlaḥ*): Is it not obvious that, once the rains have fallen in a timely fashion and the produce has grown, we then proceed to gather the produce? What additional lesson is contained in this passage?

The Talmud tackles this verse by contrasting it with the Almighty's instruction to Joshua: *This book of the Torah shall not depart from your mouth* (Joshua 1:8). From the directive to Joshua, we might conclude that we may never cease studying Torah. If this were the case, a person would be precluded from earning a livelihood. Rather, the promise of gathering produce teaches us that the obligation to study Torah retreats before the responsibility of gainful employment.

One commentator explains that those who study Torah while relying on others to provide sustenance will eventually abandon their Torah study (*Rashi*). Indeed, elsewhere our sages teach that Torah which is not combined with work ultimately comes to naught and leads to sin (*M. Avot* 2:2).

9

The relationship between Torah study and earning a livelihood might be described by borrowing a term from ecology: commensalism. This term is used to describe a situation where one organism benefits from an arrangement and the other remains unharmed. Work is beneficial to Torah study and does not adversely affect it. To ensure that the Torah shall not depart from our mouths, the Almighty tells us that we should gather our grain, our wine, and our oil. This is the approach endorsed by Rabbi Yishmael: Torah combined with work.

Rabbi Yishmael's approach is juxtaposed with an opposing view, that of Rabbi Shimon ben Yoḥai. Rabbi Shimon ben Yoḥai is concerned that if people are so busy earning a livelihood, this preoccupation with worldly matters would prevent them from studying Torah. In his eyes, the relationship between Torah and labour can only be described as parasitical, for work preys on every moment of the day and relegates the pursuit of Torah to an unrealised ideal. Rabbi Shimon ben Yoḥai therefore suggests a different *modus operandi*: "When the people of Israel do the will of God, their work is done for them by others. Then indeed Torah need not depart from their mouths."

Thus our sages suggest two conflicting models of the relationship between Torah and labour. According to one approach, earning a livelihood facilitates Torah study and both should be pursued. According to the other, working comes at the expense of Torah study and therefore should not be considered.

Let us fast-forward a number of generations and move to Babylonia. The Talmud records two responses to this argument. The first response is Abbaye's observation: "Many followed Rabbi Yishmael," combining Torah study with work, "and were successful. Many followed Rabbi Shimon ben Yoḥai, and were not successful."

The second response is Rava's entreaty to his disciples: "I beg of you, during the days of Nissan," when the grain is harvested, "and the days of Tishrei," when the grapes and olives are pressed, "do not appear before me" but rather take care of your fields and your livelihood, "so that you will not be preoccupied with your sustenance the entire year." It would appear that the Talmud concludes in favour of the approach promoted by Rabbi Yishmael.

We should not dismiss out of hand, however, the value of uninterrupted study and total devotion to plumbing the scholarly depths of a discipline without needing to worry about finances. In many institutions of higher learning, scholarships are awarded with the goal of providing the student with an environment free of fiscal stress and strain. The hope is that students freed from economic concerns will be able to reach greater heights of scholarship, and will in some way contribute to the welfare, identity, or ethics of our society.

In this vein, later commentators focus on the exact formulation of Abbaye's observation: Rabbi Shimon ben Yoḥai's course was not successful for the *many* who tried to walk that path. Yet for a chosen few, this route may well be recommended. From the standpoint of society, we desire individuals who can devote themselves totally to scholarship. It would be folly, however, to assume that this approach is appropriate for all; it is a path that should be open only to suitable candidates. Such exceptional people should be able to follow in the footsteps of Rabbi Shimon ben Yoḥai, removing themselves from this-worldly pursuits and devoting their entire existence to fathoming the depths of our tradition and unravelling its mysteries. The majority of people, however, are encouraged to see their labour as a necessary and desirable tool for Torah study.

A final word: Rabbi Yishmael might not have been describing a relationship of commensalism. While the commentators state that work can benefit Torah study, Torah study should positively impact work as well. In a poetic formulation, the sages famously declare: "If there is no flour, there is no Torah; if there is no Torah, there is no flour" (*M. Avot* 3:17). This is a description of a symbiosis between studying Torah and earning a livelihood, in which the combination of Torah and labour is mutually beneficial.

Detailed thanks

THE MISHNA DEFINES the text for the blessings over different types of produce (*M. Berakhot* 6:1). All the blessings begin the same way: "Blessed are You, God, our Lord, King of the universe," which is complemented with a phrase appropriate to the specific food. As stated above, on fruits of the tree one adds: "Creator of the fruit of the tree," on wine one adds: "Creator of the fruit of the vine," on fruits of the ground such as legumes and vegetables one adds: "Creator of the fruit of the ground," and on bread one adds: "the One Who brings forth bread from the earth."

One of the sages argues about one detail. Rabbi Yehuda suggests that when the plant itself is eaten, as is the case with cabbage, the appropriate addition is "Creator of various kinds of herbs." The Talmud cites a further stipulation of Rabbi Yehuda: for unprocessed grains and legumes where the seed, not the plant, is eaten, one should add: "Creator of various kinds of seeds" (*T. Berakhot* 4:6; *B. Berakhot* 37a). It appears that Rabbi Yehuda would agree that the addition "Creator of the fruit of the earth" is used for turnips and melons (*Ramban*). Thus Rabbi Yehuda advocated three different blessings for vegetables, whereas the mainstream opinion proposed just one.

The Talmud discusses the logic of this approach. Rabbi Yehuda advocated specific blessings for each category based on a homiletical reading of a biblical verse: *Blessed is God day [by] day* (Psalms 68:20). The repetition of the word *day* in this verse is questioned: do we make blessings only during the day and not at night? Rather the biblical repetition teaches us that on each and every day we should praise God, and that praise should reflect the particular blessings granted us on that day. The phrase employed for this approach is *"me'ein birkhotav,"* meaning "reflective of its" – the day's – "blessings" (*B. Berakhot* 40a). Thus, Rabbi Yehuda maintained that we should thank the Almighty specifically for what we have been granted, rather than employing a blessing with general language. Hence, there should be a unique blessing for each different type of produce.

Alas, Rabbi Yehuda's position was already rejected in talmudic times. The Talmud, however, is mysteriously silent on the reason for the rejection of Rabbi Yehuda's position. One commentator suggests that the words "Creator of the fruit of the ground" do indeed satisfy the *me'ein birkhotav* requirement (*Ramban*). Thirteenth-century Provençal commentators explain that the benefit of eating different types of vegetables is not significant enough to warrant different blessings (*HaMikhtam; Meiri*). Moreover, as opposed to fruits and vegetables, which are governed by different standards in many spheres of Jewish Law, there is no source for distinguishing between various types of vegetables. In addition, perhaps the level of specification proposed by Rabbi Yehuda was not accepted as normative law since it would require botanical knowledge that may not be the province of all.

Yet Rabbi Yehuda's approach is not rejected entirely. There are cases where his demand for nuanced blessings is accepted as normative law. The Mishna lists natural landmarks – such as bodies of water and impressive mountains – that warrant the pronouncement of the benediction: "Blessed are You, God, our Lord, King of the universe, Who creates the natural world." Rabbi Yehuda advocates that upon seeing the *Yam HaGadol*, "the Great Sea," a unique blessing should be recited: "Blessed are You, God, our Lord, King of the universe, Who made the Great Sea" (*M. Berakhot* 9:2). In this case the opinion of Rabbi Yehuda has been accepted as normative law, though there is some discussion as to the identity of this "Great Sea" (*Shulḥan Arukh, Oraḥ Ḥayim* 228:1).

A further instance where Rabbi Yehuda's position advocating nuanced blessings has been accepted is the case of concurrent fulfilment of multiple *mitzvot*. The Talmud quotes an opinion that if a person is about to perform many *mitzvot*, he should recite the general blessing: "Blessed are You, God, our Lord, King of the universe, Who has sanctified us with His commandments and has commanded us regarding the *mitzvot*." This non-specific blessing suffices for all the *mitzvot* about to be fulfilled (*B. Sukka* 46a). One commentator elaborates as follows. If on Sukkot one enters a *sukka* to eat, takes the four species, wraps himself in his *tallit*, and dons *tefillin* (although donning *tefillin* during *Ḥol HaMo'ed* is the subject of debate), then the one blessing suffices (*Rashi*). Rabbi Yehuda dissents. He maintains that the appropriate blessing should be recited over each *mitzva* individually. Here too the Talmud tells us that Rabbi Yehuda's position is accepted as normative law, and here too the reason given is that our benedictions should be *me'ein birkhotav.* Thus Rabbi Yehuda's rulings on specificity in the wording of blessings have been accepted as normative law in some, but not all, cases.

Rabbi Yehuda's position certainly makes sense. A descriptive, pointed, and heartfelt thank-you that specifies what we are grateful for is always more appreciated than a general, often impersonal and distant vote of thanks. True thanks means that we graciously show detailed appreciation that is *me'ein haberakhot,* giving thanks for each of the blessings that we have been granted.

This approach is also given voice in our prayers each Friday night at the end of the service when we say: "And we will give praise to His name every day, constantly, *me'ein haberakhot.*" The phrase *me'ein haberakhot,* meaning here "with the appropriate blessing," echoes the reason given for Rabbi Yehuda's nuanced texts for blessings. As we stand on Friday night reflecting on the past week, we are encouraged to thank the Almighty for the unique blessings that we enjoyed each day of the week that has just passed.

Compromise or decide

THE MISHNA RULES that on bread we recite a blessing that concludes with the words "the One Who brings forth (*hamotzi*) bread from the earth" (*M. Berakhot* 6:1). The sages consider the exact formulation of this benediction, and the discussion turns on a seemingly insignificant use of the definite article (*ha*): should we say *hamotzi* or *motzi*? The Talmud adduces scriptural support for each possibility, and concludes that all opinions recognise *motzi* as a valid formula, while one opinion adds that *hamotzi* is also justifiable (*B. Berakhot* 38a–b).

Following this discussion, the Talmud relates how the sages praised a certain scholar before the famed Rabbi Zeira. They hailed this scholar as a great person and as one who is proficient in the field of blessings. Hearing this tribute, Rabbi Zeira instructed: "When he next comes to you, bring him to me."

Sure enough, this scholar paid a visit to Rabbi Zeira, who offered him bread. Eagerly, Rabbi Zeira waited to hear the blessing that this expert would utter. The guest complied, using the word *motzi*. Rabbi Zeira was disappointed. *Motzi* was indeed a valid formula, but its use did not indicate expertise or greatness. Had the scholar employed the *hamotzi* text, he would have demonstrated that this version is also acceptable, thus teaching an invaluable lesson.

The Talmud springs to the defence of the benediction expert: He opted not to take a position on the matter; therefore, he used a term that was not subject to disagreement.

We have numerous examples in our tradition of normative compromises that are aimed at maximum position compliance (*latzet yedei kol hade'ot*). Maximum position compliance refers to the attempt to satisfy all opinions, or at least as many as possible, thereby avoiding rejection of one position in favour of another. Indeed, later in our tractate, one scholar admonishes a colleague for using a synagogue prayer text that does not accord with all opinions, saying: "You black earthenware vessel! Why do you need to get involved with the dispute?! You would have done better to use a formulation that is accepted by all" (*B. Berakhot* 50a).

In another bread-related debate, the Talmud extols one who manages to act in accordance with all opinions (*B. Berakhot* 39b): Our sages consider a case in which a person is about to eat large pieces of bread as well as a smaller loaf, and they ask whether it is preferable to make the blessing over the large slice or over the smaller but whole loaf. In other words, when deciding precedence for blessings, which is more important: size or wholeness? The Talmud suggests that a God-fearing person should accommodate both opinions by placing the slice under the loaf and holding them together while reciting the blessing.

The passage continues by relating that when this suggestion was recounted before Rav Naḥman bar Yitzḥak, he asked the speaker for his name. The speaker replied: "Shalman." Rav Naḥman bar Yitzḥak was quick to explain the name homiletically: "You are *shalom* and your teaching is whole (*sheleima*), for you have established peace (*shalom*) amongst the disciples." Thus Rav Naḥman bar Yitzḥak was full of praise for a suggestion that satisfied both opinions.

In light of these passages, Rabbi Zeira's disdain for the bene-diction specialist is puzzling. Rabbi Zeira, it would appear, was giving voice to an alternative model in which greatness is measured by resoluteness and self-confidence in the decision-making process. Though the expert chose a course that was safe, it was not one which reflected distinction. An eminent scholar need not aim to satisfy all opinions; expertise is reflected in the courage to assess divergent paths and choose between them. Hence, true scholarship is reflected in selecting the most appropriate language for a blessing, while discarding other options. With this in mind, we can understand why the sages tell us in a differ-ent context, that from the language of a blessing recited we can ascer-tain the erudition of the reciter (*B. Berakhot* 50a).

With this in mind, we can appreciate the words of one com-mentator. A person who stringently rejects any meat that is doubtfully kosher is indeed a God-fearing person, for he avoids any possible pitfalls. Such a scrupulous person surely merits reward in the World to Come, despite not being able to eat the meat in this world. Another person, who through diligent study and application establishes that the meat is in fact kosher, not only merits the World to Come, but is fortunate in this world too in that he can enjoy the meat (*Maharsha*).

This may be the thrust of another rabbinic statement in our trac-tate: "The one who derives benefit from his own labour" – referring to the scholar who carefully determines the law – "is greater than the one who fears heaven." The latter is referring to the righteous person who cautiously avoids such decision-making by trying to satisfy all opinions (*B. Berakhot* 8a).

With this in mind, it is worthwhile mentioning a fascinating law. A *shoḥet* (ritual slaughterer) who mistakenly declares meat to be kosher is sacked for misleading his customers and supplying them with non-kosher meat (*Shulḥan Arukh, Yoreh De'ah* 1:2). What about a *shoḥet* who mistakenly pronounces kosher meat as unfit? This *shoḥet*, too, is removed from his post, as he may one day make the reverse mistake, which would have serious implications (*Rivash*). This ruling appears to be harsh, for the *shoḥet* has not made anyone eat prohibited food; he has merely been too fastidious in his work. In light of our discussion, we can add that an overly cautious approach is not always the preferred route.

Thus our sages present two paradigms, each with its own merits. Seeking a normative course of action that satisfies more than one opinion – maximum position compliance – is a valiant attempt at avoiding mistaken practice. Such a course indicates a sincere concern for the law and Divine will, as the compromiser seeks to guarantee proper fulfilment of obligations. The tendency to be meticulous and fulfil all opinions simultaneously may reveal fear of Heaven; it does not, however, bespeak greatness. Choosing between two valid and compelling alternatives requires a certain fortitude and strength of character.

The Talmud acknowledges and endorses both models, recognising the relative advantages of each mode of conduct. The compromiser is distinguished by lofty fear of Heaven, while the decisor demonstrates normative courage.

BERAKHOT 39B

It's all in a name

A S MENTIONED, THE Talmud considers a case where a person is about to eat large pieces of bread as well as a smaller loaf: is it preferable to make the blessing over the large slice or over the smaller but whole loaf? Opposing opinions are offered, with the Talmud opining that a God-fearing person should accommodate both positions by placing the slice under the loaf and holding them together while reciting the blessing. The passage continues by relating how when this suggestion was recounted before Rav Naḥman bar Yitzḥak, he asked the speaker for his name. The speaker replied: "Shalman," and Rav Naḥman bar Yitzḥak homiletically explained the name: "You are *shalom* and your teaching is whole (*sheleima*), for you have established peace (*shalom*) amongst the disciples" (*B. Berakhot* 39b).

How should we understand such explications of names? Expositions of sages' names that relate to a Torah teaching they taught are common fare in the Talmud. It would seem at first blush that these are witty puns, skillfully created on the spur of the moment.

Some commentators offer a deeper insight into such deft homilies. A name is not merely a tag used for identification; a name contains within it the essence of its bearer. The character of the soul is encapsulated in the name; the destiny and mission of the name-bearer are contained within the name (*Maharal*).

In this vein, our sages recount the events that led up to Adam giving names to all the creatures (*Bereshit Rabba* 17:4). When the Almighty declared to the ministering angels the Divine intent to create humans, the angels scornfully asked: "This human – what is its nature?"

God replied: "The human's wisdom is greater than yours!" To prove this assertion, animals and fowl were brought before the ministering angels. "This one – what is its name?" inquired the Almighty in each case. Alas, the angels were unable to answer.

The creatures were then brought before Adam. "This one – what is its name?" inquired the Almighty once again. Without hesitation, Adam offered an answer in the Holy Tongue: "This is a *shor* (ox); this is a *ḥamor* (donkey); this is a *sus* (horse); this is a *gamal* (camel)." These names were descriptions of the core nature of the animals, not labels defined by collective agreement. This is indicated in the biblical account: *And God the Lord formed each beast of the field and every bird of the air, and brought them to Adam to see what he would call them. And whatever Adam called every living creature, that was its name* (Genesis 2:19). Each creature was given *its name*; that is, the name that reflected its essence.

God then turned to Adam: "And you – what is your name?"

"It is appropriate for me to be called *adam*, for I have been created from the *adama* (earth)."

"And what about Me?" inquired the Almighty, "What is My name?" "It is appropriate for You to be called *Adonai*, for You are *adon* (master) for all Your creations." Thus Adam wisely discerned the nature of each creature – including himself and even the Almighty – designating each with a name that captured its essence.

Countless times in the Talmud, our sages offer homiletic explanations for the names of biblical personalities. In our tractate, the sages provide a number of examples in which names afford a glimpse of future accomplishments (*Berakhot* 7b). Thus the name Ruth contains a hint that she would be privileged to have King David as her descendant. This was the very David who would satiate – in Hebrew *riva*, a cognate of *Ruth* – the Almighty with songs and praises.

The kabbalists go further. The mystical ability to name properly is not reserved for our biblical heroes and talmudic sages. Every mother and father is graced with a flash of Divine inspiration when they grant a name to their newborn child. This new name is no mere moniker; it is an abstract of the young child's qualities, capacities, character. Even though the name appears to be given by people in this physical world, it is the Almighty who puts the name into the mouths of the parents, and this name corresponds to the newborn's holy soul. According to this, giving a name is a momentous religious occasion in which we are blessed with Divine communication.

This explains the practice of changing a sick person's name, for a name change effectively changes a person's destiny. Following this line of thought, our sages tell us that a name change is a tool for shredding a harsh heavenly decree against a person (*B. Rosh HaShana* 16b).

Elsewhere the Talmud recounts a journey of three sages – Rabbi Meir, Rabbi Yehuda, and Rabbi Yose (*B. Yoma* 83b). Rabbi Meir, unlike his colleagues, would examine the name of the owner of the lodgings where they intended to stay. When they reached a certain place, they asked the host for his name and he replied: "Kidor." Rabbi Meir quietly cited a biblical verse: *For they are a generation* – in Hebrew *ki dor* – *of upheavals, children in whom I have no trust* (Deuteronomy 32:20). Based on this he surmised that the owner was wicked. This suspicion was proven correct when the owner later denied that Rabbi Yehuda and Rabbi Yose had entrusted their purses of money in his hands.

Given the significance of a name, we can understand the disapproval of nicknames: a pet name is a wanton attempt to change a person's essence. In fact, giving a person a nickname and calling someone by such a name are listed among the seemingly insignificant sins that our sages condemn. They go so far as to say that those who regularly transgress this injunction and are unrepentant will not have a share in the World to Come (*Maimonides*).

Thus our names are more than mere monikers; they are precious windows into our souls and our destinies. The names we carry encapsulate the tasks we must undertake in this world.

BERAKHOT 40A

Eat first

A FTER RECITING THE blessing on an item of food, one must eat it immediately. Idle chatter between saying the blessing and eating the food is proscribed. Such a disruption would require the recitation of a new blessing, for the first benediction is rendered invalid by the interruption. Our sages explain that certain pertinent phrases may be said in the interim, since they are not considered interruptions. Thus if someone has pronounced the benediction over bread but has not tasted it yet, they can pass a piece of bread to someone else and say: "Take it and recite the blessing." According to another sage, even if the person who recited the blessing said "Bring salt, bring relish," the initial blessing is not rendered void. The final opinion brought in the talmudic passage even allows one to say "Mix the food for the oxen" without voiding the initial blessing (*B. Berakhot* 40a).

Offering someone else a piece of bread or asking for condiments to season the bread are clearly connected to the task at hand – eating the meal. But surely preparing fodder for animals should be considered an interruption?

Our sages explain this rule by recalling another meal-related directive: People may not eat before they have given food to their animals. In fact, the Almighty says: *And I will give grass in your field for your animals; and you will eat and you will be satisfied* (Deuteronomy 11:15). This verse indicates that first feed is supplied for the animals, and then God ensures that humans will eat and be satisfied (see also *B. Gittin* 62a). We see that ensuring that the animals have been fed is linked to the human meal, and therefore is not considered an interruption that would require a new blessing to be made over the food.

Why must we give our animals food before we sit down to eat? Traditionally, animals have served the needs of humans. Examples abound: cows for milk, sheep for wool, chickens for eggs. In recognition of the benefit animals render humans, we are enjoined to ensure their physical welfare.

There are, however, biblical verses in which human sustenance is considered before animal fodder. When the servant of Abraham arrived to find a wife for Isaac, Rebecca first offered him a drink and only then fetched water for the camels (Genesis 24). Similarly, when Moses was instructed to bring water forth from the rock, he was told to quench the thirst of the Jewish people and of their livestock. Later in that story, when the Divine directive was carried out, the same order was followed – first the people, then the animals (Numbers 20:8, 11).

Based on these verses, the medieval pietists suggest a distinction between eating and drinking. Animals should be fed first, yet humans take precedence when it comes to beverages (*Sefer Ḥasidim*). Indeed when the servant of Abraham entered the house of Rebecca's family, first his camels were given straw and only afterward food was placed before him (Genesis 24:32–33).

While a difference between eating and drinking does emerge from a careful reading of the biblical passages, what is the logic of the distinction? One possibility is the more immediate peril of dehydration compared to the danger of starvation. Perhaps this is at the root of the opinion of one commentator, who explained Rebecca's actions toward Abraham's servant. The animals always come first, unless the human is in danger. Rebecca offered the servant a drink because he was thirsty, thus recognising the risks associated with dehydration. Once he had drunk his fill and danger had passed, she watered the camels and fed them before offering the servant food (Or HaHayim).

A different approach highlights the food chain as the explanation for the animals-eat-first rule. If there is no more available food once the animal has eaten, the humans will still not starve, for they can always slaughter the animal and eat its flesh. This logic cannot be applied to water: giving animals a drink does not increase the water supply available to humans. Moreover, the liquid inside the animal – blood – is forbidden according to Jewish law.

This approach explains the unexpected verse where the Almighty commands Noah to gather all types of food so that the ark would be stocked *for you and for them* (Genesis 6:21), that is for Noah and his family, and for the animals. Shouldn't it say that the food was first for the animals and then for the people? The answer is that permission to eat meat was granted only after the deluge. Before the flood, humans were herbivorous. Had the animals devoured the entire food supply in the ark, the humans would have starved. Hence human rations came before those of the animals in the ark.

In an unrelated biblical context, human nutrition appears to take precedence over animal nourishment. Describing *Shemita*, the sabbatical year, the verse says that the food that will naturally grow will be for us to eat and for the animals (Leviticus 25:6–7). The verse appears to go counter to the required order, giving first rights to humans before animals. We might suggest that the obligation to first give food to animals applies only when the food belongs to humans. *Shemita* produce is ownerless and therefore is not subject to the standard rules of precedence.

Here we come to a further aspect of the animals-eat-first imperative. Though the food may legally belong to us, our first obligation is to ensure that those who are our responsibility have eaten. In this spirit, codifiers extend the requirement beyond animals to our servants whose well-being is also our responsibility (*Maimonides*).

If we carefully ensure that those under our care – animals and humans – have eaten their fill before we do, we are subtly teaching ourselves the proper order of priorities. Though our stomachs may rumble, though we might claim to be famished, we are not to place ourselves at the front of the line when food is dished out. If we make sure that our animals have eaten before we do, if we ensure that our workers are satiated before we sit down to a feast, we are making the caring for others a higher priority than feeding ourselves.

Salty hands

FOR THE DESSERT menu our sages have an unusual recommendation: after eating – you should eat salt; after drinking – you should drink water (*B. Berakhot* 40a). The salt and water dessert is not a culinary recommendation, it is health advice. Salt or water effectively nullifies any possible harmful effects of the food ingested.

The passage continues with a statement that expresses the same idea in more ominous terms. If you ate food but did not follow the meal with salt, or if you had a drink but did not then drink water, then during the day you should be worried about the possibility of bad breath and during the night you should be worried about the possibility of *askera*. *Askera* is a fatal disease which results in a horrible death. It is commonly identified today as diphtheria. It involves the inflammation of the digestive tract up to the throat, which results in asphyxiation (*Rashi*).

The talmudic post-meal salt and water requirements are codified in Jewish law. We are further instructed to dip our middle finger or third finger in the salt. Dipping the thumb – we are warned – may result in burying children; dipping the pinky may bring about poverty; and dipping the forefinger may bring about severe boils (*Shibbolei HaLeket; Shulḥan Arukh, Oraḥ Ḥayim* 179:6).

Connected to the salt-eating custom, elsewhere in our tractate we are instructed to wash our hands at the end of a meal before reciting Grace After Meals (*B. Berakhot* 53b). This ritual is known as *mayim aharonim*, last water. Elsewhere in the Talmud, *mayim aharonim* is described as an obligation, and indeed it is codified as law (*B. Ḥullin* 105a;

Shulḥan Arukh, Oraḥ Ḥayim 181:1). In a third talmudic passage relating to *mayim aḥaronim*, the Talmud asks: "Why did the sages declare that *mayim aḥaronim* is obligatory?" In the Talmud's answer, the connection between the salty ending of the meal and the compulsory handwashing is stated clearly: "Because of Sodomite salt that blinds the eyes." Sodomite salt is so potent that, according to one sage, even though it is found in a concentration of just one grain per *kor* (that is, 430 litres) of ordinary salt, it is still harmful. Any other contact with Sodomite salt also requires washing the hands. Thus if Sodomite salt is measured to give to an animal, the one who served it must wash his hands even though he is not ingesting it (*B. Eruvin* 17b; *B. Ḥullin* 105b). Sodomite salt is so dangerous that the sages rule that even though a soldier at the front is released from the obligation to wash his hands before eating bread, he is still required to wash his hands at the conclusion of his meal. Evidently Sodomite salt is a clear and present danger even on the battlefield.

Sodomite salt is presumably salt from the area of Sodom, that is, the Dead Sea plain. Nowadays, the salt there has high concentrations of minerals that can be harmful to the eyes. Salt from the Dead Sea area is also extremely fine. Thus people might not be aware that a salty residue remains on their hands and may eventually reach the eyes. Nevertheless, nowadays we do not find any Sodomite salt with the power to blind upon contact with the eyes, so we need not be concerned with the danger.

Many people do not wash *mayim aḥaronim* at the end of a meal, and even fewer people are careful to have a lick of salt after eating. Codifiers explain that the salt elixir is effective even if salt is eaten as part of the meal with the food. Since our food generally has some measure of salt, this satisfies the talmudic requirement of salt at the end of a meal (*Rema*). Other authorities explain that human nature has changed and a dip of pure salt at the end of the meal is no longer sound health advice (*Magen Avraham*).

As for *mayim aḥaronim*, talmudic scholars in the Middle Ages in Western Europe explain that the salt prevalent on the Continent is from underground mines and is not the dangerous Sodomite salt. Hence it is no longer necessary to wash the hands at the end of the meal before reciting Grace After Meals (*Tosafot*).

Despite these attempts to explain why *mayim aḥaronim* is no longer necessary, some codifiers – particularly those who are conscious

of Jewish mystical tradition – state that the obligation remains. This position sees the washing as having mystical value as well as a hygienic purpose. Though this stance is favoured by mystics, its roots can be identified
in the Talmud. Our sages there distinguish between the requirements
of *mayim rishonim*, washing the hands before eating bread, and those of
mayim aharonim, washing the hands at the end of the meal. The water
for *mayim rishonim* may be poured into a vessel or onto the ground;
mayim aharonim may be poured only into a vessel, which must then be
removed from the table. Not only is the latter water repulsive since it has
been used to clean dirty hands, it also contains an evil spirit (*B. Hullin*
105a, b). Someone who steps over the used water of *mayim aharonim*
could be harmed by it. We are instructed, therefore, to dispose of the
water in a location where people are unlikely to tread (*Magen Avraham*).

Thus in broad strokes we can identify two different traditions that
have developed. Those who follow the Ashkenazic rite do not have the
custom of washing *mayim aharonim* before reciting Grace After Meals.
Those who follow the Sephardic rite and Ashkenazic Jews who are sensitive to directives of the Jewish mystical tradition are careful to wash
mayim aharonim at the conclusion of the meal.

Regardless of what tradition your family follows, it is hardly
appropriate to thank the Almighty for the food we have eaten with
soiled hands. Thus, regardless of whether your dessert is sweet or salty,
everyone agrees that if your hands are dirty they should be washed
before addressing God in the recitation of Grace After Meals.

BERAKHOT 40A

To life, to life, *lehayim!*

HAVE YOU EVER noticed that at every Jewish gathering a glass is
charged and the blessing over wine is said? Whether it is a lifecycle
event, a festival, or just the weekly Shabbat dinner, there always seems

to be a bottle of wine on the table. Sometimes the ritual opens with a glass of wine, as in the case of a wedding ceremony; at other times the wine concludes the rite, like at the redeeming of a first-born son. Every week, Shabbat is ushered in with a silver cup filled with wine, and when the holy day departs we once again fill a cup of wine. On Pesaḥ evening when the family sits down to the *seder*, we open the proceedings with the blessing over wine and then proceed to drink another three cups. Wine is poured even on Rosh HaShana, a time dedicated more to introspection and self-appraisal than to celebratory feasting. The centrality of wine to our tradition, its ritual uses, and its intoxicating properties led our sages to pronounce a ban on drinking wine produced by non-Jews.

Why is wine so central to our rituals? Wouldn't it be more appropriate to usher in momentous occasions and spiritual junctures with a short prayer, a psalm of thanks or commemoration, or a quick review of the pertinent laws? Certainly this would encourage a more pious atmosphere than drinking an alcoholic beverage! How should we understand the role of wine in Jewish tradition, a beverage that comes from cultivated grapes, a drink that has reached its current state due to human effort?

There is a Yiddish quip to the effect that the Hebrew word for water, *mayim*, is written with one *"yid"* – the Polish Jewish pronunciation of the letter *yud*. The Hebrew word for wine, *yayin*, is written with two *"yidden."* Thus when a Jew – a *Yid* – sits alone he drinks *mayim*; when two Jews are together – two *Yidden* – the beverage of choice should be *yayin*. We always celebrate Jewish occasions of note with our friends and family, and hence wine is the appropriate drink.

Rabbi Shlomo Shapira (1831–1893), chief rabbi of Munkács, which was then in Hungary and today is in Ukraine, raises this very question: Why wine? While Rabbi Shlomo Shapira did not publish his writings, his explanation is recorded by his grandson, Rabbi Ḥayim Elazar Shapira (1871–1937), who also served in the Munkács rabbinate.

The Talmud discusses the forbidden fruit in the Garden of Eden, wondering what type of fruit grew on the Tree of Knowledge of Good and Evil (*B. Berakhot* 40a; *B. Sanhedrin* 70a–b). Three opinions are presented.

According to one opinion, the forbidden fruit was wheat, for children begin to call their parents only once they have tasted grain. This suggestion is innovative since wheat stalks are not normally considered trees. The meaning of the cryptic statement regarding children may be that it is only after interacting with the physical world that people see that they have autonomy to transgress against the will of the Almighty.

A further opinion suggests that the forbidden fruit was a fig, for it was a fig leaf that was later used to hide the nudity of Adam and Eve (Genesis 3:7). According to this approach, the very item that brought about the spiritual downfall of the first couple was cobbled together to cover up their embarrassment. At the root of this approach is the idea that the very same object that can be used to wreak destruction can also be used to repair the damage. It is in this vein that the prophet tells us that in the messianic era the sharp metal of deadly swords will be made into plough-shares, which will prepare the land to provide sustenance to all (Isaiah 2:4).

However, the first opinion offered – and the one most relevant to our present discussion – maintains that the "tree" was none other than a grapevine, since the source of misery is always wine. To buttress this contention, the Talmud cites the passage where Noah partook of wine (Genesis 9:20ff). Noah and his family came out of the ark to a new, idyllic world. All evil had been eradicated, and what remained was pure. Noah quickly began life anew by working the cleansed land and by planting a vineyard. The produce of this vineyard was made into wine. When Noah drank and became intoxicated, he and his son Ham engaged in inappropriate behaviour. Thus the new beginning – just like the Almighty's initial programme – was sullied by wine.

Another biblical episode provides a similar lesson, though it is not cited in the context of our discussion (Genesis 19:30–36). After Lot and his daughters escaped the destruction of Sodom, they reached the safety of a cave. The two unmarried girls mistakenly believed that the entire world had been destroyed. In a desperate move, they concluded that they must have children with their father in order to ensure the continuation of humanity. Yet how could a father agree to such an act? The solution suggested by the older daughter and implemented by the two young women was to get their father so drunk that he would be oblivious to any misdeeds committed. This depraved plan succeeded.

Wine, therefore, has been the source of downfall since the beginning of time. In an attempt to reverse our difficulties with wine, at each festive occasion we aim to repair the damage that began in the Garden of Eden. The hope is that wine will no longer be a tool that brings about grief or that results in impropriety. Wine should be used in the service of spiritual growth.

The Almighty's creations are tools for bringing godliness into this physical world. Despite the woeful history of wine, we do not abstain from this hazardous beverage. We seek to sanctify it at moments of spiritual potential. Instead of relegating wine to the annals of vice, we elevate it and use it to open each Jewish ritual, proudly announcing that physical objects are of neutral valence. *We* choose how to employ God's creations; it is *our* lot to write their history. Will they be considered tools of vice, corruption, and sin? Or will these very objects be sources of holiness and spirituality, used as tools to repair this broken world?

BERAKHOT 41A–B

Blessings in the Land

B EFORE THE JEWISH people enter the Land of Israel, Moses urges them to keep the commandments and be faithful to the Almighty. *For God brings you into a good land, a land of water courses, of springs and of depths that come forth in the valley and in the mountain; a land of wheat, barley, vines, fig trees, and pomegranates; a land of olive oil and date honey; a land in which you will eat bread without scarceness; you will not lack anything in it* (Deuteronomy 8:7–9). Thus Moses sings the praises of the Promised Land on the eve of his own demise.

The seven species singled out in this verse – wheat, barley, grapes, figs, pomegranates, olives, and dates – have a unique status as the produce with which the Land of Israel is blessed. Our sages note that since these items were singled out, therefore they have special status when it comes to reciting blessings (*B. Berakhot* 41a). Thus if a person is presented with various foods that all require the same blessing – apples and dates, for example – the blessing is recited over the item included in the seven species, even if the person prefers the taste of the other item (*Shulḥan Arukh, Oraḥ Ḥayim* 210:1). Even among the seven species there is a hierarchy. Those mentioned earlier in the biblical verse take precedence over those mentioned later in the verse.

The Talmud relates an incident that elaborates on this rule (*B. Berakhot* 41b). Two sages, Rav Ḥisda and Rav Hamnuna, were seated together at a meal when dates and pomegranates – two of the seven species – were brought before them. The fruit may have been proffered to satisfy a desire for something sweet (*Rashi*) or perhaps as a dessert (*Tosafot*). Rav Hamnuna reached for the dates first, recited the blessing, and ate them.

Rav Ḥisda was surprised. He queried: "Don't you accept the ruling that whatever is mentioned first in the biblical verse takes precedence when reciting a blessing? You should have recited the blessing over the pomegranates – which are mentioned fifth in the verse – before the dates, which are mentioned last!"

Rav Hamnuna responded: "Though I accept that teaching, I further hold that there is significance in the proximity to the word *eretz* (land) which appears twice in the verse. Dates are mentioned as the second fruit after the second appearance of the word *eretz*, while the pomegranate appears as the fifth item after the first appearance of the word *eretz*. Thus dates take precedence over pomegranates."

Rav Ḥisda was greatly impressed by this sharp insight. He proclaimed: "O that we would have feet of steel so that we could constantly attend you and learn from you without tiring!"

With this exchange in mind, a student once approached the famed talmudist, the Brisker Rav, Rabbi Yitzḥak Ze'ev Soloveitchik (1886–1959). The student asked him how a proof could be brought from this biblical passage regarding precedence in blessings. Even if all the items had equal standing, they would have to be written in some order! The Brisker Rav was visibly displeased by such a question, and retorted that there is no "have to" in our holy Torah. Everything has a Divine reason!

After venting his anger, the Brisker Rav proceeded to answer the question: "The Midrash notes that at times Aaron's name appears before Moses' name (for instance, see Exodus 6:26), and on other occasions – even within the same biblical story – the order is reversed (for instance, see Exodus 6:27). Our sages conclude that Moses and Aaron were of equal standing and therefore the Torah purposefully alternates the order."

The Brisker Rav concluded: "Where items have no particular order, they are written in the Torah first in one order and later in a different order. The produce, however, appears in this sequence only. Perforce, the order has significance!"

The Brisker Rav was not the first authority to tackle this problem. Before him, Rabbi Yeḥezkel Landau (1713–1793), chief rabbi of Prague, posed the same question but offered a different answer. The seemingly unnecessary repetition of the word *eretz* in the biblical verse indicates that there is an internal hierarchy within the seven, with those fruits that are closer to "the land" taking precedence.

Divine blessings, however, might not be limited to the enumerated agricultural species. The Gerrer Rebbe, Rabbi Simḥa Bunem Alter (1898–1992), known as the "Lev Simḥa," was once seated at a joyous gathering with his Hasidim. With a bottle of brandy in his hand, the Rebbe was generously doling out a *leḥayim* to everyone present. With so many followers present, the liquor was soon finished; those who had not received a *leḥayim* heaved a sigh of disappointment. The Rebbe looked down at the table and saw that all that remained was orange juice.

The Lev Simḥa picked up the bottle of orange juice and began to distribute it instead of the brandy. Pouring the juice, he explained: "In the Land of Israel, even on water alone you can say '*LeḤayim!*' Our sages tell us that in the verse describing the seven species of produce with which the Land of Israel is blessed, whatever is mentioned first takes precedence when reciting blessings. The biblical verse that precedes this list says: *It is a land of water courses, of springs and of depths that come forth in the valley and in the mountain* (Deuteronomy 8:7). We see that even the water of the Land of Israel was granted as a blessing. *LeḤayim!*"

While the Land of Israel is blessed with the seven species – wheat, barley, grapes, figs, pomegranates, olives, and dates – it may be blessed with even more. Perhaps – following the example of the Lev Simḥa – we should seek out the many blessings which our land offers.

Missing our beloved deceased

WHEN THE GREAT talmudic sage Rav passed away, his students accompanied his bier as it was taken to his burial place (*B. Berakhot* 42b–43a). When they returned from the funeral they said to one another: "Let us go and eat bread on the Danak River." After they had eaten their fill, they were faced with a halakhic dilemma. The Mishna tells us that if people recline together to eat, one person recites Grace After Meals and discharges the obligation of all those present who have partaken of the meal (*M. Berakhot* 6:6). The basis of this leniency is the rule that "one who listens is like one who speaks," meaning that by listening to your peer's recitation, you can discharge your own halakhic obligation (*B. Sukka* 38b).

While this general rule applies in many scenarios, with regard to food our sages mandate an additional condition – a minimum level of commonality. In talmudic times, reclining together indicated that a meal was being shared. If people merely sat without reclining, it was as if they were eating separately and all would then recite the blessings on their own.

Later authorities add that since we do not recline today, the distinction between reclining and sitting no longer applies. Nowadays, sitting at the table together is classified as sharing a common meal for the purpose of Grace After Meals (*Tosafot*).

What was the issue that bothered the students by the Danak River? They questioned whether declaring that they would go and eat bread together at a particular location was akin to reclining together and thus met the requirement of a joint meal. The question was not theoretical, but practical: The students wondered whether one of them could recite Grace After Meals on behalf of all.

As they sat pondering the question, they realised that they had no answer at hand, and the impact of the absence of their deceased teacher was magnified.

One of the students, Rabbi Ada bar Ahava, rose and turned his shirt around so that the tear he had made previously in mourning for his teacher was behind him. He then proceeded to rend his garment in the front. This was in order to once again fulfil the stipulation for rending garments in mourning for a deceased teacher: tearing the front of the shirt while standing (*Shulḥan Arukh, Yoreh De'ah* 340).

As he tore his garment, Rabbi Ada bar Ahava lamented: "Rav has died and we have not learned the laws of Grace After Meals!" The students sat there perplexed. Eventually, an elderly man came along and pointed out that the aforementioned rule of the Mishna contradicts another rabbinic tradition that defines sitting together as a sufficient act to bind a group of diners. The elderly man resolved the contradiction by explaining that the key question was not whether they were sitting together, but whether they ate together. People who say, "Let us go and eat bread in such and such a place," have clearly decided to dine in concert. Accordingly, one person may say Grace After Meals for all participants. Thus the conundrum of the students by the Danak River was solved after they had lapsed momentarily into mourning for their deceased teacher.

One Torah commentator explains the biblical account of the mourning for Jacob in a similar vein (Genesis 50:1–14). Following the death of Jacob and a mourning period of seventy days, Joseph made plans to have his father's body taken from Egypt to be buried in the Land of Israel. A great convoy accompanied the deceased Jacob, including the servants of Pharaoh, the elders of Egypt, Joseph's entire household, and the brothers. The grand procession was accompanied by chariots and horsemen. Only the children and the livestock were left behind.

The Bible relates that when they reached the threshing-floor of Atad, a place named after a rough, prickly bramble, eulogies were once again delivered and another seven-day mourning period was observed. What happened at this mysterious threshing-floor that the great convoy was so moved? Why was another mourning period necessary? Moreover, why did the Egyptians in the travelling party mourn? Jacob's death was hardly their loss!

Rabbi Shlomo Ephraim Luntschitz (1550–1619) relates to this passage in his Torah commentary, *Keli Yakar*. Our sages tell us that the presence of a righteous person brings good fortune to the world. When the righteous person dies, however, the good fortune departs and in its place retribution may come. As long as Jacob was alive and living in Egypt, the famine was kept at bay; as soon as he died, the famine returned (*T. Sota* 10:1, 9).

The threshing-floor was unique in that it was encircled by prickly shrubs and the entrance was barred. This was a thorny situation for an area that was to be used for threshing produce. When the convoy reached this threshing-floor entirely surrounded by thorns, they recalled a time when there was no grain to be threshed, and wild bushes sprouted on the pathways to the granaries and blocked the unused entrances. This memory conjured up images of famine in the travellers' minds, reminding them that without Jacob there would be no grain and once again the paths to the threshing-floors would become overgrown. Jacob's demise was a cause for Egyptian mourning, as it led to the loss of the good fortune which this righteous person's presence had brought to their land. Thus the impact of Jacob's demise was felt anew – even by the Egyptians – when the party reached this threshing-floor. They responded appropriately by mourning once again.

Though Jewish law mandates a finite mourning period, there will always be moments that will unexpectedly remind us of our beloved deceased. It may be an image, a melody, a product on the shelf of a supermarket, a seemingly innocuous remark. Whenever that moment comes, we rightly mourn anew the loss of our dear one. Such feelings need not be quashed; even though the official mourning period has passed, it is understandable that we once again lament their loss.

Sweet scents

THE TALMUD SEEKS a source for the blessings mandated for sweet scents. It offers the final verse of Psalms: *Let every soul praise God* (Psalms 150:6). Focusing on the word *soul*, the Talmud explains: "When does the soul derive pleasure while the body does not? It must be that this refers to fragrant smells" (*B. Berakhot* 43b).

Indeed fragrances do not enter the body in a tangible form as do food and drink. There is also no noticeable organ that is satiated by a scent. The nose doesn't tingle, the cheeks do not change colour, a rumbling stomach is not quieted. Fragrances are sensed deep inside us. In fact the Hebrew word for smell – *rei'ah* – is of the same root as the word *ruḥani*, which means spiritual. This is because a fragrant smell provides spiritual delight, not physical pleasure (*Arukh HaShulḥan*).

In the creation account, the Bible describes how the Almighty imparted life to humans: *And God the Lord formed the human out of the dust of the earth and breathed into his nostrils the breath of life, and the human became a living soul* (Genesis 2:7). The nostrils – the same orifice which would be used for appreciating smells – became the channel of entry for the Divine soul to animate the physical form.

We might wonder: We recite blessings over all manner of things – food and drink, seeing special people, observing a flash of lightning, before the sounding of the *shofar*, and upon hearing the rumble of thunder. In the musical based on Sholem Aleichem's stories, *Fiddler on the Roof*, there is even a blessing over the Tsar! Naturally there should be a benediction over sweet fragrances. Furthermore, earlier in our tractate our sages tell us that it is forbidden to benefit from this world without first offering a blessing; deriving pleasure without a benediction is akin to embezzlement of sanctified property (*B. Berakhot* 35a). This statement would appear to include deriving pleasures from aromas as well.

So what makes fragrances so unique that the Talmud needs to seek another source for the blessing requirement? One commentator reminds us that the prohibition of embezzlement from the Temple did not include sounds, sights, and smells (*B. Pesaḥim* 26a). Thus the talmudic statement likening benefit without a blessing to misappropriation of holy property does not include fragrances. Therefore, we need a separate verse to teach us the requirement to make blessings over scents (*Tzlaḥ*).

A different approach suggests that since a blessing is offered by a physical movement of the lips, we might think that in cases where the physical body does not benefit, there is no need to move the mouth.

The talmudic passage teaches us that even though a scent does not involve a noticeable physical action, it nevertheless should be preceded by a blessing uttered by moving the lips (*Iyun Yaakov*).

A third, mystical approach focuses on the role of blessing in Jewish esoteric tradition. Ever since the sin in the Garden of Eden, every physical item is an admixture of good and evil. In this material world, we are charged with bringing out the good in physical objects. The recitation of a blessing is the first step in the process of harvesting the good that is encapsulated in the neutral food, elevating it from the level of the mundane to the realm of the holy. Once the food has been ingested, we can then complete the refining process by using the strength that we gain from the food for good deeds.

In the Garden of Eden account, all the senses except for one are mentioned – sight, touch, taste, and hearing (Genesis 3:6–8). Only the sense of smell is missing from this story. It appears that the sense of smell was not tainted in the Garden of Eden and instead remained in its pristine state, unsullied by sin. Thus the spiritual purity of scent is appropriate nourishment for the soul. It is for this reason that each Saturday night, as our extra Shabbat soul departs with the end of the holy day, we smell sweet spices to revive our bereft, fragmented soul (*Tosafot*).

Given the lofty status of fragrances and the assertion that olfactory powers were untainted by Edenic sin, we might presume there is no need for the process of extracting the good from smells, and hence a blessing is unnecessary. Our sages tell us that despite this assumption, there is nevertheless a need for a blessing over fragrances. We are, after all, physical beings. Even sweet fragrances have a material component, and therefore they too require some process of elevation, albeit not to the same extent as food and beverages (*Benei Yisaskhar*).

The power of scent is nonetheless of a different class to the other senses. According to Jewish esoteric tradition, the odours emitted by people reflect their iniquities (*Zohar* 3:186:1). It is recounted that the holy kabbalist, Rabbi Yitzhak Luria (1534–1572), could identify people's sins according to their smell. Moreover, Isaiah the prophet singles out the faculty of smell of the Messiah (Isaiah 11:3; *B. Sanhedrin* 93b), indicating the spiritual sensitivity which will reign during this longed-for era.

Let us return to our talmudic passage. Our sages anticipate that in the future, the youth of Israel will emit a pleasant fragrance, as it says: *His young shall go forth, his beauty shall be like the olive tree, and his aroma will be like Lebanon* (Hosea 14:7). According to one source, the reward promised to the righteous is thirteen rivers of fragrant persimmon oil (*Bereshit Rabba* 62:2).

With the spiritual standing of the power of smell in mind, blessings over fragrances take on new meaning. We are not merely thanking the Almighty for the physical benefit we derive from a sweet smell. We are opening an olfactory window into our souls, getting a whiff of a spiritual existence, and enjoying an aromatic trace of Divine sustenance.

BERAKHOT 43B

Torah with love

IN THE MORNING *sow your seed, and in the evening do not withhold your hand, for you do not know which will succeed – whether this or that, or whether both will be equally good* (Ecclesiastes 11:6). While some sages understand this verse to be offering agricultural advice, others interpret the instruction as referring to various aspects of life (*B. Yevamot* 62b; *Kohelet Rabba* 11:1).

According to one opinion, the verse is offering family planning advice. Having children while young does not preclude having children at a later stage in life, for you cannot know which child will continue your legacy.

Another opinion explains the verse in terms of Torah study, enjoining even those who studied in their youth to continue their studies in their old age.

According to Rabbi Akiva, the verse is addressing teachers of Torah and imploring them to continue training students even later in life. His understanding was born of his tragic experience as a teacher of Torah. Rabbi Akiva had an impressive 24,000 students spread over Judea. Alas, they all perished during one period between Pesaḥ and Shavuot because they did not treat each other with appropriate respect. The world was subsequently desolate of Torah study. Despite the calamity, Rabbi Akiva did not retire; rather he travelled south and taught Torah to a new cadre of pupils. Thanks to these new disciples, Torah study was revived. It was Rabbi Akiva – perhaps after this bitter experience – who coined the well-known adage that loving your neighbour as yourself is a grand principle of Torah (*Sifra, Kedoshim* 2; *Y. Nedarim* 41c).

Talmudic literature is peppered with statements from Rabbi Akiva's later disciples giving voice to this ideal. This would suggest that the later students had learned the lesson of their unfortunate predecessors and were therefore deserving of bearing the mantle of the tradition and transmitting Torah to future generations.

For instance, Rabbi Meir – one of Rabbi Akiva's students – exhorted people to be humble of spirit before every person (*M. Avot* 4:10) and we have evidence that he practised what he preached (*Y. Sota* 16d). Each week Rabbi Meir would speak in the synagogue on Friday night. One particular woman conscientiously attended. One time his sermon was longer than usual. By the time the woman arrived home, the candle she had kindled had burned out and the house was dark. As she entered her home, she was met with the gruff voice of her husband: "Where have you been?" When she told her husband that she had gone to listen to the sermon, he responded by swearing that he would not allow her to enter the house until she had spat in the face of the speaker.

A Divine message was sent to Rabbi Meir explaining the predicament. He cunningly pretended to have a sore eye and requested that anyone who knew how to heal him should come forward. A neighbour of the pious woman urged her to take advantage of this opportunity.

When the woman arrived before Rabbi Meir, he asked her: "Do you know how to heal the eye?"

As the women stood before him, she was overwhelmed and responded truthfully: "No."

Rabbi Meir told her: "Spit in my eye seven times and it will heal."

After she had dutifully spat, Rabbi Meir turned to her saying: "Now go and tell your husband that even though he told you to spit only once, you spat seven times!"

The students present were astounded. They challenged him: "Rabbi, do we disgrace Torah thus? Had you told us about this episode, we would have brought the husband and given him lashes until he forgave his wife!" Rabbi Meir calmly responded that for the sake of promoting peace between a husband and wife, one's own honour should be waived. Thus he demonstrated to his students the appropriate way to interact with others.

Another student of Rabbi Akiva, Rabbi Yose ben Ḥalafta, was extremely self-effacing. He declared that even though he knew that he was not a *kohen*, if his colleagues told him to ascend the platform and offer the priestly blessing he would acquiesce (*B. Shabbat* 118b).

Rabbi Neḥemia – another of Rabbi Akiva's later disciples – spoke of the severity of the sin of baseless hatred. He cited some of the ominous punishments that might be incurred by those guilty of baseless hatred: strife in the household, miscarriages, and the premature death of children (*B. Shabbat* 32b).

Another example of the interpersonal ideal is expounded upon by Rabbi Shimon ben Yoḥai. In our tractate he comments on the silence of Tamar when she was accused of prostitution (Genesis 38). Instead of vociferously protesting as she was being taken to be burned for her iniquity, Tamar sent a covert message to her former father-in-law Judah, indicating that he was the father of her children. Rabbi Shimon ben Yoḥai concludes that one should allow oneself to be thrown into a fiery furnace rather than publicly embarrass another (*B. Berakhot* 43b).

Knowledge is not the only prerequisite to serve as a bearer of the tradition. Passing on pure Torah is the province of those with sterling character. The thousands of students of Rabbi Akiva who died left behind no remnant of their Torah within the walls of our *beit midrash*; their books do not adorn our shelves and we do not discuss the minutiae of their statements. The grim story of Rabbi Akiva's students calls into question the value of Torah that is devoid of appropriate interpersonal behaviour.

Thankfully, there was at least a small cohort of students whose conduct was beyond reproach. Alongside their discussions of the finer points of law, they also urged future generations to refine, hone, and enhance their treatment of others. It is the Torah of these scholars, whose ethical wills are filled with love and respect for their peers (*B. Sanhedrin* 86a), which forms the basis of the corpus of Oral Law. It is their Torah which continues to animate our Torah discussions, which we continue to study today, which fills our *beit midrash*. It is the legacy of these students of Torah which we strive to bequeath to our children.

BERAKHOT 43B

Fiery furnaces

IN A NUMBER of places the Talmud makes a particularly dramatic statement: People prefer – or at least ought to prefer – to throw themselves into a fiery furnace rather than to publicly shame another person (*B. Berakhot* 43b; *B. Sota* 10b; *B. Bava Metzia* 59a). In each place the same source is cited: the story of Tamar and her father-in-law Judah (Genesis 38).

After the sale of Joseph, Judah moved away from his brothers. He married and had three sons – Er, Onan, and Shelah. When the time came, Judah found a wife, Tamar, for his oldest son Er. However, Er was not a righteous person and the Almighty brought about his death. According to the ancient custom, which later became normative Jewish law, Er's brother Onan was called upon to enter into a levirate marriage. Onan indeed cohabited with Tamar, but he knew that any children from this union would not be considered his own and thus assiduously avoided impregnating Tamar. The Almighty did not look favourably upon this course, and Onan too died.

Since Tamar still had not had any children it was up to the third son, Shelah, to perform a levirate marriage. Judah told his daughter-in-law to return to her father's home and to wait until Shelah would be old enough to do so. Judah, however, had no intention of giving his third son to Tamar, for he feared that Shelah too would die as his two older brothers had.

As the days passed, Tamar realised that Judah was not going to allow her to marry Shelah, so she devised a cunning plan to fulfil the obligation of levirate marriage. (While Jewish law would later limit levirate marriage to the brothers of the deceased, in biblical times the obligation could be fulfilled by any relative.) She dressed as a prostitute and sat where Judah would pass by. Not realising who she was, Judah propositioned her and promised her a goat as payment for her services. Judah, however, did not have a goat handy, so he deposited his signet, cord, and staff as a guarantee that he would pay later. When Judah sent someone to deliver the payment, the prostitute was nowhere to be found. In fact, all the locals denied that a harlot had ever been there. In the meantime, Tamar changed her clothes, once again wearing the garments of a widow.

About three months later, when it became obvious that Tamar was pregnant, Judah was told that his daughter-in-law had been promiscuous and was with child. Without hesitation Judah declared: *Take her out and let her be burned!* As Tamar was being led to her death, rather than announcing to all that she had been impregnated by her father-in-law, she sent him a message: *By the man to whom these belong I am with child. Please recognise who this signet, cord, and staff belong to.* Judah immediately realised what had happened and admitted his mistake. He declared: *She is more righteous than I, since I had not given her Shelah my son.*

Though she was about to be burned to death, Tamar chose not to publicly embarrass Judah, leaving in his hands the decision whether or not to take responsibility. From here the sages derive that it is preferable to be thrown into a fiery furnace rather than publicly embarrass someone.

Some of the commentators discuss in almost legal terms the sin of embarrassing another. One commentator suggests that it is as serious as the three sins which require a person to forfeit his life rather than transgress: idolatry, adultery, and murder. The commentator further suggests that the only reason that embarrassing someone is not included in this famous list of three is because it is not mentioned explicitly in the Torah (*Tosafot*).

Another commentator takes a slightly different approach. Embarrassing another does not have to be listed in addition to the three cardinal sins because it is actually a subcategory of murder. As the blood drains from the face of an embarrassed person, it is as if he has been killed (*Rabbeinu Yona Gerondi*).

An earlier mishnaic statement goes further, listing the sin of embarrassing another as one for which the perpetrator forfeits his share in the World to Come; even if the culprit is a Torah scholar and has done many good deeds (*M. Avot* 3:11).

A tale is told about Rabbi Yehoshua Leib Diskin (1818–1898). After arriving in Jerusalem in 1878 from Russia, he became one of the leaders of the Old Yishuv – the Jewish community that lived in the Land of Israel before the advent of political Zionism. Rabbi Diskin suffered from diabetic hypoglycemia in his later years. Once while the rabbi was teaching Torah, his attendant prepared him a glass of tea. To replenish the sugars in Rabbi Diskin's body, the attendant spooned a lot of sugar into the tea, and then placed the glass in front of him. Alas, the attendant mistakenly put salt instead of sugar in the tea! Rabbi Diskin did not flinch, but drank the salty tea despite the awful taste and notwithstanding the health risk for a diabetic. Later the students discovered what had transpired, and they questioned Rabbi Diskin: "How could you have endangered yourself by drinking the salty tea?" He explained that he preferred to drink the dreadful tea and risk his life, rather than embarrass the attendant.

When relating the story, the famous storyteller of Jerusalem, Rabbi Shalom Mordekhai HaKohen Schwadron (1912–1997), explained that for Rabbi Diskin it was indeed "preferable" to drink the salty tea rather than embarrass the attendant. So preferable was it that his body must not have felt the salty tea! While Rabbi Diskin's conduct might be beyond many of us, it certainly sets a standard to which we can aspire.

Perhaps we can extend the lesson of this talmudic passage. We are rarely faced with the choice of risking our lives or embarrassing another. Fiery furnaces thankfully are not a regular feature of our lives. Nonetheless, the challenge of not embarrassing others is all too prevalent. The thought of shaming another person should be so painful that it should cause our insides to burn with disgust, so much so that we would prefer to jump into a physical fire rather than embarrass someone else and spiritually scorch our soul.

BERAKHOT 43B

Walk the walk

W E A L L H A V E our own gait. Some of us amble along, saunter and meander, others march or stride, while there are still others who seem to traipse from one place to another. When our sages detail the conduct that is unbecoming of a Torah scholar they include a directive about how to walk (*B. Berakhot* 43b).

A wise person should not walk with broad strides or with an upright posture. Further in the talmudic passage, our sages explain that a large stride takes away 1/500th of a person's eyesight. Elsewhere, our sages advise all people – not just Torah scholars – to avoid large steps and thus preserve their eyesight (*B. Ta'anit* 10b). The warning against giant steps is restated in the context of Shabbat, when we try to create a special atmosphere with special foods, nice clothes, different modes of speech, and a relaxed pace (*B. Shabbat* 113b).

Tosafot, the medieval talmudic commentators from central and western Europe, wonder about this. If each broad stride takes 1/500th of a person's eyesight, then 500 large steps will render a person blind. Experience, however, suggests that this is not the case.

Tosafot, therefore, explain that with each stride people lose 1/500th of their remaining eyesight, not of their original capacity. Given this understanding, *Tosafot* ask why the first stride should inflict greater damage than subsequent steps. They explain that once the initial impairment has been wrought, people become desensitised to the harm, and the injury inflicted is progressively diminished.

The halakhic codifiers record the prohibition against walking with large strides in the context of the Shabbat atmosphere (*Rema, Oraḥ Ḥayim* 301:1). Later halakhists note that while striding and jumping on Shabbat are an infraction against the spirit of this holy day, on a weekday we must also refrain from such steps because of the potential eyesight damage (*Mishna Berura*).

Elsewhere in our tractate a third issue relating to broad strides is discussed (*B. Berakhot* 6b). The Talmud states that broad strides should not be taken specifically when exiting a synagogue, because this would give the impression that we are anxious to escape the burden of participating in the service. In this context an exception to the rule is stated. When coming to the synagogue – and indeed going to do any good deed – it is a *mitzva* to run. As the prophet says: *Let us run to know God* (Hosea 6:3).

One sage reports that when he first saw sages scurrying to hear Torah discourses on Shabbat, he thought they were transgressing against the spirit of the holy day. Once he heard the dictum that a person should always run to hear matters of halakha even on Shabbat, he too would do so! Moreover, this sage felt that the primary reward for coming to Torah discourses was for the effort exerted in running to the study hall. As one commentator explains: people who attend public lectures often cannot recap the lesson later on; all that remains is the reward for the energy spent in getting there (*Rashi*).

What is a "broad stride"? Obviously this depends on the individual, but we can nevertheless provide a general indicator of what should be avoided. A standard stride is about one cubit; that is, 48 cm or 58 cm. A step that goes beyond that would be considered a broad stride and should be sidestepped.

Poor eyesight is, however, no proof of broad strides. The Bible attributes the dimming of eyesight to another vice, accepting bribes: *Do not take a bribe, for a bribe blinds the wise and distorts the words of the righteous* (Exodus 23:8; Deuteronomy 16:19). In this context Rabbi Avraham HaLevi Ettinger (1874–1924) relates that there was a rumour that a certain Jewish judge's decisions could be purchased if the price was right. The judge happened to be lame in one foot. Rabbi Ettinger's grandfather would quip that if this judge were to become blind, he would not be able to claim that it was on account of his taking broad strides, because his limp precluded this. Thus his potential blindness would perforce be on account of his perverting justice by accepting bribes.

Is there a cure for those who have taken broad strides and seek to improve their eyesight? The Talmud tells us that eyesight can be restored with the Friday night *kiddush* wine. How does this *kiddush* cure work? According to a tradition attributed to the ninth-century Babylonian Gaon, Natronai, the medicinal properties of the *kiddush* wine take effect when the wine is placed on the eyes (*Tosafot*). The halakhists, however, recommend looking at the wine during *kiddush*; this is either to ensure concentration or to benefit from the therapeutic potential of the wine (*Rema, Oraḥ Ḥayim* 183:4, 271:10; *Mishna Berura*). Some commentators suggest that the curative powers of *kiddush* can be experienced by drinking the wine (*Rashi*).

Admittedly, the danger of broad strides and the magical properties of the holy *kiddush* wine may be difficult for the untrained eye to discern. Perhaps we can suggest a more accessible perspective: people who hurry about can often be seen taking large, rushed strides. Running around may indicate a lack of focus and perhaps even a measure of spiritual dishevelment and disarray. With no time for reflection, these people often age quickly, and naturally their eyesight deteriorates. This process can be halted or at least slowed down by taking a few deep breaths. Shabbat is the time set aside for this very purpose.

On Friday night we return from the synagogue to usher the holy day into our homes. We begin with the recitation of the *kiddush*, as we stand with our family around the bedecked table and hold a goblet of wine. We look at the cup of wine, recite the *kiddush*, and savour the taste. By doing so we create a serene atmosphere and experience a tranquillity that is unattainable as we rush around with broad strides during the hectic and demanding weekdays. In this way, the Shabbat *kiddush* wine is the perfect cure for the eyesight-damaging bustle of the work week.

Fruit of the Promised Land

O UR SAGES TELL us that if salted food is served as the first course, and bread is brought as the second course, a blessing should be made over the salted food. It is then unnecessary to recite an additional blessing over the bread (*M. Berakhot* 6:7). The Talmud questions this ruling (*B. Berakhot* 44a). If the blessing over the salted food exempts one from making a blessing over the bread, that must mean that the salted cuisine is considered the primary food, while the bread is subordinate to it. But is this really the case? Bread provides nourishment and satisfies hunger; it is the most basic form of sustenance. Therefore, it should not be considered secondary to any other food. The sages explain that the mishnaic dictum must be referring to a food that is superior even to bread. This can only be one thing: the fruit of Ginosar.

Ginosar is located in the region around the Kinneret, the Sea of Galilee. Elsewhere the Talmud identifies Ginosar with the Kinneret, explaining that Ginosar was called "Kinneret" because the fruits of this area were as sweet as a *kinor*, a lyre (*B. Megilla* 6a). The Ginosar fruit was so exceptionally sweet that according to some commentators it needed to be eaten with salt (*Ritva*). Alternatively, after eating Ginosar fruit something salty had to be brought to the table to revive those who had partaken of the sweet, syrupy fruit. The bread was then served as a condiment for the salted food (*Tosafot*). Thus the classic staple – bread – is considered subordinate to Ginosar fruit, but not to any other food.

After mentioning the sweetness of Ginosar fruit, the Talmud regales us with tales about the uniqueness of this extraordinary produce. One sage relates that when students accompanied Rabbi Yoḥanan when he went to eat Ginosar fruit, each of his students would gather fruit. If there were a hundred disciples in attendance, they would gather ten fruits each. If there were only ten students accompanying him, they would each gather a hundred fruits. Either way, Rabbi Yoḥanan would be presented with one thousand pieces of Ginosar fruit. He would devour them all and swear that he was not satiated and could eat more.

One sage ate so much Ginosar fruit that a sweet syrup oozed from the pores on his face, and a fly that landed on his forehead slipped off. Other sages so seriously overindulged in the fruit that it made their hair fall out. Reish Lakish ate so much that he became delirious, and Rabbi Yoḥanan – his mentor and colleague – had to summon help to get him home. These fruity tales, however, are not limited to the produce of Galilee.

Elsewhere in the Talmud we find lavish praise heaped on the produce of the Land of Israel (*B. Ketubot* 112a). Indeed the bountiful fruit of Israel was recognised and sampled by the twelve spies who were sent to explore the Promised Land (Numbers 13).

Throughout the Talmud, we hear of various sages who made the journey between the two Torah centres of that period – the Land of Israel and Babylonia. These travellers carried traditions and interpretations from one study hall to the other and facilitated cross-fertilisation of ideas. It should not come as a surprise that when these travellers arrived in Babylonia, they reported on the bountiful produce of the Land of Israel. Thus Rav Dimi told of one city in the Judean area of Har HaMelekh in the time of King Yannai where they would take out sixty thousand bowls of chopped salted fish each week to feed the figpickers. With so many fruit-pickers, we can only imagine how much fruit was gathered. Another traveller, Ravin, provided some insight into the size of the trees. King Yannai had one tree in Har HaMelekh where thrice monthly almost six hundred litres of newly hatched pigeons were harvested from its branches.

These extravagant talmudic descriptions defy the imagination. One commentator unabashedly states that these accounts are, in fact, exaggerations (*Ben Ish Ḥai*). The challenge for us, however, is to harvest contemporary significance from the tales – tall as they may be – that our tradition has preserved.

According to one approach, the Kinneret and its environs have an unrivalled spiritual quality and thus the fruit grown on the banks of this lake are particularly sweet. Because of this mystical quality, our sages went to great lengths to partake of the fruit of the Kinneret area (*Radal*). Another authority states that fruit from anywhere in the Promised Land is full of spiritual value; by eating fruit from the Land, we become animated and invigorated by the Almighty's Holy Presence (*Bah*).

Perhaps we can add another dimension. Our sages tell us that there are certain prerequisites which must be met for a town to be considered a worthy place of residence for a Torah scholar. A list of ten items is provided: a court of law, a mechanism for charity collection, an honest distribution method for that charity, a synagogue, a bathhouse, a lavatory, a doctor, a blood-letter, a scribe, and a schoolteacher. According to one opinion, there is a further requirement: there also must be a variety of fruits, for an assortment of fruit brightens the eyes (*B. Sanhedrin* 17b).

Medically, fruit intake affects our eyesight. Vitamin A is contained naturally in so many fruits and vegetables – most famously carrots, but also lemons, apples, apricots, melons, mangos, potatoes, pumpkins, spinach, and broccoli. A lack of vitamin A can harm vision. Luckily, the damage can be repaired by reintroducing products rich in vitamin A. Thus eating fruit can improve our eyesight, which assists us in going about so many of our daily functions and, significantly, allows us to pore over the texts of our tradition. Before the advent of eyeglasses, it was even more important for people to take care of their eyes. The instruction of our sages to eat fruit unabashedly perhaps is aimed at preserving our eyesight. And what fruit could be better than the holy and succulent fruit of the blessed Land of Israel!

BERAKHOT 44B

Rabbi M.D.

IN VARIOUS PLACES throughout the Talmud, the sages offer medical advice. Thus we find in our tractate that our sages expound on the health value of eggs. Roasted eggs are singled out, preferably lightly roasted so that they are soft and swallowed as a thick liquid, but fully roasted or boiled eggs are recommended as well (*B. Berakhot* 44b; *Rashi*).

The medicinal value of other foods is also discussed. Spleen, we are told, is particularly beneficial for teeth, yet harmful to the intestines. The sages therefore recommend chewing it and then spitting it out. Leeks have the opposite effect – they are harmful to the teeth but beneficial for the intestines, so they should be cooked until soft and then swallowed without chewing. Raw vegetables eaten after bloodletting lead to paleness, and they should not be eaten on an empty stomach. Eating anything that has not attained a quarter of its potential size stunts one's growth. To restore vitality, one should eat things that were once alive, even small fish that have fully developed. Alternatively, meat from near an animal's throat also revitalises the eater.

Cabbage is nutritious, while beets have medicinal qualities. Cabbage can also help cure the ailing, as can a soup made from dry pennyroyal. Certain parts of animals are noted for helping the sick – the innards, the womb, and the diaphragm. Turnips are particularly bad for the stomach, unless their effect is weakened either by cooking them together with fatty meat, drinking wine after they are eaten, or overcooking them.

But beware – small salted fish have fatal potential. If eaten on the seventh, seventeenth, twenty-seventh, and perhaps also the twenty-third day after being salted, they can cause death. This danger can be combated by fully roasting the fish or drinking beer after eating them.

How are we to understand these health tips that are so foreign to modern ears? Contemporary medicine does not subscribe to the majority of these guidelines. Should these health instructions be viewed as obligatory legal maxims akin to other authoritative statements of our venerable sages?

Significantly, the great codifiers do not include these passages in their halakhic works. Thus, for instance, the health guidelines offered by Maimonides – himself a physician – do not overlap with the talmudic sources. Rabbi Yosef Karo (1488–1575), in his commentary to Maimonides' halakhic work, notes that medical advice is time and location specific. The health guidelines of the Talmud – and similarly those offered by Maimonides – were appropriate to the time period and place in which they were offered. Maimonides, therefore, did not follow the talmudic health guidelines, and we need not follow them either. For that matter, we also need not follow Maimonides' suggestions.

Maimonides himself seems to suggest this approach. The Mishna records an opinion that one who vows not to eat garlic until Shabbat must refrain from garlic only until Friday evening, because we assume that he intended that his vow should be in force only until the time that people customarily eat garlic, namely Friday evening (*M. Nedarim* 8:1). In his commentary to this mishna, Maimonides notes that during the Second Temple period, it was customary to eat garlic on Friday evening because it was known to enhance male potency, and Friday night is the recommended time for scholars to have conjugal relations (*B. Bava Kamma* 82a). Significantly, Maimonides adds that garlic's therapeutic properties were effective "in accordance with their diet and their land," implying that the curative powers of garlic in his time were different. In his philosophical writings, however, Maimonides goes further and states that talmudic science was imperfect. Our sages advised their generation to the best of their abilities; however, unlike their Torah knowledge, their medical knowledge was not based on a Divine tradition.

The idea that talmudic health advice is not legally binding predates Maimonides. The Geonim of Babylonia – who lived in the same region in which the talmudic sages had lived and generally saw themselves as the authoritative bearers of the talmudic legacy – recount a tradition that talmudic health dicta do not have the status of obligatory *mitzvot* and should be followed only if they have been reviewed and approved by expert doctors.

It should be noted that there have been scholars who record these medical instructions in their halakhic compendia. Thus, for instance, Rabbi Shlomo Ganzfried (1804–1886), in his *Kitzur Shulḥan Arukh*, an abridged and accessible volume on Jewish law, dedicates an entire section to health guidelines. He draws on the code of Maimonides without entertaining the possibility that the recommendations may no longer be relevant.

The majority of codifiers, however, are conscious of the limitations of rabbinic health guidelines. In many instances they acknowledge that health dicta were context specific, and suggest that human nature may have changed so that what was once healthy may nowadays be harmful (*Magen Avraham* 173:1). Thus, for instance, our sages recommend eating salt after each meal to guarantee fresh breath during the day and protection from diphtheria at night (*B. Berakhot* 40a). One prominent codifier quotes this passage and then adds that nowadays we are not accustomed to eat salt after a meal and we experience no detrimental effects, for human nature has changed (*Shulḥan Arukh HaRav*).

One modern American scholar, Rabbi Avigdor Miller (1908–2001), proposes that the temporary nature of medical opinions teaches us something about our relationship with the Almighty. Successive generations of medical professionals discount and at times even mock the medical directives of previous generations. If past experience is any indication, even that which doctors advise today may well be disregarded in the future. Nevertheless, the health directives of previous generations must have been effective in some way when they were current, otherwise they would have been quickly abandoned.

Why did the Almighty create the world of medicine with a preponderance of fleeting "truths"? Rabbi Miller suggests that this situation leaves room for individuals to do all in their power to improve their health. Once the medicine takes effect, people then have free choice to acknowledge God's hand or to attribute their health solely to the medical counsel they received. The short-lived nature of medical truisms awakens us to the reality that medicine is merely a vehicle for the Almighty, the true Healer of all living beings.

BERAKHOT
CHAPTER SEVEN

The *ḥalla* thief

THE MISHNA DISCUSSES the *Zimmun*, the invitation to recite Grace After Meals as a quorum, and highlights situations when the *Zimmun* should not be recited (*M. Berakhot* 7:1). As a general rule, when three people eat bread together, they are required to join in a *Zimmun*. However, the Mishna states that if one of the people is eating prohibited food, he cannot be included in the *Zimmun*. The Mishna gives a few examples: consuming *tevel* – produce that has not been properly tithed; eating *ma'aser sheni* produce outside of Jerusalem; and eating *hekdesh* – food that had been consecrated for Temple use.

The Mishna addresses only the case of the post-meal *Zimmun*. Medieval scholars discuss whether a person eating prohibited food makes a blessing before eating and whether Grace After Meals is recited at all. In his legal *magnum opus*, Maimonides presents a clear ruling: Anyone consuming something that is forbidden, whether intentionally or inadvertently, does not recite a blessing before or after eating.

How does Maimonides reach this conclusion? The talmudic passage speaks only of joining a *Zimmun*! This question irked Ra'avad of Posquières, Maimonides' older contemporary in Provence. In uncompromising language, Ra'avad annotates Maimonides' text, writing: "Here he made a big mistake." He explains that the Mishna proscribes a *Zimmun* over prohibited food because we cannot say that a proper meal was eaten if the food should not have been consumed. Nevertheless, if food is eaten, blessings before partaking of it should be recited.

What then is Maimonides' source and how are we to understand his opinion? Maimonides is famous – or perhaps it would be more appropriate to say notorious – for not revealing his sources.

It could very well be that Maimonides is drawing on other talmudic passages pertinent to our discussion (*T. Sanhedrin* 1:3; *B. Bava Kamma* 94a; *B. Sanhedrin* 6b). If a thief stole wheat, ground it into flour, kneaded it into dough, baked it, and then separated the requisite *ḥalla* to give to the *kohen* (Numbers 15:17–21) – can he really recite a blessing over the separation of the *ḥalla*? For this is not blessing the Almighty but blaspheming! A proof text is offered: *A thief who recites a blessing has blasphemed God* (Psalms 10:3). If it is a blasphemy rather than a blessing, it is undoubtedly better that nothing be said.

Another talmudic passage voices a similar position. It is forbidden to make a blessing over stolen *matza* (*Y. Ḥalla* 58b). Once again the aforementioned biblical proof text is cited. These talmudic passages are a possible source for Maimonides' ruling that no blessings should be recited over forbidden foods.

Maimonides is also famous for his masterful use of the Hebrew language, often alluding to his sources with his selection of words. In the continuation of his ruling, Maimonides lists examples of prohibited foods that preclude the recitation of blessings: *tevel, ma'aser sheni* outside Jerusalem, and *hekdesh*. Maimonides' choice of examples appears to be echoing the Mishna, as if to say that his source is the mishna about *Zimmun*. It would thus appear that Maimonides conflates the talmudic sources – the *Zimmun* mishna with the *ḥalla* and *matza* thief – to reach his ruling.

Yet there is a salient difference between the ruling of Maimonides and the cases of thievery. Maimonides refers to reciting blessings before and after partaking of food, in cases when no particular *mitzva* is being performed. In the case of the *ḥalla* thief, though, the blessing is recited before performing the *mitzva* of separating *ḥalla* for the *kohen*. Even in the case of the *matza* thief, it would appear to be referring to the blessing over the *mitzva* of eating *matza* at the Pesaḥ *seder*. After all, if the passage is not referring to the *mitzva*, why specify "*matza*"? Perhaps there is a difference between one who recites a blessing before eating and one who recites a blessing before performing a *mitzva*?

This brings us to a third approach; a middle ground of sorts. It may well be that when we eat forbidden food because we are hungry, we should say blessings even though a *Zimmun* is inappropriate. This would be in line with the ruling of our mishna that refers only to *Zimmun*. However, reciting blessings over *mitzvot* – such as eating *matza* on Pesaḥ or separating *ḥalla* – is considered nothing less than blasphemy if the food has been stolen.

One commentator suggests that this distinction made between blessings before eating food for enjoyment and blessings on *mitzvot* is due to the different wording of the two types of blessings (*Korban Netanel*). Blessings before the performance of *mitzvot* include the words "Who has sanctified us with His precepts and commanded us." It is hardly appropriate to say such words after stealing wheat, for the blessing could easily be misconstrued as a Divine licence for stealing. Blessings over food do not contain this formula; they merely acknowledge God's hand in creation and in the natural order of the world. The recitation of such a blessing says nothing about sanctity or Divine command.

A further development of this idea could examine not just the wording of the blessing but also the substance. *Mitzvot* are actions that we do at the behest of the Almighty. As the text of the blessings indicates, such deeds are considered holy. We are hardly able to sanctify our existence by using stolen goods. Thus there is no place for a blessing before the performance of *mitzvot* with stolen property.

Blessings before eating for sustenance are different. They acknowledge the Almighty's ultimate ownership. One who eats food without offering a blessing is considered as having stolen from God (*B. Berakhot* 35a). It is bad enough that a person is eating forbidden food; should that person also become a thief? Though he is eating food that should really be avoided, let him at least recite a blessing so that he is not also stealing from God.

BERAKHOT 45A

A unifying response

W HEN A PERSON responds to a blessing by saying *amen*, our sages tell us that the respondent's voice should not be louder than the voice of the one who recited the benediction (*B. Berakhot* 45a). This rule is adduced from the biblical verse *Declare the greatness of God with me and let us exalt His name together* (Psalms 34:4). *"With me"* is understood to mean – equal to me. The voice of the respondent should be equal to the voice of the one who declared the greatness of God by reciting a blessing (*Ritva*).

Elsewhere in the Talmud, we seem to find a different approach. Our sages tell us that if someone responds to the *Kaddish* prayer loud and clear with all his might, pronouncing "*Amen*, may His great name be blessed forever and ever," then if there was an evil decree against him in heaven, it is torn up. The merit of a response that is "with all his might" counters whatever heavenly verdict has been rendered against him. Moreover, even if he is tainted by a trace of idolatry – a most grave sin – he is forgiven as a result of his *Kaddish* response. The Talmud continues by lauding even the seemingly negligible one-word *amen* response to blessings. The gates of the Garden of Eden in the World to Come are opened to anyone who answers *amen* with all his might (*B. Shabbat* 119b).

One commentator vividly explains the significance of the open gates for the spirit that leaves the body upon death. In normal circumstances the soul of a deserving person arrives at the Garden of Eden, and only then are the gates opened. For *amen* responders who answer with all their might, the gates are opened as soon as their souls begin the journey from this earthly world toward the Garden of Eden. The soul perceives the gates being opened from a distance and gains significant satisfaction from knowing that it has merited entering without hesitation (*Ben Ish Ḥai*).

The value of an *amen* response may be reflected in the meaning of the word "*amen*," which is an affirmation of the blessing just said. Moreover the word may be understood as an acronym for *El melekh ne'eman*, meaning "powerful God, trustworthy King" – an affirmation of the Almighty's sovereignty and trustworthiness. According to one commentator, every time we respond by saying *amen* we should meditate on the meaning of this acronym (*Tosafot*).

Let us return to the phrase "with all his might" – what does that mean? Some commentators explain that the response to *Kaddish* should be said as loudly as possible (*Ri*). Such a thunderous pronouncement is said in order to focus ourselves and indicate that we are devoting our entire being to blessing the Almighty (*Ritva*).

How loud should we say "*Amen,* may His great name be blessed forever and ever"? One authority limits the volume of the response. There is no need to answer with such a loud voice that others present will laugh (*Rabbeinu Yona Gerondi*). While such a booming response may be well-intentioned, it may in fact cause others to sin (*Mishna Berura*).

This limitation – so that others will not laugh – is a far cry from the aforementioned restriction of the volume to no louder than the one who recited the blessing. Perhaps in consideration of the more limited volume restriction, other authorities understand "with all your might" to be referring to power of concentration rather than volume. A person should respond to the *Kaddish* with the utmost attentiveness (*Rashi*).

What is the reason that a volume restriction is placed on the *amen* respondent? We recall that one opinion advocates shouting the response in order to increase our concentration. Another opinion states the exact opposite, namely that the volume restriction is designed to facilitate our focus on the previous words. Since we must listen attentively to the prayer leader to ascertain the permitted volume level, we are likely to meditate on the content of the prayer – the appropriate course considering we are about to affirm what the reciter is asserting. Moreover, shouting in a communal situation is hardly conducive to concentration; our sages therefore declare that the maximum volume of the response is defined by the volume of the leader. This commentator adds that, in addition to the goal of improving concentration, equalising the volume also conveys the comparative importance of the two acts: both the recital of the blessing or *Kaddish* and the response are of comparable value (*Ben Ish Ḥai*).

A different approach that also contrasts volume with concentration suggests that a loud response is an external expression that at times may hide an internal abyss (Rabbi Moshe Tzuriel). A shouted *amen* is no substitute for a heartfelt *amen*. To avoid the folly of a loud but heartless response, a cap is placed on the volume.

Perhaps we can suggest a further explanation that is not based on the tension between volume and concentration, but that focuses on the forum where this responsive *amen* takes place. The responsive "*Amen,* may His great name be blessed forever and ever" can only be recited in the presence of a *minyan,* a quorum of ten. Even the minimal *amen* requires more than an individual, for it is almost invariably said in response to the blessing of another. Thus the *amen* response bespeaks community.

A communal prayer effort is not a competition; it is a joint undertaking. The respondent should strive to complement the one who offered the blessing; not compete against him. There is little value accorded to an individual standing out, while standing with the congregation. At this time audible conformity is called for, in an attempt to foster a cooperative spirit of kinship. The community responds in unison so that the experience is truly a shared spiritual endeavour.

The power of our People lies in that elusive unity for which we so yearn. Perhaps a response that is "with all our might" is a fulfilment of this ideal, declaring our faith and fidelity in one voice.

BERAKHOT 45A

It loses something in translation

FROM THE BABYLONIAN exile through mishnaic and talmudic times the prevalent custom was for the Torah reading to be coupled with a translation in the Aramaic vernacular. As with all translations, the Aramaic translation of the Torah was also an elucidation. After the Torah reader read each biblical verse in the original Hebrew, the translator rendered it into Aramaic (*M. Megilla* 4:4; *B. Megilla* 23b–24a). The purpose of this supplement was clear: to ensure that those present understood what was being read. The Talmud offers a rule about the relative volume of two synagogue functionaries: the translator of the Torah reading is not permitted to raise his voice above that of the reader (*B. Berakhot* 45a).

While this custom was codified as Jewish law, it is practised today only in select communities. This ritual faded as its utility became limited, when the Aramaic vernacular fell into disuse and people no longer understood the translation (*Shulḥan Arukh, Oraḥ Ḥayim* 145).

The Talmud offers the following biblical source for the volume rule, a source which – as we will presently see – is puzzling: *Moses would speak and God would respond to him with a voice* (Exodus 19:19). The verse appears in the context of the Ten Commandments. The Jewish people heard the first two commandments from the Almighty, while the remaining eight were transmitted by God to Moses, who relayed them to the people. The Talmud notes that in the biblical verse the word translated *with a voice* is superfluous; the verse is perfectly comprehensible without it. The Talmud goes on to explain that the added word indicates that the Almighty responded to Moses in a voice equal to that of Moses.

Why did the Almighty need to suit His voice to that of His translator-transmitter, Moses? The talmudic rule, it would appear, would indicate that it is the responsibility of the translator-transmitter to check his volume. The Almighty – as the reader of the original Torah verses – could have spoken as loud as He wished; all Moses needed to do was to ensure that his voice was no louder than God's!

One possible explanation is that Moses needed to speak loudly so that all the people assembled at Mount Sinai could clearly hear what he was saying. True, God needed to speak only to Moses; but had the Almighty just whispered, then Moses as the translator-transmitter would not have been permitted to speak loudly. God therefore raised the volume of the Divine voice, so that Moses too could speak loudly (*Tosafot*).

One of the commentators suggests – albeit with great hesitation – that maybe Moses was the reader and the Almighty was his translator, and that is why God's voice needed to suit Moses' voice. Explaining this possibility, the commentator notes that Moses would have read the Torah in Hebrew, yet not all present would have understood the language. Elsewhere in the Talmud it says that whenever God spoke, the words were miraculously heard in seventy languages (*B. Shabbat* 88a). Thus the Almighty served as a translator for Moses, the reader, and it was God who needed to lower the volume of the Divine voice (*Maharsha*).

While this explanation fits the talmudic interpretation of the biblical verse, it is certainly surprising to think of the Almighty as Moses' translator, and even more startling to think of Moses as the original reader. Indeed, in a number of biblical passages Moses is described as explaining the Torah; that is, serving in the classic role of the translator-transmitter (Deuteronomy 1:5, 27:8).

Considering the notion that the volume of God's voice took stock of the volume of Moses' voice, another commentator proposes that not only must the translator-transmitter check his voice, but the reader too must aim to use the same volume level as the translator-transmitter (*Iyun Yaakov*). This approach is buttressed by the continuation of the talmudic passage, which cites a slightly different version of the volume rule: "The translator is not permitted to raise his voice above that of the reader. If it is not possible for the translator to match the voice of the reader, then the reader should reduce the volume of his voice to the level of that of the translator." Why must the reader lower his voice? Up until now we have been working under the assumption that the reader should be louder than the translator! The codifiers indicate that there may be an omission in the talmudic text. After stating that the translator must not be louder than the reader, the text should read that likewise the reader must not be louder than the translator. If the translator is unable to match the reader's volume level, the reader should lower his voice so that both the reading and the translating are at the same volume (*Maimonides*).

Thus we see that it is incumbent upon both reader and translator to speak at the same level of volume. The Almighty therefore lowered the Divine voice as reader so that it matched the human voice of Moses as translator-transmitter when he presented the commandments to the people.

What is the reason for these volume directives? According to one commentator, the rules have a hierarchical purpose. The congregation should not mistakenly think that the translator-transmitter is greater than the reader. To avoid such an error, the translator-transmitter may not be louder than the reader (*Ben Ish Ḥai*).

We might develop this idea further. Each of the two functionaries – the reader and the translator – represents a different value. The job of translator was introduced because the sages recognised the importance of understanding what was being read. In instituting this office, our sages were striving to provide access to the tradition even for those who could not comprehend the text in its original language.

By limiting the volume of the translator, however, the sages were hinting that while it is true that ideas may transcend the boundaries of language, nevertheless, there is no substitute for hearing the original text. Any translation, perforce, contains an element of interpretation. The translator-transmitter is an intermediary; for an unmediated encounter with the text it is imperative to gain access to the original.

By demanding that the translator-transmitter and the original reader speak at an equal volume, the Talmud is balancing two values: access and authenticity. On the one hand, it is important to provide everyone with an opportunity to explore the Torah. On the other hand, we should not abandon or forgo the ideal of being able to access the original, primary sources of our heritage.

BERAKHOT 46A

I will bless those who bless you

WHENEVER WE GATHER together to eat a formal meal, there is always the question of who should recite the blessing over the bread. Should the host honour one of the guests with leading all present, or is it the host's obligation to recite the benediction? The Talmud recounts a tale that focuses on this very question (*B. Berakhot* 46a).

Rabbi Zeira was once in poor health. His colleague Rabbi Abahu paid him a visit. Rabbi Abahu made a vow, saying: "If the small man with the singed thighs" – a nickname for the diminutive Rabbi Zeira, who had once been scorched in an oven (*B. Bava Metzia* 85a) – "recovers, I will make a party for the rabbis." Rabbi Zeira indeed recovered and Rabbi Abahu organised a feast for all the rabbis. When all were seated and the meal was about to start, Rabbi Abahu turned to Rabbi Zeira and invited him to recite the appropriate blessing, break the bread, and begin the meal. Rabbi Zeira declined, asking: "Don't you follow the ruling that the host should recite the blessing and break the bread?"

The Talmud explains that Rabbi Abahu indeed adhered to the opinion that the host should break the bread. Why then did he ask Rabbi Zeira to begin the meal? Commentators explain that since the meal was in honour of Rabbi Zeira, Rabbi Abahu considered his colleague to be the host and therefore expected him to start the meal (*Rashba*).

Our sages explain why the host should be the one to begin the meal: so that the host will break the bread with "a good eye," generously offering the guests large portions.

Based on an exchange between two Hasidic personalities, perhaps we can suggest a further reason why the host is the most appropriate person to break the bread.

Rabbi Meir Yeḥiel HaLevi Halstock of Ostrowiec (1852–1928) was once visited by the Gerrer Rebbe, Rabbi Avraham Mordekhai Alter of Góra Kalwaria (1866–1948). As was the custom, the host asked for fruit and beverages to be brought for his honoured guest. When the refreshments were served, Rabbi Avraham Mordekhai did not touch the food.

Rabbi Meir Yeḥiel was somewhat surprised: "Why won't you taste anything?" he inquired.

Rabbi Avraham Mordekhai astutely answered by referring to a talmudic passage (*B. Berakhot* 35a–b). Our sages declare that it is forbidden to benefit from this world without first reciting a blessing. Eating with no prior benediction – or for that matter, deriving any benefit from this world without acknowledging the Almighty – is akin to stealing. Indeed the Psalmist says: *The earth and all that is in it belong to God* (Psalms 24:1). The talmudic discussion continues, comparing the verse that attributes all to Divine ownership with another biblical verse: *The heavens are the heavens of God, but the land He gave to humans* (Psalms 115:16). Do the earth and all that it contains belong to the Almighty, or did God give them to humans? The Talmud explains that the two verses are referring to two different junctures. Before a blessing is recited, all belongs to the Almighty; once the appropriate benediction has been said, the rights to the object are granted to humans by God. Thus partaking of any item requires asking leave of the true owner, God, and this permission is obtained by saying a blessing.

Returning to the two Hasidic masters: Rabbi Avraham Mordekhai explained to his host, Rabbi Yehiel Meir, "Until you recite a blessing, you are offering me fruit and drink that is not yours! Only after you recite the blessing do the rights to the food transfer to you, at which point you can honour me as your guest!"

Without hesitating, Rabbi Meir Yehiel picked up a fruit, made a blessing, and ate. This was no trifling matter, for Rabbi Meir Yehiel was known to favour asceticism. He did not change his clothes during the weekdays nor did he listen to music, even though he greatly loved it. Days would pass when Rabbi Meir Yehiel would remain silent, not saying a word. Hasidic lore records that Rabbi Meir Yehiel fasted for forty years, eating only in the evenings. Thus joining his guest in partaking of the refreshments was no small matter.

Once Rabbi Meir Yehiel had recited the blessing and tasted the fruit, Rabbi Avraham Mordekhai also ate from the food that had been placed before them.

Here we see a further reason why the host must break bread first. If hosts seek to honour their visitors, they can do so only with their own food. The host recites the blessing, effectively acquiring the rights to the food, and then proffers the food to the visitors.

At the end of the meal, however, the honour of leading Grace After Meals is different. Let us return to Rabbi Abahu and Rabbi Zeira. At the conclusion of the feast, the host Rabbi Abahu invited Rabbi Zeira to lead Grace After Meals. Once again Rabbi Zeira demurred. He queried: "Don't you follow the ruling that the one who breaks the bread should also recite Grace After Meals?" Unlike their conversation at the beginning of the meal, here Rabbi Abahu did not agree with Rabbi Zeira. He felt that it was most appropriate for a guest to lead Grace After Meals so that the guest could include a blessing for the host. Following this line of thought, Jewish law suggests that the guest who recites Grace After Meals should offer a blessing for the host, even though it is the host's prerogative to forgo this blessing and lead the recital (*Shulhan Arukh, Orah Hayim* 201:1).

One further law bears mentioning. We are told that if someone is asked to lead Grace After Meals and refuses, his days are shortened (*B. Berakhot* 55a). Our sages derive this forbidding rule from the more positive Divine pledge to Abraham: *And I will bless those who bless you* (Genesis 12:3). Blessing the host – a descendant of Abraham who has generously shared his meal with you – merits a Divine blessing in turn.

After you, sir

NORMALLY, WE ARE instructed to accord honour to people who are greater than us, by inviting them to go first. However, our sages teach us that there are three cases in which we need not accord honour by inviting a greater person to proceed first (*B. Berakhot* 46b–47a): when travelling on roads, when crossing bridges, and when washing dirty hands after eating. Why is honour not accorded in these three cases?

With regard to soiled hands, it is hardly an honour to proffer a basin of water and a towel, intimating that the recipient needs a wash.

With regard to travelling and passing over bridges there are at least two possible explanations. Elsewhere, the sages state that all roads should be considered dangerous (*Y. Berakhot* 8b). In talmudic times bandits lay in wait at every turn; any lapse in concentration or restful respite could be fatal (*M. Berakhot* 1:3). In our times too, driving on the road is fraught with danger: unsafe roads, careless drivers, faulty cars. With hazards lurking at every junction, it is hardly safe to stop and consider who is the most worthy person at any given intersection. It is far wiser to focus on road safety.

One commentator offers a different reason, also focusing on the practical perspective. He suggests that the public good overrides the protocol of according honour (*Meiri*). If each meeting of travellers were accompanied by an "after you" ritual, traffic would come to a standstill. Travel time would increase exponentially and few would reach their destinations. Imagine a latecomer offering the excuse: "I'm sorry I'm late, but I met a few worthy people on the road and was forced to pull over and let them pass."

When codifying the law, Maimonides adds a further qualification. Inviting a worthy person to proceed first is relevant only when entering somewhere; there is no honour in exiting first.

The Talmud illustrates the principle of according honour when entering by recounting a tale of two sages: Abbaye, who served as the head of the talmudic academy at Pumbedita during the fourth century, and Ravin, who had arrived in Babylonia from the Land of Israel. As the two scholars were travelling, Ravin's donkey overtook Abbaye's. Seeing the junior scholar overtake him without inviting him to go first, Abbaye muttered to himself: "Since this scholar has come from the west" – meaning from the Land of Israel – "he has become haughty."

When the two travellers reached the entrance to the synagogue, Ravin stopped and turned to Abbaye: "Let the master enter first."

Abbaye was surprised. He questioned this sudden show of respect: "Wasn't I the master until now?" Why had Ravin invited Abbaye to proceed only when they reached their destination?

Ravin explained why he had not accorded Abbaye honour during the journey, by quoting a teaching of Rabbi Yoḥanan, the head of the talmudic academy in the Land of Israel. "Thus said Rabbi Yoḥanan: 'We accord honour only at an entrance that has a *mezuza*.'" Accordingly, Ravin did not render honour while on the road, but he invited Abbaye to enter first once they reached a doorway.

The Talmud is a bit surprised by Ravin's justification. Strictly speaking, if a house of prayer is used for no purpose other than prayer, it need not have a *mezuza* since it does not serve as living quarters (*Shulḥan Arukh, Yoreh De'ah* 286:3). Following Rabbi Yoḥanan, then, Ravin need not have accorded Abbaye the honour of entering first, even once they reached the synagogue.

To explain this, the Talmud qualifies Rabbi Yoḥanan's statement by explaining that honour should be accorded at a place that could have a *mezuza* – namely, a doorway – even if for some reason that particular entrance does not require a *mezuza*. Thus the doorway to a synagogue, though it might not have a *mezuza*, is nevertheless an appropriate place to accord honour. In contrast, travelling along the road or entering through a breach in a wall does not necessitate according honour.

What is the connection between according honour and the *mezuza*? Rabbi Yoḥanan could have said that the right of first entry is granted in doorways. Why did he mention the *mezuza*?

The Talmud relates that the famous Roman convert, Onkelos (c. 35–120), once pointed out that a human ruler sits inside and has his subjects stand outside guarding the entrance to his chambers. Not so the Almighty, for God's name is placed on the doorpost outside each Jewish house and provides protection for each person within (*B. Avoda Zara* 11a). Indeed, the Hebrew word *mezuza* has the same numerical value as *Adonai*, one of the names we use for the Almighty. Since the *mezuza* is a sign that God honours us with Divine protection at the entrance to our homes, we attempt to imitate the Almighty by according respect at these same places.

Upon examining this talmudic exchange, one commentator feels that the core of the passage is not concerned with where honour must be accorded; rather, the focus is on where honour is superfluous (*Ben Ish Ḥai*). We are informed that there is no need to accord honour while travelling. On the highways of life, as we cross the bridges we chance upon during our journeys, an intent focus on who deserves honour can soil the soul. It is certainly appropriate to accord honour to those deserving this distinction, yet we should not become preoccupied with such matters. We spend more time inside rooms than entering them, and we would be mistaken to devote a disproportionate amount of energy to matters whose significance is momentary and fleeting.

A person once complained that no one accorded him the honour he deserved. A wise confidant advised him that honour graces only those who flee from it. Some time later the person returned and insisted: "I have been running from honour for some time now, yet it has not caught up with me." The wise person explained: "Though you may have been running from honour, you kept looking over your shoulder to see if it was following you!"

Competing values

THE TORAH MANDATES that produce be tithed before being eaten. The tithing process involves allocating portions of produce for designated parties or purposes. Produce that has not been properly tithed is termed *tevel* and is forbidden to all. One who eats *tevel* incurs the punishment of *mitah bidei shamayim*, death by the hands of God, as opposed to execution by a human court.

The Mishna tells us that during the Second Temple period there was no longer a need to inquire whether produce had been properly tithed, due to certain assumptions regarding the status of produce (*M. Sota* 9:10). What were these assumptions?

The Talmud recounts that Yoḥanan the *Kohen Gadol* did a survey and found that some of the uneducated people were not fulfilling all the tithing requirements (*B. Sota* 48a). The unlearned were indeed scrupulous about separating *teruma gedola*, the heave-offering awarded to *kohanim* from an Israelite's produce. They were, however, less meticulous about other tithing obligations. Their care in giving only *teruma gedola* stemmed from the mistaken impression that one incurred the heavenly death penalty only by eating produce from which *teruma gedola* had not been separated.

Yoḥanan the *Kohen Gadol* explained to them: "My children, just as eating *teruma gedola* is a sin punishable by Divinely decreed death, the same is true for eating *tevel* or *terumat ma'aser*" – the heave-offering that the Levite gives to the *kohen* and that may not be eaten by non-priests.

Due to the gravity of this sin, Yoḥanan the *Kohen Gadol* legislated that all produce of doubtful status should be tithed just in case. A new category of produce was created called *demai*, produce of uncertain tithing status which had to be tithed before being eaten. The term *demai* comes from the Aramaic *da mai*, meaning "What is this?" The word possibly has a Greek root, coming from the word *demos*, meaning people or masses.

From *demai* produce, *ma'aser rishon* – a tenth of the produce after *teruma gedola* has been separated – must be apportioned to the Levite. While the Levite normally receives the *ma'aser rishon*, in the case of *demai* the burden of proof lies with the Levite, who must show that the produce had indeed been untithed. Until the Levite can produce such proof, the *ma'aser rishon* remains in the hands of the owner. While it is in the hands of the owner, however, the subsequent *terumat ma'aser* – the heave-offering normally apportioned by the Levite – must be transferred to the *kohen*.

After *ma'aser rishon* has been separated, an additional tenth of the remaining produce is separated. During the first, second, fourth, and fifth years of the seven-year *Shemita* cycle, this second tithe – known as *ma'aser sheni* – is brought to Jerusalem and eaten there. Alternatively, *ma'aser sheni* may be redeemed, and the money taken to Jerusalem and spent on food in the capital city.

During the third and sixth year of the *Shemita* cycle, instead of *ma'aser sheni*, a tithe for the needy is apportioned – *ma'aser ani*. As with the Levite claiming a tithe from *demai*, the needy must prove that the *demai* produce has previously not been tithed in order to claim the *ma'aser ani*.

While *demai* produce must be tithed before being eaten, the Mishna states an exception to this rule. *Demai* may be given to the needy or to guests without tithing it first (*M. Demai* 3:1).

The Talmud quotes this mishna and records a dissenting opinion on the matter which maintains that we do not feed the needy or guests with *demai* (*B. Berakhot* 47a; *B. Eruvin* 17b, 31a–b). This second opinion is cited in the name of the School of Shammai and has not been adopted as normative law. Rather, Jewish law rules in accordance with the opinion cited in the Mishna, the opinion of the School of Hillel: *demai* may be offered to guests or the poor.

Commentators discuss the identity of these guests. According to one opinion these guests are regular visitors whom we invite into our homes (*Maimonides*). According to another opinion the guests are soldiers who are being billeted in people's homes. The responsibility to feed these foreign legions falls on the hosts. Since these soldiers are away from their own homes, they are classified as needy, as is anybody who leaves his domain (*Rashi* following *M. Pe'ah* 5:4). Elsewhere, the sages teach that *demai* is one of four things from which soldiers are exempted entirely during a military campaign, even if there is no danger in tithing *demai* before consuming the produce (*M. Eruvin* 1:10).

Since *demai* is normally forbidden, why may it be given to the needy? From a legal standpoint, the *demai* decree is a rabbinic enactment, and as such it is subject to consideration of various extenuating circumstances. Because the majority of the unlearned did tithe produce, and the *demai* decree of Yoḥanan the *Kohen Gadol* was legislated only in consideration of a significant minority, the sages relaxed the law in certain cases (*Rashi*).

Probing this exception, we can suggest that the sages employed this legal mechanism in a bid to assist those who bear the communal burden of supporting the needy. This law, therefore, reflects the value of helping the underprivileged and the importance of hosting guests (*Maimonides*).

This leads us to what is perhaps the most striking aspect of the exception to the *demai* decree: the value system reflected by the permitted uses of *demai*. As we noted, *demai* is produce whose tithe status is uncertain. On the one hand, this suspicion is taken seriously. The religious severity of eating untithed produce necessitates corrective action, and the produce must be tithed in case it is indeed *tevel*. On the other hand, providing assistance to the needy and hosting others in our homes are paramount values in our tradition. When weighing competing objectives, our sages declare that helping the needy and hosting others override the reservations we have about the status of the produce. Our concern about tithing recedes in the face of the need to assist the poor and to open our homes to others.

BERAKHOT 47B

Enfranchising the unlearned

THE SEVENTH CHAPTER of *Tractate Berakhot* deals extensively with *Zimmun*, the invitation to recite Grace After Meals as a quorum of three. The Mishna outlines the rules for the *Zimmun*: the text of the call to recite the blessings, the quorum requirements and limitations, and who may join in the *Zimmun*. Although *amei ha'aretz*, the unlearned, need to form a *Zimmun*, the Talmud states that Torah scholars should not form a *Zimmun* together with the unlearned (*B. Berakhot* 47b; *Shitta Mekubetzet*).

If three unlearned people are eating together, they must use the *Zimmun* formulation to introduce Grace After Meals. Similarly, if unlearned people are sitting with three scholars who are about to recite the *Zimmun*, they cannot excuse themselves before responding to the call. If, however, to form the minimum quorum of three, one or two scholars would have to join with one or two of the unlearned, a *Zimmun* should not be formed.

This rule excluding the unlearned is surprising and distasteful. There is no such limitation on the unlearned being counted in a quorum of ten for public prayer. Some halakhists grapple with this exclusion by recasting someone unlearned as a public sinner. A person who publicly eats pork – a known and stigmatised prohibition – should not be dined with, nor should such a person be included when the afterblessings are recited (*Mishna Berura* 199).

While this approach may explain the harsh ruling, the original wording used is *am ha'aretz*, "the unlearned," a far milder term than "public sinner."

A different approach to the exclusionary nature of this rule is to explain that it is not referring to those who never had the opportunity to study. The rule refers to those who never bothered to exert the effort to study. It does not behoove Torah scholars to join with those who have consciously declined to take part in the learning endeavour (*Rosh*).

The identification of an *am ha'aretz*, however, is no simple matter. The Talmud offers a plethora of opinions as to who falls into this category and should therefore be excluded from a *Zimmun*. One opinion sets a particularly high standard: An *am ha'aretz* is anyone who is not particular to eat even normal, unconsecrated food in a state of ritual purity. Another opinion suggests that the law itself, not added stringencies, should be the benchmark. Thus an *am ha'aretz* is one who does not properly tithe produce.

Other yardsticks that are not food-related are suggested as well. One sage maintains that a person who does not recite *Shema* in the evening and in the morning is categorised as an *am ha'aretz*. Another sage understands the term to mean a man who does not don *tefillin*. A third opinion proposes that an *am ha'aretz* is a man who does not wear the fringed *tzitzit*, while a fourth sage cites the failure to fulfil the *mezuza* requirement as the defining parameter.

Other approaches focus not on the fulfilment of specific commandments, but on the general attitude toward Torah study. Thus one sage suggests that people who do not provide Torah education for their children are to be classified as *amei ha'aretz*. A final opinion suggests that an *am ha'aretz* is a person who studied Bible and learned the oral tradition, but did not take education to the next level by serving Torah scholars and acquiring true comprehension of the material. A later talmudic sage rules that this last definition is accepted as normative when determining whom to exclude from a *Zimmun*.

Despite discussing who might be classified as an *am ha'aretz* for purposes of exclusion from a *Zimmun* with the learned, commentators cite a tradition dating back to Hai Gaon (939–1038) that this rule is no longer applied. Indeed Jewish law no longer prevents the learned and the unlearned from joining together to form a *Zimmun* (*Shulḥan Arukh, Oraḥ Ḥayim* 199:3). The talmudic rule seems to be clear and undisputed. Why then is it rejected by later scholars? The commentators offer a number of explanations for this sharp change of direction.

A first approach focuses on the possible negative consequences of such a rule. In a different context in the Talmud, an opinion is expressed that *amei ha'aretz* should not be excluded because it might arouse their animosity (*B. Ḥagiga* 22a). So too, barring segments of the population from the *Zimmun* ritual is likely to result in hostilities within the community, with possible dire consequences for communal institutions.

A second approach highlights the problem with allowing a group to exclude someone on the grounds that that person is an *am ha'aretz* (*Tosafot*). Such a determination is not based upon a candid self-assessment of the barred person. It means the group handing down the decision is declaring themselves to be learned scholars, and on that basis barring the unlearned. Is a group really qualified to make such a determination?

A final approach suggested by one of the halakhists looks at the communal consequences of this rule. If the learned exclude the unlearned, it is likely that the unlearned will withdraw entirely from the community (*Magen Avraham*).

Let us explore this approach further. Excluding the unlearned was the result – not the goal – of the talmudic law. The purpose of the law was to encourage wider participation in Torah study and eliminate the phenomenon of *amei ha'aretz*. The hope was that by excluding the unlearned from *Zimmun*, they would be goaded to study so that they could be included. Indeed, the aim of promoting Torah study for all is an objective with which we strongly identify today.

It is not hard to imagine, however, that this rule may have had the opposite effect. Instead of aspiring to join the ranks of the learned, *amei ha'aretz* would have felt excluded and disenfranchised from the Torah enterprise. The gulf between the scholarly and the unschooled would have widened when they stopped eating together and joining together for *Zimmun* and Grace After Meals.

Sidelining the original talmudic dictum sends an inclusive and encouraging message of shared membership and participation in a joint venture. Normative halakha conveys that we are not a people divided into two classes – the learned and the unlearned, the educated and the illiterate – rather we are one people, one community, joining together to praise God.

BERAKHOT 47B–48A

Auspicious signs

THE MISHNA DECLARES that a minor cannot join a *Zimmun* (*M. Berakhot* 7:2). Despite this rule, the talmudic sages discuss possible scenarios in which minors could be included in the *Zimmun* (*B. Berakhot* 47b–48a). The Talmud concludes that of the various suggestions, there is only one licence for leniency that is accepted as normative law. A minor who understands that we recite blessings to the Almighty may be counted for *Zimmun* purposes. The prevailing custom, however, is that minors are not counted in the *Zimmun* until they come of age and are obligated to fulfil the commandments (*Rema, Oraḥ Ḥayim* 199:10).

The Talmud recounts an incident in which two minors showed that they understood to whom we direct blessings. Abbaye and Rava were two of the most prominent talmudic scholars. They grappled with inconsistencies in earlier rabbinic texts and offered resolutions for the discrepancies. Their dicta are regularly quoted and their rulings form the basis of further discussion. In fact, talmudic discussion as a whole is referred to as "the inquiries of Abbaye and Rava" (*B. Sukka* 28a; *B. Bava Batra* 134a).

The Talmud relates a tale from the early childhood of these talmudic heroes. The two of them were sitting before their teacher Rabba, and he asked them: "To whom do we recite blessings?"

The two children answered: "To the Merciful One."

Probing further, Rabba asked: "And where does this Merciful One dwell?"

The two children were too young to fully articulate an answer to such a deep question, but Rava pointed up at the ceiling of the *beit midrash*, while Abbaye ran outside and pointed to the sky. Their master Rabba was satisfied and felt that their answers heralded greatness. He predicted: "Both of you will grow up to be sages!"

The Talmud concludes the tale by quoting a popular adage: "Small pumpkins can be known from their sap." As soon as a sprouting pumpkin begins to bud, a trained eye can discern whether it will ripen into a good pumpkin. So too, a perceptive observer can tell from budding youngsters whether they are destined for greatness.

Not only did Rabba's astute comment prove to be accurate – indeed these two children went on to become talmudic sages of note – but the way Abbaye and Rava answered the question hinted at their individual futures as well. Abbaye, it appears, was more connected to God in heaven, while Rava was more in tune with the Divine Presence in the *beit midrash*.

The Talmud relates that Abbaye was greeted by the heavenly academy each Friday. Rava was granted such a privilege only once a year, on the eve of Yom Kippur. Another person – Abba the blood-letting surgeon – received such a greeting each day. Abbaye was distressed that he did not merit such frequent heavenly acknowledgment. After being told of the greatness of Abba the blood-letter, Abbaye decided to learn more about the surgeon and observe his conduct firsthand. The Talmud adds that Rava too felt distressed, since he did not merit a weekly salutation from heaven. Rava worried that he was less worthy than his colleague Abbaye, and he was placated only when told that he should not be concerned since the entire city was protected in his merit (*B. Ta'anit* 21b–22a). Significantly, Rava did not feel the need to investigate further those who received regular heavenly communiqués; once reassured of his righteousness, Rava was apparently satisfied with his annual salutation from heaven.

Whenever the two sages are mentioned together, Abbaye's name always precedes Rava's name. This may be because Abbaye served as the head of the talmudic academy before Rava (*B. Horayot* 14a), or it may be connected to Abbaye's unique heavenly connection.

In contrast to Abbaye, Rava was more in tune with the Divine Presence in the *beit midrash*. Thus normative law favours Rava's opinion over Abbaye's position, with only six exceptions (*B. Bava Metzia* 22b).

Elsewhere in the Talmud we find a typical argument between Abbaye and Rava that reflects the different foci of these two sages (*B. Rosh HaShana* 18a; *Rashi*). The Talmud tells us that a heavenly decree against a community can always be overturned by heartfelt remorse, unless the decree is coupled with a Divine oath. In such a case, even repentance cannot reverse the judgment. The source for this declaration is found in a biblical episode relating to Eli, who served as *Kohen Gadol* and judge. While Eli himself was righteous, his sons Hophni and Phinehas were not. Hophni and Phinehas disgraced their office by sending attendants to seize portions of slaughtered offerings to which they were not entitled (1 Samuel 2:12–17). Their misconduct went further and included licentious behaviour (ibid., 22–25; *B. Shabbat* 55b; *B. Yoma* 9b). A man of God came to Eli and told him that because of their behaviour, *There will not be an old man in your family line* (1 Samuel 2:31). The iniquity was so great that young Samuel prophesied in the name of God: *Therefore I have sworn concerning the House of Eli, that the sin of the*

House of Eli will never be atoned for by sacrifice or meal offering (ibid., 3:14). Thus the decree was irrevocable as it was accompanied by a Divine oath.

Rava and Abbaye agreed that while the verdict against the family could not be nullified, it could be mitigated in the case of specific descendants. Rava – who as a youngster had identified the Divine Presence inside the *beit midrash* – suggested that the decree could be negated through the study of Torah. Abbaye – who had perceived God beyond the confines of the *beit midrash* – suggested that the verdict could be ameliorated not only with Torah study, but also with acts of kindness.

The Talmud shows how the theoretical positions of Rava and Abbaye were expressed in their lives. Both sages were descendants of Eli. Rava, who dedicated his life to the study of Torah, avoided the dire verdict for twenty years. He lived to the age of forty – twenty years beyond the age of twenty when a person is considered liable for punishment (*B. Shabbat* 89b; *Y. Bikkurim* 2:11). Abbaye, who engaged in both Torah study and in acts of kindness, lived for sixty years.

Our children may seem like they are merely playing, waiting their turn to join the *Zimmun*. Yet in their actions, in their questions, and in their responses lie hidden signs of their destiny.

Mutual responsibility

THE JEWISH PEOPLE have a strong sense of mutual responsibility. We have a long and proud tradition of helping others and we rightly feel a duty to look after our brothers and sisters. Our sages have termed this sense of shared responsibility "*areivut*," and they often repeat the adage that *kol Yisrael areivim zeh bazeh*, all Jews are responsible for one another (*B. Shevuot* 39b).

The concept of *areivut* is not just a nebulous ideal; *areivut* has tangible legal implications. Even people who have discharged their own obligation to fulfil a Torah commandment – for instance, to say *kiddush* on Shabbat – still have a broader duty to facilitate others' discharging their obligation. Thus even if they have already made *kiddush* they are permitted to recite it a second time in order to facilitate others fulfilling their *kiddush* requirement (*B. Rosh HaShana* 29a). One commentator describes the *areivut* situation clearly: as long as your peers have not discharged their obligation, it is as if you have not discharged your own obligation since part of your obligation is that your peers fulfil their duty (*Ran*).

There appear, at first blush, to be exceptions to this rule: blessings recited over food, drink, and scent. In these cases, the law requires that the one who recites the blessing also partakes of the substance. A blessing reciter who has no intention to eat, drink, or smell cannot say the blessing for others. This rule, which appears to run contrary to the theme of *areivut*, is actually rooted in the *areivut* principle. Since there is no obligation to smell a rose, therefore there is no duty to facilitate that act by reciting the appropriate blessing for someone else (*Rashi*).

There is another qualification to the *areivut* principle. The legal status of the obligation of the facilitator needs to be equal to or weightier than that of the one who is being assisted. Thus a minor, fool, or deaf-mute – all of whom Torah law exempts from fulfilling the precepts – cannot blow the *shofar* for others on Rosh HaShana (*M. Rosh HaShana* 3:8). This principle is formulated in the Talmud as follows: one who is not obligated cannot discharge the obligation of others.

This limitation is at the root of a question asked in the Talmud (*B. Berakhot* 20b): Is a woman's obligation to recite Grace After Meals a Torah obligation or a rabbinic one? Without answering the question, the Talmud pounces and challenges: What difference does it make? Regardless of the source of the law, a woman must recite Grace After Meals! The Talmud explains that we need to categorise the requirement so that we can determine whose obligation she can discharge. If her obligation is on the level of Torah law, then she can discharge the obligation of another person who has that level of obligation. If, however, her obligation is the product of a rabbinic decree, she cannot discharge someone else's Torah-level obligation.

This limitation is colourfully illustrated in a talmudic tale (*B. Berakhot* 48a). Yannai, a Hasmonean king and *Kohen Gadol* in the Temple, was dining together with the queen and members of the court. Yannai had previously massacred the rabbis after one of them had suggested that he was not halakhically fit to serve in the Temple. Thus, as the meal drew to a close, there was no one to be found who could recite Grace After Meals (*B. Kiddushin* 66a).

Turning to his wife, Yannai lamented: "Who can bring someone who is able to recite Grace After Meals?"

The queen responded: "Swear to me that if I bring you someone, you will not persecute him." The king gave his word.

The queen brought her brother, Shimon ben Shetaḥ, the former head of the Sanhedrin who had been in hiding since the execution of the other rabbis. Yannai offered Shimon ben Shetaḥ the seat between the two monarchs.

"Do you see how much honour I am according you?" he pointedly asked the sage.

Citing a biblical verse – *Exalt her, and she will promote you; she will bring you to honour, when you embrace her* (Proverbs 4:8) – Shimon ben Shetaḥ sharply responded: "It is not you who accords me honour, rather it is the Torah!"

The ruler turned to his wife and exclaimed: "You see that he does not accept authority!" Yannai was intimating that massacring the rabbis was justified (*Rashash*).

A cup of wine was brought to the table, and Shimon ben Shetaḥ was expected to recite Grace After Meals with the cup in hand. The assumption was that the sage would discharge the obligation of those who had dined. Yet Shimon ben Shetaḥ had not partaken of any food.

"How should I recite the blessing?" he enquired impudently. "Shall I say 'Blessed is He of Whose bounty Yannai and his friends have eaten'?" The sage promptly drank that cup of wine, and another one was brought on which he could recite Grace After Meals. The Talmud objects to Shimon ben Shetaḥ's conduct, stating that in order to recite Grace After Meals drinking wine is insufficient; the reciter must have eaten bread. Despite this objection, it is apparent that the principle of *areivut* holds true: we have a shared responsibility to discharge each other's obligations.

So far we have explored the legal implications of the *areivut* principle. *Areivut*, however, demands far more than the mere discharging of obligations.

The forerunner of the Hasidic movement, Rabbi Yisrael Ba'al Shem Tov (c. 1700–1760), known by the acronym Besht, is often quoted as offering a deeper explanation of the rule that one who is not obligated cannot discharge the obligation of others. Leaders who are "not obligated" – meaning, they are not truly committed to their constituents – cannot liberate others from their quagmires. Only if the leaders are with the people in the trenches can they hope to fulfil their duties and provide for their constituents.

Mutual responsibility is not just about discharging legal obligations on behalf of others. If this was the sole expression of *areivut*, then *areivut* would be a rather formal and shallow principle. *Areivut* involves much more. The Besht is credited with a vivid description of *areivut*: You cannot pull someone from a muddy bog by standing at a safe distance, intent on not getting dirty. A deep concern for our brothers and sisters may at times require us to muddy ourselves as we help others. This is true *areivut*.

BERAKHOT 48B

Grace After Meals

AT THE CONCLUSION of every meal we thank the Almighty for the nourishment we have been given. *Birkat HaMazon*, Grace After Meals, is not just an expression of thanks. Rather, the text of this prayer reflects central Jewish themes and recounts key historical episodes. The Talmud records the history of the composition of Grace After Meals, highlighting the historical context of each of its four sections (*B. Berakhot* 48b).

The first section speaks of God-given sustenance. The Talmud tells us that this paragraph was instituted by Moses when the manna fell from heaven in the desert and nourished the wandering Jewish people. In this section we thank the Almighty for the continued nourishment bestowed upon us, and indeed upon all living things. Thus the blessing concludes: "Blessed are You, O God, Who gives sustenance to all."

The second section was instituted by Joshua when the fledgling nation entered the Land of Israel. This passage recognises the Divine gift of our homeland. It recounts the Exodus from Egypt, tells of our covenant with the Almighty, and mentions the Torah that serves as the hub of our relationship with God. The culmination of our liberation, of the covenant, and of the Torah is possession of our own land, where we can flourish as a people following the Almighty. This blessing thanks God for everything and concludes: "Blessed are You, O God, for the Land and for the food."

The third part of Grace After Meals is attributed to two authors: King David and his son King Solomon. The Talmud explains that David composed the first part of this blessing, which refers to the Jewish nation and its central city, Jerusalem. When referring to the nation's capital, the Bible merely mentions *the place that God, your Lord, will choose* (Deuteronomy 12:5), without specifying the location of the chosen place. King David was the first Jewish sovereign to make Jerusalem his capital. While Jerusalem lay on the border of two tribes – Judah and Benjamin – King David chose this border city as the capital, broadcasting that the Jewish people are not a conglomerate of different tribes descended from one ancestor; they are a united nation. Jerusalem is therefore not a border town on the seam between the lands of two tribes; it is a city deep in the heart of a nation.

King David's son and successor, King Solomon, continued the work of his father by building the Temple in the capital city. To the blessing of his father, King Solomon added a mention of the Temple: "The great and holy House over which Your name is proclaimed." This blessing signs off with the words: "Blessed are You, O God, Who in His compassion rebuilds Jerusalem."

Later authorities note that the text which we have before us could not have been the text recited by King David and King Solomon, for they had no need to request the rebuilding of Jerusalem. Instead, they prayed for continued peace and tranquillity in the land, stability in government, and permanence of the Temple (*Tur*). David and Solomon – according to one codifier – concluded their blessing with the phrase: "Blessed are You, O God, Who sustains Jerusalem" (*Abudraham*). Thus the two rulers set the theme for this third part of Grace After Meals without coining the exact words that we say.

While the first three sections of Grace After Meals reflect central themes of our existence and destiny, the fourth part refers to a particular historic episode. During the reign of Hadrian, a Roman emperor in the second century, Bar Kokhba led an uprising against Roman rule. When the Roman overlords crushed the rebellion, they took revenge by massacring innumerable people in the city of Beitar. The reprisal did not stop there. The Romans also forbade the burial of the slaughtered people. Their bodies were left strewn in the streets of Beitar to be scavenged by vultures.

Some time later, the rabbinic court in Yavne under the leadership of Rabban Gamliel, fasted and prayed for a reversal of this cruel decision. At great personal expense, Rabban Gamliel bribed the Roman oppressors to permit the burial of those killed in Beitar. Finally permission was granted. When the Jews went to bury the murdered people, they found that their bodies had not decayed. The Yavne rabbinic court then instituted the fourth section of Grace After Meals, entitled *HaTov VeHaMetiv* – "[God] Who is good and Who confers good." The Talmud explains the double language. We say "Who is good" because miraculously the bodies did not decompose; we say "Who confers good" because ultimately the slain people were accorded a proper burial.

Why was this blessing included in Grace After Meals? One commentator explains that the massacre at Beitar damaged the dignity of Israel. Our honour will be restored when Jerusalem is rebuilt. Thus this fourth section is a continuation of the previous benediction's request for the reconstruction of Jerusalem (*Rosh*).

Another commentator suggests that the thankful benediction of *HaTov VeHaMetiv* befits the joyous atmosphere of a feast (*Abudraham*). Appropriately, a shortened form of this blessing is recited upon propitious rainfall or upon hearing good news (*M. Berakhot* 9:2). The shortened form is recited even if someone drinking wine is brought a second glass of wine that is of better quality than the first one (*B. Berakhot* 59b).

A final explanation of the inclusion of the *HaTov VeHaMetiv* blessing offers an insight into the symbolism of this benediction (*Tzlaḥ*). The bodies of the slaughtered did not decompose. Similarly, though we are physically exiled, we do not decay. The spirit of our people retains its vitality, even as we pray for a complete redemption. We say "Who is good" thanking the Almighty for ensuring that we do not rot in physical exile; we say "Who confers good" thanking the Almighty for ensuring that we will be granted a spiritual reprieve in the future.

BERAKHOT 48B

Thank you

JEWISH TRADITION MANDATES blessings before and after eating. By sincerely reciting blessings we acknowledge God's role in providing sustenance, thereby elevating the mundane, physical necessity of dining to a Divine plane. *Birkat HaMazon*, Grace After Meals, is the only food-related blessing for which the Talmud (*B. Berakhot* 48b) identifies a biblical source: *And you will eat and you will be satisfied and you will bless the Lord your God for the good land that He has given you* (Deuteronomy 8:10). As such, Grace After Meals is the prototypical blessing.

A legal requirement to give thanks would seem to reflect a sorry state of affairs. If there is truly abundant goodness, shouldn't we thank God reflexively? A close reading of the biblical passage from which the obligation to say Grace After Meals is derived may bolster our question. As the Italian scholar and poet Shmuel David Luzzatto (1800–1865) – commonly known by the acronym Shadal – points out, the verse is not phrased as an instruction. Rather, the Bible is notifying us that our goodness will be so bountiful and our success so unbridled that we will recognise God's kindness and be naturally inspired to bless the Almighty.

The appropriate response to prosperity is to thank and bless the provider of that goodness. Common courtesy dictates an expression of thanks whenever we receive something.

If thanking is the obvious response to the granting of goodness and if there is no biblical source requiring a blessing, why did the sages mandate Grace After Meals?

Reading on in the biblical passage, we are immediately confronted with a warning: *Beware lest you forget the Lord your God.... Lest when you have eaten and are satisfied and have built fine houses and dwelled in them, and when your herds and your flocks multiply, and your silver and gold have increased and everything you own has prospered, your heart will be haughty and you will forget the Lord your God* (Deuteronomy 8:11–14). While a show of gratitude is the fitting response, it is not always the actual one. Even if it is human nature to bless God for Divinely provided goodness, with the passage of time that goodness may be taken for granted. Those who have prospered may find it challenging to recall another reality.

Not realising how privileged we are is not the only possible negative consequence of prosperity. An even worse state of forgetfulness can ensue, whereby the affluent dismiss God's providing hand and credit themselves for their good fortune. The Bible warns against this as well: *And you will say in your heart, "My own power and the might of my own hand have attained this wealth for me"* (Deuteronomy 8:17). A verse in Moses' final poetic speech to the Jewish people traces the progression from prosperity to rejection of God: *But Yeshurun* – referring to Israel – *grew fat and kicked; / you grew fat and thick and gross. / Then he forsook the God Who made him / and spurned the Rock of his deliverance* (Deuteronomy 32:15).

In truth, giving thanks is never an easy task. Our sages note that from the time of the world's creation there was no one who thanked God until our foremother Leah came along and thanked the Almighty (*B. Berakhot* 7b). This declaration is based on Leah's statement when she named her son Judah: *Now I will thank the Lord* (Genesis 29:35).

Extolling Leah for thanking God is surprising, as she expressed her appreciation only after her fourth son was born. Moreover, even this expression of thanks seems somewhat tainted: the phrase "*Now I will thank*" implies that she did not feel compelled to thank God for her fortune in bearing the first three boys. Surely her co-wife Rachel, who was pining for offspring, would have been devastated to hear her sister thank God only for her fourth child.

Our sages explain that Leah prophetically saw that Jacob was to father twelve sons, and she presumed that each of his four wives would bear three sons. Upon the birth of her fourth son, Leah thanked God for granting her more than her allotment (*Bereshit Rabba* 71:4).

Though we can understand Leah's elation at bearing a fourth son, this hardly mitigates her lack of an expression of gratitude upon the births of three healthy children!

Alas, expressions of appreciation may not always be the natural response to good fortune. The biblical notion of blessing God in the wake of feeling nourished and satisfied might not be describing an instinctive reaction; it might be giving voice to the ideal response. With this understanding we can appreciate why the sages translate the biblical description of eating, being satisfied, and blessing into the commandment to recite Grace After Meals.

As parents we encourage our children to develop the good habit of saying "thank you." Even though this may be an emotionless and mechanical expression, we aim to increase our children's sense of appreciation, encouraging them to be grateful for what they receive. Similarly, the sages mandate blessings, not because they are in favour of cold and detached words of thanks, but rather because they are trying to inculcate feelings of gratitude for the goodness that God bestows upon us.

BERAKHOT 48B

Part of the Divine plan

WHEN THE TIME arrived for the appointment of the first king of Israel, the Bible describes a Divinely orchestrated series of events that led to Saul's coronation (1 Samuel 9). The donkeys of Kish, Saul's father, went missing. Kish asked his son to go with one of the servants to look for them. Saul and his companion undertook a long search; their quest, however, bore no fruit. Saul was prepared to return empty-handed to his father. Before giving up, the attendant suggested that they make a final attempt at locating the missing donkeys: *Behold now, there is in this city a person of God and he is an honourable person; all that he says is sure to come true. Now let us go there, perhaps he can show us the way that we should go* (verse 6).

After some coaxing, Saul agreed. As they neared the city, they met girls going to draw water. *"Is the seer here?"* they enquired of the girls (verse 11).

The girls responded: *He is. Behold he is before you; make haste now, for today he came to the city, for the people are making a sacrifice today at the high place. When you come into the city you will find him, before he goes up to the high place to eat; for the people will not eat until he comes, because he blesses the sacrifice and afterwards those who are invited eat. Now go up, for about this time you will find him* (verses 12–13).

This long-winded answer intrigues the sages. Was such a lengthy response necessary? The Talmud presents three explanations for the drawn-out answer (*B. Berakhot* 48b).

First, the Talmud suggests that women are generally chatterboxes. The girls were merely gossiping and there is no deeper meaning to be sought in the biblical exchange. This approach may offend modern sensibilities. More importantly, it goes against the grain of our understanding of the Bible, where every passage, every phrase, every word, and even every letter contains some lesson.

A second approach explains that the girls wanted to gaze at Saul on account of his striking appearance. The biblical verse describes Saul's physical features: *From his shoulders up, he was taller than any of the people* (verse 2). Saul's height was his most prominent feature, and it would be conspicuous at his coronation (1 Samuel 10:23). Seeing this handsome man before them, the girls sought to detain Saul by engaging him in conversation. This explains why the girls' lengthy response is recorded. As part of the biblical description of Saul's eye-catching appearance, it is an integral part of the narrative. Alas, it still does not paint a positive view of the women who were captivated by mere external appearances. In fact, a later midrashic compilation records a somewhat forceful rejection of this approach (*Yalkut Shimoni*, Samuel 108): "If this is your approach, then you have relegated the daughters of Israel to the level of harlots!"

This incident gives rise to conflicting opinions in Jewish law as to the propriety of women looking at men. The issue is relevant in various contemporary scenarios. May a mother supervise her son at a swimming pool during the time set aside for men's swimming? Is it appropriate for a female photographer to photograph men?

The Talmud does not seem to condemn the girls. It records their conduct using neutral language. The Midrash, on the other hand, clearly deems women watching men as inappropriate. Thus the Midrash renders the principle: "Just as men should not feast their eyes on women whom they are not permitted to be with, so too women should not feast their eyes on men who are not theirs."

The symmetry expressed by the Midrash is taken up by later sources. Rabbi Yehuda HeHasid (1140–1217), in his work *Sefer Hasidim*, states that just as a man should not listen to a woman's voice, so too a woman should not listen to a man's voice. He adds that whatever is forbidden to a man is also forbidden to a woman. Similarly, *Sefer HaHinukh*, the thirteenth-century Spanish work by an anonymous author, takes an egalitarian position and asserts that women should not think about men other than their husbands. This path – states *Sefer HaHinukh* – is appropriate for upstanding Jewish girls.

As opposed to this, many halakhists – following the accepted rules of halakhic decision-making – have opted for the position of the Talmud over that of the Midrash. Thus, for instance, Chief Rabbi Ovadia Yosef (1920–2013) writes that women not looking at men is classified as a *humra*, a stringency rather than a law.

Besides the halakhic implications, the different understandings of the Talmud and Midrash describe the nature of women's attraction to men. It is therefore unsurprising that our male sages express differing opinions on the matter!

Let us return to our sages' discussion. A third approach to the longwinded answer is suggested in both the Talmud and the Midrash. The delay was Divinely arranged since the reign of one ruler must not encroach upon the reign of another, even by a mere hair's breadth.

At that time the leader of the Jewish people was Samuel the prophet, who served as judge. At the upcoming meeting of Samuel and Saul, the mantle of leadership would pass to Saul. Samuel's responsibilities, however, had not yet been completed, so the time for the propitious meeting had yet to arrive. The Almighty had the girls deliver a lengthy response so that the encounter and leadership transfer would occur at exactly the designated moment.

Even if the girls were chatterers, even if they were intent on gazing at Saul's beauty, their actions weren't meaningless. While the girls may have been unaware of it, they were in fact fulfilling a God-determined mission. The invisible Divine hand was guiding every move, so that the first sovereign of Israel would be anointed at exactly the right time, in exactly the right place. The thrust of the entire biblical account with the innocuous lost donkeys seems to fit well with this.

What a refreshing approach! All of us – women and men – have a role to play in the Divine plan. We may not even be aware of our mission. God, however, is.

BERAKHOT 49B

Olive-sized

WHEN IS A nibble or a taste defined as eating? We may recall as children being warned not to snack before dinner so as not to ruin our appetites, but for halakhic purposes this is hardly a standardised yardstick for what might be considered "eating." In normative terms, when is eating deemed eating?

The practical implication of this question lies in the requirement to intone Grace After Meals. How much must one eat in order to be obligated to recite Grace After Meals? Our sages dispute this minimum amount (*B. Berakhot* 49b). Should it be the volume of an average olive? Or should it be double that amount; that is, the volume of an average egg with its shell?

An extension of this dispute is reflected in the mishna that discusses *Zimmun* (*M. Berakhot* 7:2). There are two opinions as to when a person has sufficiently partaken of the meal such that he can be included in a *Zimmun*. Normative law rules that the standard volume is the mass of an olive (*Shulḥan Arukh, Oraḥ Ḥayim* 184:6).

The question of a benchmark is not only a culinary issue; other laws also use the olive measure as a gauge. For instance, contracting ritual impurity from a dead body can occur only by touching this minimum standard amount of human flesh (*M. Oholot* 2:1).

While an olive is the most common measure, it is not the only volume standard in Jewish law. Transgressing the grievous sin of eating on Yom Kippur is defined using a different measure: the average volume of a plump date – an amount that is larger than an olive but smaller than an egg. While eating less than that amount is not permitted, punishment can only be incurred once the prescribed volume has been ingested (*B. Yoma* 73b–74a). The reason that punishable eating on Yom Kippur is defined by the larger measure – the date and not the olive – is because the biblical verse does not specify a prohibition against eating. The Bible requires a person to feel afflicted on Yom Kippur (Leviticus 23:29), and this is understood to mean that people should be hungry such that they have difficulty concentrating. According to tradition, average people remain in this state until they have eaten the volume of a date (*B. Yoma* 80a–b).

Nevertheless, the volume of an olive is the most widely used standard and defines almost all matters of eating (*B. Berakhot* 41a–b). For instance, on Pesaḥ we eat at least an olive's worth of *matza* and of *maror* to fulfil the obligations of the *seder* night.

One Hasidic master, Rabbi Avraham Yehoshua Heshel of Opatów (1745–1825), comments on the olive measure. The *Ohev Yisrael*, Lover of Israel – as he is affectionately called on his epitaph and as the compilation of his talks is entitled – was a large person. Later Hasidic masters used to say that the Ohev Yisrael was able to serve the Almighty by eating, just as others did by fasting. No stranger to food, the Ohev Yisrael sought the deeper significance of the olive as the minimum eating standard.

The Ohev Yisrael discusses two mystical properties of the olive that are mentioned in the Talmud. On the one hand, the sages tell us that eating a plethora of olives can precipitate forgetfulness. On the other hand, liberally using olive oil is an elixir for memory. According to one of the sages – just as olives can make a person forget seventy years of learning, so too olive oil can restore seventy years of study (*B. Horayot* 13b; *B. Menaḥot* 85b).

The mystical polarity of the olive is reflected in the nature of the fruit. As long as an olive remains in its original form, it has a bitter taste. It is at this acrid stage that the olive causes forgetfulness. The precious oil that can be extracted from the olive, however, is among the most prized of liquids and can serve as a memory potion.

After surveying the properties of the olive, the Ohev Yisrael goes on to explain why the olive is the fruit that defines eating. If a person who is eating considers the exterior nature of the food only, then such a meal is a bitter experience, for the food answers only a base need and has no spiritual valence. In contrast, when a person looks past the raw food and considers the concealed potential of the substance – namely, the power of a physical object to animate us – then eating suddenly takes on a new spiritual dimension. Our eating, therefore, is akin to olives. It is a quest to discover the value of the food; value which is invisible to the insensitive eye.

The olive plays an important role not only in Jewish law, but also in Jewish lore. The dove returned to Noah with an olive branch in its mouth as a symbol that the destructive waters of the deluge had begun to recede and that life was sprouting anew (Genesis 8:11). This dove and olive branch would later be adopted as the international symbol of peace. Further in the Bible, the Land of Israel is called the land of olive oil and honey (Deuteronomy 8:8), and the olive is among the seven species with which the Land of Israel is blessed.

Significantly, the shield of the modern State of Israel – chosen on the eleventh of Shevat 5709, February 10, 1949 – is a *menora* bordered by two olive branches. This mirrors the prophetic vision of Zechariah: *I have looked, and behold a* menora *entirely of gold with a bowl on the top of it… and two olive [trees] by it, one on the right of the bowl and one on its left* (Zechariah 4:2–3).

Perhaps we can offer a broader perspective, inspired by the Ohev Yisrael's perspective on eating. The symbol of the State of Israel invites us to look beyond the physical entity of the modern state. As bitter as it sometimes may seem, the State of Israel has a rich, hidden dimension. We are beckoned to focus on the deeper significance of the independence we have in our ancestral homeland, with the hope of taking the raw, olive-like product and extracting the rich Divine essence contained within.

The wicked child

THE MISHNA DISCUSSES the impact that the number of participants has on the wording of the *Zimmun*, the invitation to recite Grace After Meals as a group (*M. Berakhot* 7:3).

First, to what extent should the mention and praise of God reflect an increase in the number of participants? The first opinion in the Mishna presents a two-tiered *Zimmun* system. For three to nine diners the opening line of the *Zimmun* formula is: "Let us bless the One Whose food we have eaten." If ten or more diners are present, we add the Almighty's name and say: "Let us bless our Lord Whose food we have eaten." The mention of God's name is appropriate when a congregation of ten is present (*M. Megilla* 4:3).

We are familiar with this approach because it is the accepted halakhic practice. As Rabbi Akiva explains in the Mishna, it is reflected in all our prayer rites: Once the threshold of ten is reached, more participants do not further affect the wording of the prayer.

The alternative opinion suggests that for each significant increase in the number of people participating in the *Zimmun*, the language of the *Zimmun* is altered. Whereas the first opinion acknowledges only the difference between fewer than ten and ten or more participants, this view recognises multiple tiers – three, ten, one hundred, one thousand, and ten thousand. Each increase justifies its own unique *Zimmun* formulation. Thus for one hundred diners the *mezamen,* the one who initiates the invitation to recite Grace After Meals, says: "Let us bless God, our Lord." If there are one thousand diners, the wording changes to: "Let us bless God, our Lord and the Lord of Israel." If we have a myriad of people eating together, the *Zimmun* formula is even more expansive in mentioning God: "Let us bless God, our Lord and the Lord of Israel, Lord of hosts, Who dwells by the cherubim."

A second aspect of the *Zimmun* formula is also discussed in the Mishna. The *mezamen* must check to see if the quorum includes him or if there is a quorum besides him. If there are three diners then the formula, as we have seen, is: "Let us bless." If there are three in addition to the *mezamen,* he turns to them in second person and instructs: "You should bless."

The Talmud declares that this second rule – changing the wording if there is a quorum besides the leader – should not be implemented. The Talmud explains that it is rejected since a person should never exclude himself from the group. Thus when there are four diners the *mezamen* should use the inclusive language of "Let us bless" (*B. Berakhot* 49b–50a; *Y. Berakhot* 54b).

Similarly, concluding the *Zimmun* by saying *uvetuvo ḥayinu* – "through Whose goodness we live" – reflects wisdom, while saying *uvetuvo ḥayim* – "through Whose goodness they live" – reflects ignorance, for this wording excludes the one reciting the words from the group of those who live through Divine goodness.

The principle that one should not exclude oneself from the group also appears in other contexts in the Talmud (*B. Ta'anit* 11a). Our sages praise people who minimise their eating during years of famine. Similarly, those who already have children and choose to refrain from marital relations during years of famine are lauded as well. The self-imposed abstinence reflects solidarity with the plight of the community and is therefore acclaimed.

The Talmud goes further, offering a vivid depiction of those who choose to do the opposite. At a time when the people of Israel are steeped in distress, if a person separates himself from the community and does not share their pain, the two guardian angels that accompany this person place their hands on his head and declare: "This person who has separated from the community shall not witness the consolation of the community when salvation arrives." The Talmud concludes on a more positive note by stating the opposite as well: Anyone who suffers together with the community will be privileged to witness its future consolation. This adage is quoted in codes of law (*Shulḥan Arukh, Oraḥ Ḥayim* 574:5).

In his code, Maimonides points out that one who separates from the community is effectively locking the door to the path of repentance, for when the community repents, the loner is not with them and does not have a share in their merits.

In this context it is worth mentioning an approach that is found a number of times in the Zohar. If one separates from the community, then he is judged alone. This judgment is exacting and involves scrutinising his every move. Alas, a positive outcome is unlikely (*Zohar* 1:69b, 1:160b, 2:33b, 2:44b).

The severity of leaving the group is starkly portrayed in the Pesaḥ Haggada, in the famous passage that describes the four children: the wise, the wicked, the simple, and the one who knows not how to ask. The Haggada tells us that the wicked child asks: "What is this service to you?" What is so wicked about this question? It would appear that the child is confounded by the Pesaḥ rites and turns to his parents for an explanation. Why then is this second child labelled as the wicked child? The Haggada does not detail any other conduct of the second child that would justify calling him "wicked"; in fact, he appears to be participating in the *seder* together with the rest of the family.

The Haggada immediately explains. The problem is the child's attitude, which is reflected in the language of the question. The child asks "What is this service *to you*," indicating that this service is relevant "to you" but not to him! "Since he has excluded himself from the community, it is as if he has denied that which is fundamental." The wicked child commits one cardinal sin: he excludes himself from the community.

It is no wonder, then, that the sages laud those who feel the pain of the community in its most distressing times. Our *Zimmun* formula – and indeed all our liturgy – advocates inclusive language and communal solidarity. We eat together, we pray together, and hopefully we are answered together.

The giver, not the gift

HAVING DISCUSSED THE appropriate phrases for the *Zimmun*, the Talmud turns to the exact wording of these phrases (*M. Berakhot* 7:3; *B. Berakhot* 50a). The final words of the *Zimmun* acknowledge the Almighty's goodness in granting us sustenance.

One sage comments: "From a person's recitation of blessings, it is discernible whether that person is a Torah scholar or not." The passage continues, saying that if the one reciting the *Zimmun* says, "Let us bless the One Whose food we have eaten and through Whose goodness (*uvetuvo*) we live," this indicates that the person is wise. If an ever so slightly different wording concludes the statement, "and from Whose goodness (*umituvo*) we live," this is a sign of an ignoramus.

What is the difference between the two phrases: *uvetuvo* – "through Whose goodness," as opposed to *umituvo* – "from Whose goodness"? In Hebrew it is a difference of only one letter. What does this one-letter variation reveal about the reciter?

One commentator explains that "through Whose goodness we live" indicates the Almighty's unbounded goodwill. In contrast, saying "from Whose goodness we live" suggests that from amidst God's unlimited ability to bestow goodness, the Almighty chooses to grant us only a fraction, perhaps even a minimal amount, to enable us to live. This one-letter variation reflects whether we praise the Almighty in a maximal or minimal fashion (*Rashi*).

The Talmud questions this assertion by citing a verse from a prayer of King David: *And from Your blessing, may the house of Your servant be blessed forever* (11 Samuel 7:29). King David, it seems, used a similar phrase to the *Zimmun* recitation of an ignoramus. The ignoramus says *umituvo* – "from Whose goodness," and King David turns to the Almighty and requests *umibirkhatkha* – "from Your blessing." What is the difference between King David and the ignoramus? The Talmud answers that when thanking the Almighty for His goodness – as in the case of a *Zimmun* – there is no need to limit our praise; when asking for God's benevolence – as in the case of King David – we should be unassuming and present a modest request.

Citing a further biblical verse, the Talmud offers an exception to the rule of modest requests. *Open your mouth widely* – says the Almighty in reference to our requests – *and I will fill it* (Psalms 81:11). This verse, the Talmud explains, refers to grasping the depths of Torah, and in this area we are encouraged not to limit our appeals.

Thus the bottom line is that when we are acknowledging the Almighty's beneficence we should not limit our praise; when petitioning God we should be more reserved, unless we are asking for assistance in comprehending Torah. Apart from the realm of Torah study, the unlimited nature of God's philanthropy should not be called upon; it should only be acknowledged after the fact.

The beloved Hasidic master Rabbi Levi Yitzhak of Berdyczów (1740–1810) was a leader known to flout propriety in his conversations with God. He suggests an entirely different structure, recommending that we indeed call on the Almighty's unbounded benevolence when making our requests.

Rabbi Levi Yitzhak explains: On the High Holy Days, as we stand in prayer beseeching the Almighty, what should we ask for? The primary request of each person should be that God grant goodness to all. The basis of our request should not be because we are deserving; rather, we base our request on the notion that the Creator is merciful and bestows goodness and unlimited kindness upon us. Before the Almighty King we should stand as paupers asking for beneficence, even if we are undeserving. We should ask for all God's goodness, not just a minimal measure.

Why is this the recommended course? Rabbi Levi Yitzhak continues: If we stand before the Almighty on our own merits, we may be found lacking. Since our merits are certainly measurable and finite, there is the unfortunate possibility that they may not suffice for our requests. However, when we simply throw ourselves on the mercy of the Almighty, we are not limited by our worthiness, and so we can ask for the unlimited.

Rabbi Levi Yitzḥak offers a proof text: *I will mention the acts of God's kindness and the praises of God, according to all that God has bestowed upon us, and the great goodness toward the House of Israel which He has bestowed on them according to His mercies and according to the abundance of His kindness* (Isaiah 63:7). When is there *great goodness toward the House of Israel?* Rabbi Levi Yitzḥak answers: when it comes from *the abundance of His kindness.*

Another Hasidic source may be expressing a similar sentiment with regard to daily prayers. In his early eighteenth-century kabbalistic prayer book, Rabbi Shabbetai of Raszków writes that at the end of the *Amida*, the silent prayer, a person should "not expect any favour, heaven forbid." This may indicate that the basis of the *Amida* entreaties should not be the merits of the supplicant.

Let us return to Rabbi Levi Yitzḥak. He continues with a parable. A king gave the same gift to two of his subjects. The first recipient was excited, because the gift was truly valuable; the second was thrilled as well, but for a different reason. "How lucky I am to receive a present from the king," he thought. For the second recipient, the present indicated a special relationship with the king. The first recipient's enthusiasm was defined by – and limited to – the value of the gift. The excitement of the second beneficiary was unbounded, for he valued the giver rather than the gift.

As we stand before the Almighty in prayer, we can choose our path. We can follow the talmudic outline, modestly requesting the minimum and lavishly heaping blessings for the Almighty's past kindnesses. Alternatively, we can follow the suggestion of Rabbi Levi Yitzḥak, standing before God not on the basis of our own limited merits, but relying on God's boundless benevolence and asking for all of God's goodness. Regardless of which path of prayer we choose, we should look to the Giver and not to the gift.

Wisdom at the dinner table

L ET US CONTINUE the discussion of the language used in the
Zimmun. As we have seen, the sages declare that from one's choice
of words it can be discerned whether that person is wise or not. A few
salient examples – discussed in greater depth above – are offered: If a
person reciting the *Zimmun* says in reference to God: *uvetuvo* – "and
through Whose goodness" – this is a sign of wisdom, for the statement
does not limit the Almighty's goodness. However, if the person says:
umituvo – "and from Whose goodness" – this is a sign of an ignoramus,
for the use of the term "from" seems to minimise the measure of
Divine goodness we enjoy. Along the same lines, saying: *uvetuvo
ḥayinu* – "through Whose goodness we live" – reflects wisdom; while
saying: *uvetuvo ḥayim* – "through Whose goodness they live" – reflects
ignorance, for the latter version excludes the one reciting the words from
the group of those who live through Divine goodness (*B. Berakhot* 50a).

Rabbi Yehuda Tzadka (1910–1991) expands the scope of these
talmudic dicta. Born in Jerusalem to a prominent rabbinic family from
Baghdad, Rabbi Tzadka went on to become the head of Yeshivat Porat
Yosef. In this position, he taught the most prominent Sephardic rabbis
of our day, including former Chief Rabbis Ovadia Yosef (1920–2013)
and Mordekhai Eliyahu (1929–2010).

Once, a person seeking a certain rabbinic post came to Rabbi
Tzadka to obtain a letter of recommendation. The young applicant
assumed that Rabbi Tzadka would test his Torah knowledge so that he
could confirm the candidate's appropriateness for the position. To the
candidate's surprise, Rabbi Tzadka simply invited him in and offered
him a cup of tea.

The young man took the cup of tea and began to recite the
blessing. As he did so, Rabbi Tzadka leaned forward to observe closely
whether he would recite the blessing with concentration. When he

realised that the recitation of the blessing was merely lip service and did not come from the heart, he refused to sign the letter of recommendation attesting to the candidate's scholarship. "Wisdom is reflected in a person's blessings," asserted Rabbi Tzadka.

Scholarship is not usually measured by eating. Yet our sages are telling us that in addition to noting people's table manners and eating habits, conduct at the table may be used to gauge wisdom. As examples, the Talmud refers to the choice of words used for the invitation to recite Grace After Meals, while Rabbi Tzadka used the blessings recited before eating as a yardstick.

We might suggest that even conduct during the meal – unrelated to the recitation of blessings before and after eating – can tell us much about the wisdom of our dinner company.

The Bible states *A wise person's eyes are in his head* (Ecclesiastes 2:14), meaning that a wise person looks ahead. The sages tell us that Alexander the Great posed ten questions to the Elders of the South (*B. Tamid* 31b–32a). One of the questions he asked was: "Who is considered a wise person?"

The Elders of the South responded: "Who is a wise person? One who perceives future developments."

When we sit down to dinner we may be famished and tempted to pile far too much delicious food on our plates. Wise people, however, have a good idea of how much they are going to eat. To decide how much food to take, they use their heads rather than their stomachs.

There are other character traits that our sages highlight as heralding a lack of wisdom. While these mannerisms are not directly connected to eating, they are often revealed when we dine together. Our sages tell us that wise people who act haughtily will lose their wisdom. Similarly, wise people who get angry are also prone to losing their wisdom (*B. Pesaḥim* 66b). Exhibiting haughtiness or displaying anger at the dinner table portend a lack of wisdom.

Choosing to sit with others may also diagnose the level of wisdom. The Talmud tells us that wise people who study alone are likely to become foolish since they have no one to challenge their assumptions or correct their mistakes (*B. Berakhot* 63b). Perhaps the same may be said of those who eat alone.

The dinner table is hardly the place to assess intellectual faculties. Yet our blessings, our eating habits, our conduct, and even the company we choose are all indicative of our wisdom.

Open wide your little mouth

A S W E H A V E seen, the Talmud suggests guidelines for relating to the Almighty's beneficence (*B. Berakhot* 50a). First, when thanking God we should be expansive in our praise, with profuse appreciation for all God's benevolence. Second, when petitioning God we should humbly beseech the Almighty, limiting our requests rather than audaciously asking for huge favours. Third, when petitioning God for assistance in Torah we need not be reserved at all.

This final recommendation, which at first blush appears to contradict the rule about modest requests, is based on the verse which cites the Almighty as saying: *Open your mouth widely, and I will fill it* (Psalms 81:11). The instruction *open your mouth widely* is understood to mean that we should request unlimited Divine goodness in Torah matters. Thus when asking God for physical well-being our requests should be modest. Not so when we ask the Almighty for Torah; regarding spiritual pursuits, we may ask for bountiful blessing.

In truth, we have biblical precedents for not limiting our requests of the Almighty when it comes to the spiritual realm. After Moses was banned from entering the Promised Land, he repeatedly beseeched the Almighty to revoke the decree (Deuteronomy 3:23–25). One of the talmudic sages asks: Why did Moses so desperately desire to enter the Land of Israel? Did he need to eat the fruit of the land? Did he need to sate himself with the bounty of the land? Undoubtedly it was not for these physical benefits that Moses sought to enter the Land of Israel! Rather, Moses said to himself: "There are many *mitzvot* that the Jewish people have been commanded and that can be fulfilled only in the Land of Israel; I need to enter the land so that I will have the opportunity to fulfil those commandments" (*B. Sota* 14a). According to tradition, of the 613 commandments only 270 *mitzvot* – the numerical value of the Hebrew word *ra*, meaning evil – can be fulfilled in the Diaspora; the remaining 343 *mitzvot* – the numerical value of the Hebrew word *geshem*, meaning rain – apply only in the Land of Israel.

Alas, Moses' request to enter the Land of Israel where he would have the opportunity to fulfil more *mitzvot* was not granted. However, not all such requests are rejected.

When the first commemoration of the Exodus approached, some of the Jews wandering in the desert were ineligible to offer the Pesah sacrifice. Everyone took part in this festival except for those who were ritually impure because they had come into contact with the body of a dead person (Numbers 9:6–14).

Our sages ask: Who were these people and why were they impure? The sages offer three possible answers. First, they may have been the pallbearers who were carrying the coffin of Joseph from Egypt to the Promised Land. A second suggestion identifies the ritually impure as the two sons of Aaron, Mishael and Elzaphan, who had recently buried their brothers Nadab and Abihu. A third approach does not identify the ritually impure or the deceased as any known personalities, but rather says they were merely people who had performed the *mitzva* of burying the dead (*Sifrei, Beha'alotekha* 10). One medieval commentator explains that with such a large population wandering through the desert, it would be nigh impossible for a day to go by without someone dying (*Ibn Ezra*).

All these reasons have a common theme. Those who were ritually impure were not culpable for their state and therefore could be excused for missing the Paschal sacrifice. Elsewhere the Talmud acknowledges this when discussing the case in the context of the principle that one who is involved in performing a *mitzva* is exempt from the obligation to fulfil other *mitzvot* (*B. Sukka* 25a–b).

Nevertheless, these people came to Moses with a heartfelt petition: *Why should we be disadvantaged in that we cannot bring the sacrifice of God at its appropriate time together with the Children of Israel?* (Numbers 9:7).

Moses turned to the Almighty, Who instituted a new law: *Pesaḥ Sheni* – exactly one month after Pesaḥ, there would now be a second opportunity to offer the Paschal sacrifice, specifically for those who were ritually impure or too far away to be part of the Pesaḥ festivities.

The opportunity of *Pesaḥ Sheni* is unique and fascinating; it is the only *mitzva* in the Torah that was created as a result of the demand of the people. Thanks to those who *opened their mouth wide* – to borrow the phrase from Psalms – *Pesaḥ Sheni* was instituted for generations to come.

Normally, the requests for blessing that we submit to God should be modest. Not so with regard to the spiritual pursuits of Torah and *mitzvot*. When asking the Almighty for spiritual sustenance, it is appropriate to ask for our heart's desires. The more we ask for, the more we may be granted.

From the mouths of foetuses

AFTER THE FLEDGLING Jewish nation crossed the Reed Sea, escaping the clutches of the pursuing Egyptians, the people were moved to sing a song of praise, the Song of the Sea. Our sages discuss the manner in which this *shira* (song) was sung (*M. Sota* 5:4; *B. Sota* 30b–31a). Three opinions are offered.

According to the first opinion, Moses sang the verses and the people responded with a refrain taken from the opening line: *I shall sing to God* (Exodus 15:1). A second opinion suggests that the people repeated the words that Moses sang, verse by verse. A third opinion explains that Moses merely prompted the people to begin the song; once he said the opening words, they joined in and continued singing instinctively (*Rashi*). Alternatively, Moses recited the first half of each sentence and the people responded in unison with the second half (*Tosafot*). Either way the Divine creative spirit rested on all present, and each person spontaneously composed the same words to this *shira*.

Continuing with the line of thought in this third opinion which maintains that the spirit of the Almighty was perceived by all those present, our sages describe the miracles relating to those who were involved in singing the *shira*. Not only did the adults sing, but even infants sitting in their mothers' laps and babies suckling at their mother's breasts joined in this *shira*. Once they perceived the Holy Presence they lifted up their heads and declared: *This is my God and I will glorify Him* (Exodus 15:2). One sage, Rabbi Meir, adds that even foetuses in their mothers' wombs joined in the singing (*B. Berakhot* 50a; *B. Ketubot* 7b). Rabbi Meir cites a biblical verse to support his dictum: *In assemblages bless the Lord, God, from the source of Israel* (Psalms 68:27). *The source*, he explains, refers to the starting place of each person, that is, the womb; *assemblages* refers to the gathering of Israel at the sea (*Rashi*).

The Talmud questions Rabbi Meir's assertion. Since the foetuses could not see the Holy Presence from within the womb, how then could they have said *This is my God*? The Talmud explains that their mothers' abdomens became like clear glass and the foetuses were able to see through it, perceive the Almighty, and declare *This is my God*.

Seeing the Holy Presence from within the womb would not have been the only challenge these yet-to-be-born babies would have faced when they were moved to sing. With undeveloped faculties of speech, how could they have recited the *shira*?

The Maharal of Prague (1512?–1609) acknowledges that we are clearly not talking about *shira* where words are formed with the physical mouth and given sound by the vocal cords. Rather, we are describing a visceral desire to transcend the physical world and cleave to the Almighty. Such silent *shira* expresses a sense of yearning for the Divine which emanates from the depths of consciousness and is not bound by physical words. In the adults this yen took the form of the Song of the Sea, while in the infants it remained a tacit, unspoken feeling. Both expressions – the audible and the silent – are termed *shira*.

Speaking in 1913, one Polish Hasidic master – Rabbi Shmuel Bornsztain of Sochaczew (1855–1926), commonly known by the title of his work *Shem MiShmuel* – suggested that the infants, babies, and foetuses did in fact sing! How could it be that everyone present spontaneously chose the same poetic words to praise the Almighty for their salvation? It must be, explains the Shem MiShmuel, that they were all animated by the spirit of prophecy. Just as the Divine voice spoke through Moses despite his speech impediment, so too the Divine voice radiated from the mouth of the infants, babies, and foetuses after the splitting of the Reed Sea.

The approach suggested by the Shem MiShmuel raises a question in his mind. If the entire *shira* was really the Divine voice, why is this song of praise attributed to the liberated Jewish people? The Shem MiShmuel explains that the Divine voice does not coercively take over one's vocal cords. It is only after the heart is spiritually ready to be a conduit for God's word that the Almighty's voice will emanate from the mouth. The Jewish people standing at the other side of the sea – adults, children, infants, babies, and even foetuses – sought to acknowledge the miraculous salvation they had just experienced and to express their praises to the Almighty. That heartfelt desire opened the door for the Divinely inspired *shira*. While it may have been God's voice, it was the people's yearning that triggered the *shira*.

Without referencing the Maharal, the Shem MiShmuel essentially returns to the idea that the key element of the *shira* was the people's hearfelt yearning to express praise and thanks to the Almighty.

The Jewish people were moved to sing not only after the splitting of the Reed Sea but also later on, when they praised the miraculous well that provided them with water during their desert travels (Numbers 21:17–18).

Why did the people not burst forth in song when they received the Torah? Certainly the Torah and its commandments – the lifeblood of our people – are worthy of such a wholehearted response?

According to one commentator, the *shira* for the well was really sung for the Torah (*Or HaḤayim*). Indeed, Torah is often compared to water.

Perhaps we could suggest another approach: the Torah itself is referred to as *shira*. Thus the instruction to write the Torah is derived from the verse *And now write for yourselves this shira* (Deuteronomy 31:19). To recite *shira* over *shira* would be a never-ending loop. Just as we do not recite a blessing over another blessing – for example, we do not recite a blessing before we begin Grace After Meals – so too we do not sing *shira* over *shira*.

When we study the *shira* of Torah, the song of our people, we seek a spiritual connection to the Almighty. We are not coerced into being a conduit for *shira*. Rather we open our hearts, yearn to hear this song, and prepare our souls so that the Divine voice of Torah can speak through our mouths.

Sweet redemption

WHEN A GROOM is called up to the Torah in honour of his marriage, an army of children usually cluster around his feet waiting for lollies to be thrown. As the sweets come raining down on the groom, there is a mad scramble as each young gatherer dives for every candy that hits the floor.

The Talmud discusses using food not to eat but merely to add to the joy of a bride and groom: "We may let wine flow through pipes before a groom and before a bride" (*B. Berakhot* 50b). Nowadays this custom is not practised; it is nonetheless intriguing to understand the significance of the flowing wine.

One commentator explains that this procedure is meant to be a good omen (*Rashi*). Alas, this does not explain the symbolism of the custom. A later halakhic authority elaborates: just as the wine is drawn through the pipes, flowing evenly and smoothly, so too tranquillity and goodness should flow with ease for the young couple (*Levush*). According to another commentator, the symbolism focuses on the liquid, which is wine and not water (*Ben Ish Ḥai*). Wine improves with age, and we bless the newlyweds that their mutual love should be like wine. As the years pass, their love should only be enhanced. An aged wine is not like a young wine; and a relationship that has stood the test of time is enriched by the joint experiences and by the couple's grappling together with the vicissitudes of life.

What happens to the wine once it flows through the pipes? We find two approaches amongst the commentators. According to one commentator, the flowing wine is central to the joy of bride and groom. Even though the wine is rendered unusable, it is not considered wasteful, for it serves its purpose in promoting the happiness of the new couple (*Rashba*).

Another explanation offered is that the wine flows through the pipes into a vessel and is then drunk. Thus the wine is not wasted (*Rashi; Shulḥan Arukh, Oraḥ Ḥayim* 171:4). This approach fits with the continuation of the talmudic passage, which discusses other food-related customs aimed at delighting the young couple. During the summer we throw toasted grain and nuts in front of the bride and groom, but not during the winter. Baked rolls, however, are never thrown before the newlyweds, regardless of the season. These guidelines are based on what effect being thrown has on the food. Baked goods become unappetising once they are thrown, and certainly once they hit the ground. Toasted grain or nuts can still be eaten if they fall on a dry floor; not so if they fall in the wintry mud. In the same vein, our sages allow the flowing wine, since people would still drink the wine after its symbolic journey through the pipes.

The grain and nuts which were once thrown before the bride and groom may be the source for the current custom to throw sweets at the groom when he is called up to the Torah. Even throwing confetti may have similar roots. Though nowadays confetti is made of small pieces of paper or plastic, the Italian word *confetti* refers to almonds with a hard sugar coating.

One halakhic authority records the practice of throwing raisins before the groom on the Shabbat before his marriage when, according to the Ashkenazic rite, he is called up to the Torah. This custom, however, is frowned upon, for raisins are soft and become unappetising when they fall on the ground (*Mishna Berura*).

Throwing items in honour of the bride and groom may be problematic for reasons other than wasting food. First, it may hurt them. Significantly, none of the sources record throwing things *at* the bride and groom; anything tossed is done so *before* them for their enjoyment and not to injure, hurt, or even sting them in any way. A hard candy pitched at a young groom as he nervously reads the blessings over the Torah reading is hardly a formula for causing him delight! Perhaps for this reason, Italians no longer throw the sugar-coated almond *confetti*; rather they throw little pieces of paper called *coriandoli*. Italians do, however, give out little tulle bags of *confetti* at weddings.

The mess made may also be a concern. One halakhic authority implores those who throw the toasted wheat before the bride and groom to sweep up afterward so that the wheat will not be stepped upon and crushed by passers-by (*Levush*).

Rabbi Avigdor Nebenzahl (b. 1935), rabbi of the Old City of Jerusalem from 1973 until 2008, raises a further problem with throwing candies. It is likely that when they are hurled, they will strike the Torah scroll – hardly a respectful way to treat our holiest book. Rabbi Nebenzahl does note that no previous authorities were concerned with this issue. The sweets are thrown with good intentions, not to show disrespect toward the Torah scroll. Nevertheless, Rabbi Nebenzahl questions the value of the practice of throwing candies, and praises congregations that instead of throwing them, distribute the sweets in little bags to the children.

While Rabbi Nebenzahl's suggestion solves certain problems, it is unclear how such distribution achieves the goal of bringing joy to the bride and groom. Perhaps they take pleasure in the children's happiness.

A Jewish wedding is certainly a cause for communal celebration. A particular focus of the festivities is the responsibility of the participants to facilitate the joy of the newlyweds. Two of the seven blessings recited at the wedding in honour of the newlyweds refer to making the groom and bride revel in their new status (*B. Ketubot* 8a). Furthermore, the sages tell us that delighting the groom and bride is akin to rebuilding one of the ruins of Jerusalem (*B. Berakhot* 6b). Thus there is an element of national redemption in making the new couple happy.

While we undoubtedly seek to increase the joy of newlyweds as they embark upon building a new home, other considerations may place limitations on what we do as we seek to rebuild the ruins of Jerusalem.

Garlic breath

GARLIC IS MENTIONED only once in the Bible. When the rabble tire of the manna and lust for meat, they bemoan their situation, recalling days of old before the Exodus: *We remember the fish we freely ate in Egypt, and the zucchini and the melons and the leeks and the onions and the garlic. Alas, now our soul has withered; there is nothing at all beside this manna before our eyes* (Numbers 11:5–6). Despite this dubious start to the career of garlic in Jewish collective memory, later generations lauded its medicinal properties.

In the Second Temple period, Ezra the Scribe advised that garlic be eaten on Friday evening because of its potency as an aphrodisiac (*Y. Megilla* 75a). Other sages note five properties of garlic: it satiates, it warms the body, it brightens a person's countenance, it increases semen, and it kills parasites in the intestines. Others note that garlic also affects a person's mental health, as it gladdens the heart and therefore eliminates jealousy (*B. Bava Kamma* 82a).

Following Ezra's rule that garlic should be eaten on Friday evening, the Talmud lists it among the foods – cooked beets, large fish, and cloves of garlic – that are recommended to fulfil the *mitzva* of *Oneg Shabbat*, delighting in Shabbat (*B. Shabbat* 118a–b). While halakha rules that any food that is especially prepared or set aside for Shabbat fulfils the obligation of *Oneg Shabbat*, garlic is particularly favoured in the eyes of our sages.

Eating garlic has been such a part of Jewish identity that the Mishna rules that if someone took a vow prohibiting benefit from "those who eat garlic," the one who pronounced the vow may not derive benefit from any Jew (*M. Nedarim* 3:10). This vow is recorded together with two other vows. If someone vowed not to benefit from "those who rest on Shabbat" or from "those who ascend to Jerusalem" – these particular vows prohibit benefit from any fellow Jew. Just as the Jewish people were known to ascend to Jerusalem on the pilgrimage festivals, and just as they were known for refraining from work and resting on the seventh day, so too they were known as garlic munchers.

Despite garlic's medicinal properties, its use as an aphrodisiac, its status as a delicacy, and even its position as a "Jewish food" of sorts – there is no denying that it has a powerful odour. This pungent smell is referred to unfavourably in the Talmud.

The Talmud recounts a number of episodes where people took the blame for actions they did not do, in order to save someone else from embarrassment (*B. Sanhedrin* 11a). Rabbi Yehuda the Prince – simply known as Rebbi because of his piety and his contribution to the canonisation of the Mishna – was once sitting and teaching his students. As he expounded the lesson, the odour of garlic assaulted him. The stench may have been strong, or perhaps Rebbi did not like garlic; either way he could not continue the lesson.

"Whoever ate garlic – leave," instructed Rebbi. One of his star students, Rav Ḥiyya, stood up and walked out. Seeing this, all the other students rose and followed Rav Ḥiyya out, leaving Rebbi sitting there alone.

Next morning Rebbi's son, Rabbi Shimon, met Rav Ḥiyya and spoke to him in an accusatory tone: "Was it you who irritated my father with your bad breath?"

"Heaven forbid," replied Rav Ḥiyya without hesitation. "There should be no such thing in all of Israel!" No one should eat garlic before coming to the *beit midrash*, and certainly Rav Ḥiyya hadn't. He had left only to save the guilty garlic eater from embarrassment, for he knew that if he left the other students would follow out of deference to him, and the culprit's identity would be hidden (*Rashi*).

In our tractate it is reported that one sage was presented with a case of someone who ate and drank but did not recite a blessing beforehand. The question arose: if one realises in the middle of a meal that he has forgotten to recite the blessing over the food, can it be said at that moment? The sage responded: "If one has eaten a garlic clove such that his breath smells, should he go and eat another garlic clove so that his breath will smell even more?" The smell of garlic is likened to the odour of sin. One iniquity should not encourage a further wrongdoing.

Thus the person who mistakenly began to eat without reciting a bene-diction is enjoined to pause and recite a blessing before continuing to eat (*B. Berakhot* 51a).

Elsewhere in the Talmud a similar reference to garlic appears. Our sages discuss a cryptic biblical verse: *Do not be excessively wicked* (Ecclesiastes 7:17). They question whether the verse could really be suggesting that it is acceptable to be a little wicked. One sage explains the meaning of the verse by way of the garlic analogy. If someone has eaten a garlic clove which has given him bad breath, should he go back and eat another so that his breath will smell even worse?! Simi-larly, it is a shame to commit a sin, but one wrongdoing should not lead a person to despondency. One should not get accustomed to liv-ing with the stench of sin and should not allow oneself to get bogged down in a quagmire of his own making. This would serve only to per-petuate the unfortunate situation and encourage further wrongdoing (*B. Shabbat* 31b).

Garlic has many uses. In our tradition – as well as in other cultures – its culinary and medicinal properties have been extolled. In the Talmud, garlic serves an additional function that should not be over-looked: Garlic serves as a pedagogic and andragogic tool to illustrate olfactorily a point about the aftermath of sin. Accordingly, even if you are repulsed by the pungent odour of garlic and religiously avoid garlic breath, this simple plant need not be tossed aside. It may serve as an educational tool that vividly and pungently conveys a message.

BERAKHOT 51A

Spitting in your face

MANY TALMUDIC DISCUSSIONS refer to realities that are not part of our world. Nonetheless, the hallowed texts of our tradition contain timeless messages. As we read seemingly irrelevant talmudic passages, the challenge before us is to plumb their depths as we explore how our sacred texts talk to us.

The Talmud discusses the medicinal value of *ispargus* (*B. Berakhot* 51a). Not to be confused with asparagus the vegetable, *ispargus* refers to the juice of a cabbage marinated in undiluted wine or beer. Due to its therapeutic properties, *ispargus* is drunk in the morning on an empty stomach. According to the sages, *ispargus* is beneficial for the heart, valuable for the eyes, and certainly good for the intestines. The whole body benefits from a daily regimen of *ispargus*. But beware: getting drunk on this beverage is harmful to the entire body.

The sages offer further *ispargus* counsel. *Ispargus* should be prepared with undiluted wine only, imbibed from a full cup, received from the pourer in the right hand, but drunk with the left. Sipping the potion should not be interrupted by chatter; and even after it has been drunk, speaking is not recommended until the cup is returned to the one who first proffered it. *Ispargus* made from wine differs from that fermented in beer. As a chaser, bread should be eaten after wine-*ispargus*, while after beer-*ispargus* foods similar to the beer base should be ingested. Moreover, the therapeutic value of wine-*ispargus* is hindered if we spit after drinking this elixir. Not so beer-*ispargus*, which can be harmful if we don't spit after taking a swig. The damage can be so serious that we are enjoined to spit after beer-*ispargus* even in the presence of a king.

While we don't drink *ispargus* today, the discussion still has relevance. The respected halakhic authority Rabbi Shlomo Zalman Auerbach (1910–1995) had recourse to this passage when exploring a spitting custom.

Spitting after reading a Torah verse is considered an odious act. Thus one who recites a scriptural verse over an injury or for the benefit of a sick person and then spits has no portion in the World to Come (*Shulḥan Arukh, Yoreh De'ah* 179:8). One of the commentators records the practice to spit in the middle of the *Aleinu* prayer. After saying "for they prostrate themselves to vanity and emptiness," some people spit before continuing "but we bow and prostrate ourselves and give thanks before the King, King of kings, the Holy One blessed be He." How could we spit before referring to the Almighty? The answer, of course, is that the spittle is a response to the previous statement about idol worship.

Since the spitting was out of revulsion at the thought of bowing down to idols, the normally repulsive act can be cast as a way of honouring God (*Taz*).

Seeking support for this custom, Rabbi Auerbach recalls that the Talmud mandates spitting after drinking beer-brewed *ispargus* even if we stand before a king. Spitting in this forum is advised, rather than endangering our health by leaving the *ispargus* saliva in our mouths. Similarly, during *Aleinu* – we feel sick to our stomachs at the thought of bowing to idols, so we are permitted to spit in order to avoid endangering our physical, spiritual, mental, and emotional health.

Moving away from the literal meaning of the *ispargus* discussion, for non-*ispargus* drinkers we can read this passage metaphorically. Rabbi Yosef Ḥayim of Baghdad (1834–1909) suggests that the passage can be read as referring to Torah study. Why would Torah be referred to as *ispargus*? Rabbi Yosef Ḥayim explains the etymology of the term: *ei-sefer-gus*, meaning "this lofty book." Thus in the morning we shouldn't be drinking alcoholic cabbage on an empty stomach, rather we should start our day by studying from "this lofty book," namely Torah.

Before we become weighed down by the pressures of earning a living, before our minds become distracted by the day's challenges and before our stomachs churn as we grapple with the world – we should harness our morning energy and direct our faculties towards Torah study. This is good for our hearts, our eyes, and our innards. Indeed, a daily regimen of morning Torah study is beneficial for our entire being.

Rabbi Yosef Ḥayim continues the analogy, applying it to the next line of the talmudic passage which states that getting drunk from *ispargus* is detrimental to the entire body. Rabbi Yosef Ḥayim understands "getting drunk" as mixing Torah learning with the study of non-Torah disciplines. He suggests that such a programme of study reflects badly on the Torah we study, for it appears that we are driven by a mere thirst for knowledge, rather than the lofty goal of communing with the Divine.

Perhaps we can offer an alternative metaphor for getting drunk on *ispargus*. When we are drunk we are not in full command of our faculties; our vision is blurred and our deeds unchecked. Such an intoxicated state removes us from reality. Reality requires us to care for the physical well-being of our families – a task which often necessitates reluctantly closing the tome of Talmud, leaving the intoxicating world of Torah study, and soberly accepting responsibility. If we are so inebriated with Torah study that we neglect our worldly responsibilities, this is hardly beneficial to us.

While a morning shot of *ispargus* on an empty stomach is no longer part of our diet, commentators discover contemporary significance in the *ispargus* discussion – some using it to understand a prayer custom; others offering a metaphoric reading. Those of us who are on-the-wagon, teetotallers, who prefer to wake up with a glass of milk rather than a stiff *ispargus*, can still find relevance in the timeless texts of our tradition.

Mystical Talmud

SOME OF THE sages, besides being legal scholars and bearers of our tradition, also experienced mystical encounters and reported them. Rabbi Yishmael ben Elisha was no stranger to mystical experiences (*B. Berakhot* 7a), and he once related that a certain highly stationed angel called Suriel shared three instructions with him (*B. Berakhot* 51a).

First, when getting dressed in the morning, do not take your shirt from the hand of the butler. Rather, take your shirt personally from wherever it is to be found. Second, upon arising in the morning, do not let someone who has not washed his own hands wash your hands for *netilat yadayim*, the ritual hand-washing. Third, do not return the *ispargus* cup – that morning drink of cabbage fermented in wine – to the one who proffered it to you. These directives are designed as protection against *takhsefit*, a group of demons, or against *istalganit*, a group of harmful angels. These otherworldly factions eagerly wait for a person to do one of these three things and thus fall into their clutches.

The Talmud further relates a mystical encounter that Rabbi Yehoshua ben Levi had with the angel of death. Rabbi Yehoshua ben Levi had previously met and bested the angel of death (*B. Ketubot* 77b). This time the angel of death offered Rabbi Yehoshua ben Levi three pieces of advice. The first two directives were identical to the first two given to Rabbi Yishmael ben Elisha. The third directive was not to stand in front of women returning from a funeral. The angel of death explained: "I dance before them with my sword in my hand and I have licence to harm."

The Talmud offers advice to the unfortunate soul who perchances upon women returning from a funeral with the angel of death merrily leading them: Jump four cubits from where you are standing. If there is a river – cross it; if there is another road – take it; if there is a wall – stand behind it until the procession passes. If you are in an unfortunate situation where none of these options is viable, you should turn away and recite the biblical verse *And God said to Satan: "God will denounce you, O Satan"* (Zechariah 3:2). Citing this biblical verse is effective because elsewhere the Talmud states that "Satan is the same as the evil inclination which is the same as the angel of death" (*B. Bava Batra* 16a).

While these mystical directives may be beyond the ken of most, two of them are codified in halakhic treatises. First, one who has not washed his hands in the morning should not pour the water for someone else's *netilat yadayim*, though it may be permissible for him to pass the water (*Shulḥan Arukh, Oraḥ Ḥayim* 4:11; *Magen Avraham*). Second, female participation in funeral processions is discouraged (*Shulḥan Arukh, Yoreh De'ah* 359:2).

The *ispargus* directive does not appear in the codes, probably because we no longer partake of this beverage. The instruction not to take your shirt from the butler in the morning is not recorded either, yet some scholars still attached supreme importance to this guideline. Thus the Klausenburger Rebbe, Rabbi Yehuda Yekutiel Halberstam (1904–1995), related the following tale of his great-grandfather, the Tzanzer Rebbe, Rabbi Ḥayim Halberstam of Nowy Sącz (1797–1876).

Once, one of the members of the Tzanzer Rebbe's household hung the aging Rebbe's *bekishe*, the long silk coat favoured by Hasidim, on a high peg so that it would not be trampled on. When the Rebbe awoke from a nap, he found his *bekishe* out of reach. The Tzanzer Rebbe called his attendant, Reb Rafael, and asked for a table and chair to be aligned against the wall below the *bekishe*. Reb Rafael hastily did the bidding of his master.

When the chair and table were in place, the Tzanzer Rebbe climbed onto the chair and from there onto the table. Alas, the master still could not reach his *bekishe*. "I will get it for you," the attendant offered, but the Tzanzer Rebbe adamantly refused.

Reb Rafael offered to place the chair on top of the table. The Tzanzer Rebbe gingerly climbed up onto the chair and reached for the *bekishe*. Alas, he still could not reach the coat.

Once again Reb Rafael proposed to retrieve the *bekishe*, and once again the Tzanzer Rebbe obstinately rejected the offer.

Finally Reb Rafael offered a solution. Since he was a strong man, he would climb onto the table and from there onto the chair, and he would lift the Tzanzer Rebbe up so that the master could take the *bekishe* with his own hands. This proposition was acceptable to the Tzanzer Rebbe.

Commenting on the episode, the Klausenburger Rebbe noted the deference of his great-grandfather with respect to the words of our sages. Meticulously, the Tzanzer Rebbe followed the heavenly directive as communicated by the angels to our sages. Despite the fact that he was elderly and weak, and despite the fact that many would have been honoured to hand him his *bekishe*, the Tzanzer Rebbe was unwilling to take his *bekishe* from the hand of an attendant as he chose to exert every possible effort to avoid deviating from the angels' instruction.

The Klausenburger Rebbe added that we are certainly dealing with a noteworthy matter. After all, a ministering angel felt it worthy to warn Rabbi Yishmael ben Elisha. Moreover, the Talmud went to the trouble of recording the incident. We might add that we, as a people, have preserved this talmudic account.

The Talmud is generally read as a text which addresses reality in this world. It offers legal instruction and ethical guidelines presented in the forms of aphorisms, maxims, and stories. In our passage, another facet of this great work is revealed. The Talmud is a text that preserves supernatural encounters and strategies for dealing with the esoteric world. As such, the Talmud provides a window into the mystical world of the sages.

BERAKHOT
CHAPTER EIGHT

Enticing the body to join the soul

THE EIGHTH CHAPTER of *Mishna Berakhot* opens with a list of meal-related legal disputes between the School of Shammai and the School of Hillel. The first concerns the *kiddush* over wine recited at the beginning of the first meal on Shabbat and festivals. *Kiddush* is comprised of two blessings: the benediction over wine and the blessing acknowledging the sanctity of the day. This second blessing is called *kiddush*, meaning sanctification, and the entire ritual is named for this benediction.

The two schools dispute the sequence of these two blessings. The School of Shammai proposes that the blessing over the sanctity of the day be recited first, followed by the blessing over the wine. The School of Hillel disagrees, opining that the blessing over wine should precede the blessing sanctifying the day. The Mishna records the different positions, while the Talmud quotes an early source that explains them both (*B. Berakhot* 51b–52a).

The School of Shammai maintains that the only reason wine is being consumed is because of the special holy status of the day. Therefore, it is appropriate that before we partake of the wine, we give voice to the importance of the day. Moreover, the holy day is ushered in before the wine is brought to the table, and therefore the obligation to recite the *kiddush* blessing precedes the obligation to recite the wine blessing.

The School of Hillel demurs, also offering two explanations. The *kiddush* blessing can be recited only over wine or a wine substitute, namely bread. Thus it is the wine that enables us to recite the *kiddush* benediction. As such, the blessing over wine or its substitute should precede the *kiddush* blessing. Furthermore, there is a general principle in Jewish law that when something which is more frequent competes with something which is less frequent, the frequent takes precedence over the infrequent (*B. Zevaḥim* 89a, 91a). Frequency here is not measured in terms of the optional regular consumption of wine but by its obligatory consumption. Drinking wine is mandated not only when we usher in Shabbat and festivals, but also at the conclusion of these holy days, as part of Grace After Meals, and during a wedding ceremony. The blessing over the wine is therefore said more frequently as part of Jewish ritual than the *kiddush* blessing, which is recited only at select junctures during the year. Hence the frequent blessing over wine should precede the relatively infrequent blessing over *kiddush*.

As we know from common practice, normative law follows the opinion of the School of Hillel. On Shabbat and festivals we recite the blessing over wine before the *kiddush* blessing sanctifying the day (*B. Eruvin* 89a).

Rabbi Barukh Yitzḥak Lipschuetz (1812–1877), son of the famous Mishna commentator Rabbi Yisrael Lipschuetz (1782–1861), in his addenda to his father's commentary weaves a colourful parable to explain the root of the disagreement between the two schools. A wealthy householder needed to embark upon an arduous journey for business purposes. He woke up early, keen to set out, only to find the attendant who was to drive the wagon still fast asleep. The businessman understood his attendant. He, the businessman, was driven by the profit he would make from this journey. In anticipation, he industriously arose to prepare for an early departure. His attendant, however, had no such incentive. There was no appealing reward waiting for him at the end of the long journey. He would merely receive his keep, just as he did when he completed chores around the estate. He was in no hurry to begin this trip.

Understanding this, the businessman prepared some food and beverage for the attendant. When the light meal was ready he called to the attendant: "Come and have something to eat." The attendant woke with a start and jumped out of bed in excitement at the prospect of a prepared breakfast. Thus the businessman began his journey in a timely fashion. He was awake in anticipation of eventual profit, while his attendant was ready thanks to the early breakfast.

Rabbi Barukh Yitzḥak Lipschuetz unpacks the parable. Our soul is like the businessman and our body is its servant. As Shabbat and the festivals enter, our soul desires to soar to the loftiest heights, to seek the wealth of distant spiritual realms. Alas, the body cannot understand the soul's eagerness to set out; it is tired and seeks just a few more minutes of slumber. Without the attendant body, whose task it is to drive the vehicle, we cannot go far. We are stuck, with no way of embarking upon the alluring spiritual journey. If we want to encourage the attendant body to join our soul on this voyage, we need to offer the body something that will appeal to its sensibilities, something that the body will appreciate. Proclaiming the sanctity of Shabbat and the festivals is a foreign language to the body. It knows not of spiritual gratification, of Divine pursuits. The appeal of wine, however, can jump-start the body.

It is at this point, that the Schools of Shammai and Hillel part ways. The School of Shammai feels that the primary purpose – the spiritual heights of the holy day – should be mentioned first. The physical wine, whose only purpose is to encourage the attendant body to join the soul on its exciting journey, is clearly of secondary significance and therefore should be relegated to second place.

The School of Hillel, however, feels that before embarking on this spiritual voyage, the body needs to be enticed from slumber. For this reason the blessing over wine should be recited first. Once the body has been charmed into action, once it is ready to stand as a faithful attendant to do the bidding of its master, only then may our soul begin the journey that promises great spiritual wealth.

A moment of silence

AT THE CONCLUSION of Shabbat, when we are once again permitted to use fire, we recite a blessing over a flame. If there is a group of people in the *beit midrash* at the conclusion of Shabbat and a candle is brought before them so that they can recite the appropriate benediction, there is a dispute as to the proper procedure to follow (*B. Berakhot* 53a).

According to the first opinion presented in the Talmud, that of the School of Shammai, everybody present should recite the text of the blessing on their own. The School of Hillel dissents. One person should recite the blessing publicly, thereby discharging the obligation of all present. The School of Hillel adduces biblical support for its position. The verse states: *In the multitude of the people is the glory of the king* (Proverbs 14:28). This indicates that a glorification of the King of kings in a public forum, in the presence of numerous people, is a greater expression of honour than if each individual privately articulates the same sentiments.

The ensuing talmudic discussion scrutinises these two conflicting opinions, noting that only the School of Hillel offers a reason for its position. What is the logic of the position of the School of Shammai? The Talmud explains that the School of Shammai is concerned that a public recital of the blessing would constitute *bitul beit hamidrash*, a disruption of learning in the study hall. When one person recites the blessing for others, all present must momentarily pause in their studies, attentively listen to the recitation, and appropriately respond by saying *amen* (*Rashi*). This would constitute an unjustified interruption of learning. The School of Shammai feels that it is preferable for each person to recite the benediction privately at a convenient time.

To buttress this position, the Talmud offers a source that relates to another type of interruption. The household of Rabban Gamliel would not say the customary word *marpe* – meaning "health," the equivalent of "bless you" – after someone sneezed in the *beit midrash* because this would disrupt learning.

What type of disruption is the pronouncement of *amen* or *marpe*? It is one solitary word said in a fraction of a second!

We can offer three possible explanations of the nature of this one-word disturbance. The most prevalent approach among the commentators focuses on the importance of not taking even a moment away from Torah study (*Anaf Yosef*). The primary difference between an individual recital of the flame blessing and a public recital is the word *amen*. Similarly, after someone sneezes, even the word *marpe* should not be said so that a moment of Torah study is not lost. Following this line of reasoning, the Klausenburger Rebbe, Rabbi Yehuda Yekutiel Halberstam (1904–1995), notes the value of each and every moment of a twenty-four hour day, each hour with sixty minutes and each minute with sixty seconds. This demanding approach places a premium on each and every study moment in the *beit midrash*. Not a second should be wasted on responding with *amen* or offering someone the one-word *marpe* blessing.

The flip side of concern for each moment wasted is the concern for the merit of each lost word of Torah which would have been spoken in the *beit midrash* if not for the interruption. One of the most outstanding Torah scholars of recent centuries, Rabbi Eliyahu of Vilna (1720–1797), known as the Gaon of Vilna or the Gra, suggests that a single word of Torah is so powerful that with one word a person can discharge his minimal obligation of Torah study.

At first blush this may appear to be a surprising statement coming from someone who was wholly committed to Torah study. Yet on closer examination we can understand that the Gra, who recognises the value of every single word of Torah, would want to dedicate every single moment to engaging the texts of our tradition, never diverting his attention for a second. The Gra maintains that studying a single page of Talmud is the equivalent of fulfilling a myriad of *mitzvot*. It is not only the sum of the arguments, reasoning, thoughts, and ideas encountered while learning which is valuable; each and every word of Torah has great value.

We may offer a second explanation for why our talmudic passage is concerned with a one-word interruption. The concern of the School of Shammai and of Rabban Gamliel's family is not merely with the length of time it takes to say a word, but rather with the disruptive nature of responding to outside stimuli – a blessing or a sneeze – while studying. While it may only take a fraction of a second to say a word, the cost of this interruption may be far greater. In-depth and meaningful Torah study is something that requires concentrated focus and application. Even the shortest stoppage distracts the mind and the heart from the noble task at hand.

A final possible explanation of the talmudic passage focuses on the term used in justifying the positions of both the School of Shammai and Rabban Gamliel's household – *bitul beit hamidrash*. While each person may recite the blessing over the flame, and while any person may randomly sneeze while learning, a total cessation of study is an unthinkable scenario for the *beit midrash*. The *beit midrash* must be – as its name suggests – a house of learning; at each and every moment the hum of

Torah study must reverberate within its walls. A pause in study effectively cancels the very nature of this sacred space, albeit momentarily. Such a cessation is unconscionable.

The School of Hillel would not deny the essential nature of the *beit midrash*, and undoubtedly would demand uninterrupted Torah study. Nevertheless, the School of Hillel might suggest that there are valid reasons for a moment of silence in the *beit midrash*, namely a public, unified expression that glorifies the Almighty.

Let us return to the verse cited by the School of Hillel – *In the multitude of the people is the glory of the king*: The veneration of the King is not only in the public nature of the statement, nor is it only due to the presence of the masses. Perhaps the glorification of God can be found in the unity, commonality, and solidarity – albeit fleeting – of all the King's subjects. For this lofty value, the School of Hillel advocates a momentary disruption of study.

Location, location, location

FORGETFULNESS IS A common human frailty. As such the halakhic system provides guidance for the times when we forget to fulfil a religious obligation. Our sages dispute the correct course of action if someone forgets to recite Grace After Meals and remembers the omission only after leaving the place where the food was consumed (*M. Berakhot* 8:7).

According to the School of Shammai, the person must always return to the site of eating and recite the Grace After Meals on location. In principle, the School of Hillel agrees that Grace After Meals should be recited at the place of eating. Moreover, an intentional change of location necessitates a return to the original place of food consumption. In one scenario, however, the School of Hillel disagrees with the School of Shammai. The School of Hillel maintains that in the case of an inadvertent change of location, Grace After Meals may be recited at the new location when the forgetful diner remembers the omission.

A parallel source quoted in the Talmud elaborates on the debate between the two schools (*B. Berakhot* 53b). The School of Hillel sought to demonstrate the absurdity of the opinion of the other school, and challenged: "According to your approach, O School of Shammai, someone who ate at the top of a towering mansion and descended without reciting Grace After Meals would have to climb back to the top to recite it!"

The School of Shammai was not dissuaded, and responded: "Indeed that is the case. For if someone forgot a wallet full of money at the top of a towering mansion, wouldn't he ascend to retrieve it? If he is willing to ascend for his own benefit, shouldn't he be even more willing to ascend for the honour of heaven?"

While there is a disagreement between the two schools regarding an inadvertent change in location, all agree that there is a time limit on the recitation of Grace After Meals. The blessings can be said only as long as the food in one's stomach has not been digested.

The early commentators discuss whether the requirement of reciting an after-blessing on location applies only to the full Grace After Meals recited after bread (*Rashba*). Some opinions maintain that the talmudic discussion also refers to the after-blessings for other foods made from the five grains – wheat, barley, spelt, rye, and oats – even if they are not bread (*Rosh*). Other authorities hold that the discussion is not limited to grain products, but includes wine and the species of fruit with which the Land of Israel is praised (*Maimonides*). After consuming any of these non-bread products, a shortened after-blessing is recited that encapsulates the three principal blessings of the Grace After Meals in one short text. All agree that there is no location requirement after consuming other foods, such as fruit, vegetables, and beverages, when the shortest form of after-blessing is recited.

Normative halakha appears to follow the opinion that requires an on-site after-blessing for any grain product, even if it is not bread (*Mishna Berura* 178:45).

The Talmud continues with a colourful incident that illustrates the issue. Rabba bar bar Ḥana was travelling in a caravan. At one stop, he ate and forgot to recite Grace After Meals. Only once the caravan had continued on its journey did Rabba bar bar Ḥana realise his omission.

"What should I do?" he wondered. "If I say to them" – that is to his fellow travellers – "that I forgot to say Grace After Meals, they will tell me: 'Recite it here, for wherever you recite Grace After Meals you are blessing the Merciful One.'"

Rabba bar bar Ḥana therefore hatched a cunning plan: "I will say that I forgot a golden dove." Such a claim would convince the convoy to halt and allow him to return to the last rest stop, ostensibly to retrieve the valuable forgotten item.

Thus Rabba bar bar Ḥana turned to his travelling companions and requested: "Wait for me, for I forgot a golden dove." The caravan stopped and he retraced his steps with the goal of reciting Grace After Meals where he ate. When he arrived at the location he indeed found a golden dove!

Let us explore two aspects of this passage. First, we will try to understand the significance of the location requirement. Second, we will try to understand Rabba bar bar Ḥana's course of action. The passage also raises the question of *ḥumra*, the stringent application of law. We will deal with this issue in the next chapter.

1. TIME AND SPACE

The claim that Rabba bar bar Ḥana placed in the mouths of his travelling party sounds convincing. Surely thanking the Omnipresent for sustenance is not site-specific. Why then do the sages insist on reciting Grace After Meals where the food was consumed?

The existence of the Jewish people can be plotted on both a time axis and a space axis. In the realm of time, the Jewish calendar accompanies us through the seasons, focusing our energies toward different themes over the year. Each week we seek rest and restoration on Shabbat, regardless of where we find ourselves. On Pesaḥ, the world over, we discuss the Exodus and how God formed us into a nation. As the northern hemisphere winter approaches we think about the protective cocoon of the Almighty's Presence as we sit in the *sukka*. These time-associated events transcend any physical location; they are not limited in space. Alas, for so long the exilic reality has forced us to focus on the time continuum, while the spatial focus has been but a dream and a longing for most Jews.

Grace After Meals affords us the opportunity to relate to both axes of our existence. First, the blessings must be recited within a time frame, namely before the food is digested. Second, location is a feature of the blessings as well. The species of fruit with which the Land of Israel is blessed requires a special form of after-blessing. If the actual fruit eaten – not just the species – was grown in the Land of Israel, the text of the blessing is adjusted to reflect this. Moreover, the focus of the second blessing of the full form of Grace After Meals is the Land of Israel.

In this context we can understand the requirement to recite Grace After Meals on-site. Not only does it remind us of the importance of location in our tradition, but it indicates that every location has the potential for sanctification even if it is beyond the boundaries of our Land.

2. WINGS OF A DOVE

As noted, the School of Shammai and the School of Hillel dispute whether a diner who forgot to recite Grace After Meals must return to the location of his meal. In most cases of disagreement between the two schools, normative law follows the School of Hillel. Nevertheless, in this case the Talmud seems to indicate that acting in accordance with the School of Shammai is praiseworthy. Certainly Rabba bar bar Ḥana, who presented a tall tale about a golden dove, sought to act in accordance with the School of Shammai. Consequently, normative law on this point is far from clear (*Shulḥan Arukh, Oraḥ Hayim* 184:1).

It is rather surprising – to put it mildly – to find Rabba bar bar Ḥana concocting this fanciful story. The opinion of the School of Hillel provides sound legal basis for not inconveniencing the entire convoy. Following the opinion of the School of Shammai may be laudable, but should it be encouraged at the cost of a lie? How are we to understand Rabba bar bar Ḥana's chosen course of action? Perhaps more importantly, how are we to fathom the Divine approval or even encouragement of his behaviour?

Perhaps we can suggest that Rabba bar bar Ḥana was merely speaking metaphorically. In the continuation of the talmudic passage, Israel is compared to a dove. Just as a dove protects itself with its wings, Israel protects itself with the commandments it performs (Psalms 68:14). Furthermore, in the Bible, the Torah is compared to gold (Psalms 19:11). Rabba bar bar Ḥana was bemoaning his loss: "I lost a golden dove," meaning: I lost part of my identity, the opportunity to fulfil the Torah requirement of reciting Grace After Meals where I ate.

His travelling companions of course did not understand the metaphor. Blinded by the thought of a glittering gold dove lying abandoned in the desert, they agreed to facilitate his detour. The Divine reward was not for the tale invented by Rabba bar bar Ḥana, but for his feeling of heartfelt loss at the prospect of losing the golden opportunity to recite Grace After Meals *in situ*.

This explanation departs from the initial reading of the talmudic text and makes an important point. Forgetting to recite Grace After Meals involves more than just the pure halakhic question of what should be done. True, the practical, legal question of whether the forgetful diner needs to return to where he ate must be addressed. But beyond that issue lies a deeper question: whether the forgetfulness truly bothers the diner.

How upset do we get if we forget to thank the Almighty for the sustenance with which we have been blessed? Do we feel as Rabba bar bar Ḥana did that we have lost something valuable? Would we be willing to inconvenience others – or even just ourselves – to return to where we ate so that we could properly recite Grace After Meals?

Rabba bar bar Ḥana's desperation suggests the importance of location. The incident conveys the spirit of the law which requires reciting Grace After Meals where we partook of the food. This story complements the second blessing of Grace After Meals, which is all about location – the location of our people in the Land of Israel. Thus the sages encourage us to take note of location: the location where we eat and the location from which our nation draws its sustenance.

On stringencies

THERE ARE THOSE who prefer the path of *ḥumra*, stringency in the application of Jewish law. This tendency may be driven by a religious desire to ensure the fulfilment of the Almighty's will. In the quest to fulfil God's word, taking the strict approach is a small price to pay in order to avoid any doubts. Adopting the stringent approach may also have a social aspect: membership in a group may be dependent on certain halakhic positions or a general halakhic approach that prefers *ḥumra*. To what extent is this approach rooted in the Talmud? There are two stories in our tractate which relate to this question and deserve consideration: the Golden Dove and the Reclining Sage.

We have just discussed Rabba bar bar Ḥana's choice to adopt the opinion of the School of Shammai and return – or rather trick his entire travelling party to allow him to return – to the site of his meal so that he could recite Grace After Meals where he ate. The precious discovery of a golden dove seems to reflect Divine approval for adopting the stringent position of the School of Shammai (*B. Berakhot* 53b). This passage, therefore, appears to extol *ḥumra* adoption.

This approach, however, does not seem to be reflected in the case of the Reclining Sage. There is a debate between the Schools of Hillel and Shammai regarding the appropriate posture for the recitation of *Shema* (*M. Berakhot* 1:3). Rabbi Tarfon opted to act in accordance with the strict opinion of the School of Shammai, rather than the normative position of the School of Hillel. Rabbi Tarfon reported that when he did so he endangered himself. His peers responded harshly: "You deserved to forfeit your life, for you transgressed the words of the School of Hillel!" This unsympathetic reply is startling, for Rabbi Tarfon's choice could easily be viewed as a decision to adopt a *ḥumra*.

The two tales seem to reflect conflicting values. The Golden Dove appears to laud those who adopt a *humra* position, while the Reclining Sage seems to condemn those who prefer a *humra* over the accepted normative position. What is the preferred course?

A careful reading of the two tales suggests a possible distinction. In the case of the Reclining Sage there is a fundamental argument as to the interpretation of a biblical verse which dictates the posture for *Shema* recitation. Once the normative position has been concluded, no quarter should be given to the opposing opinion. Adopting the dissenting position is not a case of *humra*; it is defying the rabbinic authority that has decided how the halakhic community should act.

In the case of the Golden Dove all agree that in principle Grace After Meals should be recited where the meal was eaten. The two Schools differ only in the case of a mistake. While normative law follows the lenient position, adopting the other position as a *humra* is not an act of defiance, since all agree that it is the preferred course.

This distinction offers a nuanced approach to the possibility of adopting a *humra*. There are occasions when adopting a *humra* is laudable though not normative, and there are other cases when preferring the *humra* is not only discouraged, but should be perceived as flouting halakhic authority.

Humra, therefore, is of dual nature: at times praiseworthy, at times contemptible. The key is to evaluate each *humra* independently, and to establish the appropriate course of action on a case-by-case basis.

BERAKHOT 53B

Amen, brother!

FROM WIDESPREAD CUSTOM, we are familiar with the practice of responding *amen* after hearing someone recite a blessing. Our sages discuss the value of the responsive *amen* and how it compares with the value of the original blessing (*M. Berakhot* 8:8; *B. Berakhot* 53b; *B. Nazir* 66a–b).

According to one sage, the one who answers *amen* is greater than the one who precipitates the response by reciting a blessing. One commentator explains that this is part of the broader principle that credit for an entire *mitzva* is bestowed upon the person who completes the act (*Rosh*).

Illustrating this point, another sage offers a parable from the battlefield. Beginning with the exclamation "By heaven it is so!" this sage explains that in a skirmish, the common soldiers go first to engage the enemy in battle. Later the mighty warriors join the fight to seal the victory. The triumph is credited to those later warriors who finish the job (*Tosafot*). Unpacking the parable, we can say that the reciter of the blessing begins the proceedings, but the responder seals the act by pronouncing *amen*. Accolades are reserved for the one who responds with the final word.

This, however, is not the final word on the issue. There are other sages who do not subscribe to this approach; they declare that the *amen* response – though a worthy act – is not greater than the recitation of the original benediction. According to this approach, it is better to be a reciter than a responder.

Following this line of thought, two sages are recorded as instructing their sons to grab – or at least adroitly try to gain possession of (*Rashi*) – the cup at the end of a meal and to recite Grace After Meals on behalf of all present. This is preferable to allowing someone else to recite Grace After Meals and merely listening attentively and responding *amen* at the conclusion of each blessing. The Talmud further states that the heavenly emissaries hasten to bestow reward on the reciter before the respondent. To be sure, both the blessing-reciter and the *amen*-responder receive reward, yet the reciter is given preference and hence one should prefer this role.

The codifiers adopt the approach that one should aspire to lead Grace After Meals. One should position oneself in such a way as to be offered the honour, so as to be able to recite the blessing over the wine at the conclusion of Grace After Meals (*Shulḥan Arukh, Oraḥ Ḥayim* 201:4). This preference appears to have broader implications. With regard to any blessing, it is preferable to be the reciter rather than the respondent, not just blessings associated with Grace After Meals (*Rosh; Magen Avraham*).

Commenting on this talmudic passage, the Munkatcher Rebbe, Rabbi Ḥayim Elazar Shapira (1871–1937), offers an entirely different explanation of the issue at hand. The Munkatcher Rebbe notes that the two sages who advocated snatching the cup to recite the blessings were both talking to their sons. The Talmud, it would appear, presents a lesson specific to educating one's child, or more broadly to educating the next generation. The focus of the directive of these fathers was not the seizing of the cup, but the recitation of the blessing. They were exhorting their sons to be proactive: take the cup and loudly pronounce the benediction.

The Munkatcher Rebbe continues, contrasting the value of a blessing whispered quietly with a blessing publicly proclaimed. When people privately serve the Almighty, away from the public eye, we can be sure their motives are pure. Such people are not liable to perform in order to satisfy societal pressures. Their deeds can truly be for the sake of heaven.

In contrast, when people's conduct is seen by all, they may be subject to acting out of peer pressure. However, public action has a different advantage. Children and students see the conduct and can mimic it. Future generations, acting upon what they have seen, will also serve the Almighty publicly and in turn their disciples will observe and learn. Thus the chain of tradition is continued from generation to generation.

These two approaches can be read into the biblical verse: *The concealed matters belong to God our Lord, whereas the revealed matters are for us and for our children forever, that we may fulfil all the words of this Torah* (Deuteronomy 29:28). Those who are concealed in their service of the Almighty act for God alone; those whose service is revealed to all bequeath their conduct to their children and future generations, ensuring the continuation of the tradition.

How then should we understand the opinion that seems to advocate the passive approach of waiting patiently for the opportunity to respond *amen*? Here the Munkatcher Rebbe creatively explains the sage's unexpected exclamation "By heaven it is so!" Sitting quietly and responding with a heartfelt *amen* is indeed a path that is treasured by heaven. Torah, however, is not in heaven. In this world it is preferable to express ourselves and declare the Almighty's blessings.

A final word on the one who recites the blessing and the one who responds *amen*: the biblical verses which deal with blessing the Almighty relate to both the reciter and the respondent. Thus the verse (Nehemiah 9:5) begins: *The Levites… said, "Arise, bless God your Lord."* This refers to the recitation of the blessing. The verse continues: *"and let them bless Your glorious name, which is exalted upon every blessing and praise."* This indicates that for each blessing there should be a praise rejoinder – the *amen* response (*B. Berakhot* 63a; *B. Ta'anit* 16b). Another verse that is quoted in this context also mentions both parties (Psalms 34:4): *Declare the greatness of God with me* – denoting the reciter of the blessing – *and let us exalt His name together* – adding the respondent to the scene.

The texts used when discussing blessings refer to both the recitation and the response. A blessing is not merely a private obligation incumbent on the individual. A blessing is a joint venture, a partnership, whose goal is the communal recognition of the Almighty.

BERAKHOT 53B

When meaning is lost

THE TALMUD TELLS us that before reciting Grace After Meals, one's hands must be clean and fragrant (*B. Berakhot* 53b). Dirty or reeking hands disqualify a person from reciting Grace After Meals. According to one sage, this is patterned on the Temple. Just as an offensive odour disqualifies a person from serving in the Temple, so too hands that have an offensive odour disqualify a person from reciting Grace After Meals. The requirement to wash the hands at the end of the meal is called *mayim aharonim*, meaning "last water," and is codified as Jewish law (*Shulḥan Arukh, Oraḥ Ḥayim* 181:1). As mentioned above, there are authoritative medieval sources that justify the custom of those who do not wash their hands before Grace After Meals (*Tosafot*). Nevertheless, *mayim aḥaronim* is practised by many.

One of the most fascinating aspects of *mayim aḥaronim* is the lack of clarity surrounding the reason for the original requirement. From various talmudic statements, we can identify three possible reasons for the ritual (*B. Ḥullin* 105a–b).

At first glance, *mayim aḥaronim* is aimed at cleansing the hands from food residue accumulated while eating. Following this approach, the Talmud tells us that only cold water should be used for *mayim aḥaronim*. Washing with hot water may soften the hands and result in the dirt being absorbed further rather than being washed away. Additionally, the sages note that the obligatory nature of *mayim aḥaronim* stems from the fear of Sodomite salt that has the power to blind if it comes in contact with the eyes. While the precise identity and nature of Sodomite salt are unclear to us today, it would appear that washing *mayim aḥaronim* serves to rid the diner of any traces of this potent substance.

Our sages also note that *mayim aḥaronim* should not be poured onto the floor, apparently because water used to clean dirty hands becomes vile and repulsive, and may even give off a foul odour (*Rashi*). It would seem, however, that the disquiet is not merely one of propriety and practicality; mystical concerns are also in play. Water used for *mayim aḥaronim* is considered to be the repository of an evil spirit. Thus the used water of *mayim aḥaronim* should not be poured onto the ground, lest a passerby tread on it and be harmed. This is the second reason for *mayim aḥaronim*: to combat the mystical dirt associated with evil spirits.

This brings us to the third explanation. Rav Dimi returned to Babylonia after visiting the Land of Israel, and upon his return he recounted laws and opinions he had heard, discussions he had participated in, and practices he had witnessed while in the west. Among his reports, Rav Dimi related that because of a particular person's failure to wash *mayim aḥaronim*, he ended up divorcing his wife. Ravin, another rabbinic traveller who transmitted traditions from the Land of Israel to Babylonia, related another tradition: because of a particular person's failure to wash *mayim aharonim*, murder was committed (*B. Hullin* 106a).

It is not clear from this source why there would be a connection between washing *mayim aharonim* and having a happy marriage, or between washing *mayim aharonim* and not committing murder. Fortunately, the tale is told elsewhere in the Talmud (*B. Yoma* 83b).

Three scholars – Rabbi Meir, Rabbi Yehuda, and Rabbi Yose – stayed at a certain inn one weekend. Before the onset of Shabbat two of the party – Rabbis Yehuda and Yose – deposited their money purses with Kidor the innkeeper for safekeeping. When they came to retrieve their money after Shabbat, Kidor denied ever having been entrusted with it. The sages persuaded Kidor to join them for a drink, hoping that the alcohol would loosen his tongue and he would reveal where he had hidden their money (*Maharsha*). The sages then noticed that there were lentils on Kidor's moustache, and they hurried to Kidor's home to talk to his wife.

When they met her, they said: "Your husband said that you should return our purses. To assure you that we are telling the truth, he told us to mention that the two of you ate lentils today."

The ploy worked. The couple had indeed eaten lentils, and based on this sign, Kidor's wife returned the purses. When Kidor discovered what had transpired, he was enraged. According to one version, he killed his wife; according to another version, he divorced her. Had Kidor washed *mayim aharonim*, he presumably would have wiped his moustache and his relationship with his wife would not have been harmed. (While the codes do not mention the need to wipe one's moustache as part of *mayim aharonim*, it is common practice to do so.) Thus *mayim aharonim* is a reminder of a frightening historical episode.

One early codifier states that while the harmful Sodomite salt may no longer be part of our diet, this tale nevertheless indicates the continuing need for *mayim aharonim* (*Rif*).

To sum up, the Talmud and commentators suggest a number of possible reasons why we wash *mayim aharonim*: hygienic, mystical, and commemorative. The different reasons offered reflect the attempt by our sages to find meaning in a prevalent practice with hazy origins.

In this sense, *mayim aharonim* may be paradigmatic. Whenever we are faced with an established practice of our tradition, our first course should be to try to understand it. As can be expected, different people will connect to different possible reasons. Those raised with an emphasis on good manners and hygiene may view hand-washing at the end of the meal as necessary in order to remove dirt. Mystically-minded people will likely seek the esoteric meaning behind the practice. And those with a keen sense of history will turn to events of the past that are commemorated by practice in the present.

Beyond the actual *mayim aharonim* practice, the discussion suggests a model for approaching our time-honoured traditions. Even when the original motive has been lost, we are charged with seeking the reasons for and relevance of our hallowed traditions.

BERAKHOT
CHAPTER NINE

Seeing the sea

THE MISHNA LISTS various natural landmarks that warrant the recitation of a blessing. "Upon seeing mountains, hills, seas, rivers, and
deserts one recites the benediction, 'Blessed are You, God, our Lord, King
of the universe, Who creates the natural world'" (*M. Berakhot* 9:2). The
commentators note that not just any hillock or stream merits the blessing.
The benediction is limited to phenomena whose extraordinary appearance
captures our attention and indicates the might of the Creator (*Abudraham*).

Some commentators suggest that only the four rivers listed in Genesis 2:10–14 call for the recitation of the benediction: *And a river went out of
Eden to water the garden and from there it parted and became four heads. The
name of the first is Pishon … and the name of the second river is Gihon … and the
name of the third river is Tigris … and the fourth river is the Euphrates* (*Tosafot*).
Later commentators understand that the four biblical rivers are examples
and the list is not comprehensive. The blessing should also be recited over
other major waterways around the world, such as the Rhine and Volga Rivers,
and over mountain ranges like the Alps or the Pyrenees (*Arukh HaShulḥan*).

The Mishna continues with the opinion of Rabbi Yehuda. As we
have seen, Rabbi Yehuda generally advocates nuanced texts for blessings,
so that benedictions recited accurately express the precise circumstances
of the blessing (*B. Berakhot* 40a; *B. Sukka* 46a). In this vein, Rabbi
Yehuda proposes that upon seeing the *Yam HaGadol*, the Great Sea, a
unique blessing be recited: "Blessed are You, God, our Lord, King of
the universe, Who made the Great Sea."

The identification of Rabbi Yehuda's *Yam HaGadol* is the subject of discussion amongst authorities. Which body of water is the *Yam*

HaGadol? The most obvious candidate for Rabbi Yehuda's blessing is the Mediterranean Sea, for the Bible refers to this body of water as *Yam HaGadol*. For instance, when defining the borders of the Land of Israel, the Almighty tells Moses: *And as for the western border – you will have the* Yam HaGadol, *and this border will be your western border* (Numbers 34:6; see also Joshua 9:1; Ezekiel 47:15).

Some commentators, however, feel that the Mediterranean Sea barely justifies the appellation *Yam HaGadol*. The Mediterranean may be a significant body of water from the vantage point of the Land of Israel, but it hardly stands out in relation to other bodies of water around the globe. It is unlikely that Rabbi Yehuda would suggest a special blessing for a body of water that only has local significance. *Yam HaGadol* must therefore refer to the ocean (*Rosh*).

A third opinion seeks a middle ground. *Yam HaGadol* refers to the vast body of water that encircles the planet. All waters that are connected to this body are to be considered part of *Yam HaGadol*. Seeing the oceans of the world or the Mediterranean Sea would therefore justify the recitation of the blessing. Only landlocked bodies of water, such as the Caspian Sea or the Dead Sea, would not be included under the *Yam HaGadol* rubric.

In 1976 Rabbi Joseph B. Soloveitchik (1903–1993) delivered a eulogy in memory of Rabbi Moshe Dovber Rivkin, a follower of the Lubavitcher Rebbe who had been the head of Mesivta Torah Vodaas in Brooklyn. Rabbi Soloveitchik related that as a child growing up in Russia he had never seen a major body of water. One spring he travelled with a cousin to Danzig (today Gdansk, Poland). In 1976 he vividly described the experience:

"I remember that the water was blue, deeply blue. From afar it looked like a blue forest. It resembled the aboriginal forests near Pruzhana, where I was born. When I came close and realised it was the Baltic Sea, I was overwhelmed by its beauty. Spontaneously, I began to recite the psalm of *Bless the Lord, O my soul* – I did not plan to do this, yet the words flowed from my lips – *O Lord, my God, Thou art very great; Thou art clothed with glory and majesty* (Psalms 104:1). *There is the sea, vast and wide* (verse 25). It was a religious reaction to viewing the majesty of God's creation. When I recited the blessing upon seeing the sea, I did so with emotion and deep feeling. I deeply experienced the words of the benediction: 'Blessed be He Who wrought creation.'"

The experience described by Rabbi Soloveitchik is inspiring. He understood that this was a momentous occasion. He continued: "Not all the blessings that I recite are said with such concentration. It was more than simply a blessing, it was an encounter with the Creator. I felt that the *Shekhina* (Divine Presence) was hidden in the darkness and vastness of the sea. The experience was unique and unforgettable; the blessing welled out of me."

A few years earlier, in 1969, Rabbi Soloveitchik described this encounter as "one of the greatest religious experiences I have ever had."

Alas, for Rabbi Soloveitchik the experience could not be replicated and he was well aware that not every visit to the beach is an encounter with God. He concluded wryly: "Since then I have seen the ocean many times. I still recite the benediction if thirty days have elapsed since I last saw it. Nevertheless, since that first time it has become a routine blessing, a cold blessing (*misnagdisher berakha*)" (Aaron Rakeffet-Rothkoff, *The Rav*, vol. 2, pp. 164–166).

Recognition of God's hand should not be limited to the circumstances dictated by the strictures of the halakhic system. Appreciating Divine handiwork should ideally be a natural process stemming from a religious awakening that comes from within us. Alas, we cannot control such experiences. It is not in our power to simply turn on the tap of religious experience. Halakha provides structured opportunities to acknowledge the Almighty's power of creation. At the same time, we hope that reciting blessings will not remain a mere formality; rather, we aspire to use these moments as springboards, triggers, or catalysts for true spiritual encounters.

BERAKHOT 54A

Blessings for the bad

IT IS NATURAL to thank the Almighty when we are favoured with good fortune; it is more difficult to acknowledge God's hand after a misfortune. Our sages tell us that just as one blesses God for the good, so too one must bless God for the bad (*M. Berakhot* 9:5).

The source for this idea is the biblical verse: *And you shall love God, your Lord, with all your heart, with all your soul, and with all your might* (Deuteronomy 6:5). The sages use a wordplay to expound the Hebrew word *me'odekha*, meaning "your might": "Whatever measure (*midda umidda*) the Almighty metes out (*moded*) to you, you are to give thanks (*modeh*) very much (*me'od me'od*)."

Thus one blessing is mandated for good tidings: "Blessed are You…Who is good and Who confers good." Another blessing is for bad news: "Blessed are You…the true Judge" (*M. Berakhot* 9:2).

The Talmud clarifies that even though the blessings are different, we are expected to accept both the good and the bad happily, for both are the Almighty's will (*B. Berakhot* 60b). This may be a tall order: Can we truly expect someone to joyfully give thanks to God for the bad just as for the good?

Hasidic lore recounts the attitude of the beloved Rabbi Meshulam Zusha of Annopol (1718–1800). His teacher Rabbi Dov Ber (d. 1772), the *maggid* (preacher) of Mezrich (Międzyrzec Korecki), was once asked: How is it possible to accept the good and the bad with true equanimity, thanking the Almighty for both to the same extent?

The Maggid responded: "Go and ask my student, Reb Zusha."

The questioners sought Reb Zusha and found him sitting in a corner, in torn rags, a picture of pain and suffering. They addressed him: "Reb Zusha, the Maggid sent us to you. How is it possible to accept the good and the bad with true equanimity?"

Hearing the question, Reb Zusha was surprised. He responded: "You must be mistaken; I am not the person to ask. Thank God, I have never experienced anything bad!"

Reb Zusha was able to see the Divine hand in everything. From God's perspective all is good; seeing things as bad is only a human assessment. Reb Zusha was able to see past the temporal perspective and recognise everything as the Almighty's will – that is, to view it from God's point of view.

The level of Reb Zusha is truly lofty, perhaps out of reach for many of us who grapple with the vicissitudes of life. A later Hasidic master, Rabbi Yitzhak Friedman (1835–1896) of Bohush (Buhuşi, Romania), suggests a more attainable goal. The Talmud offers further proof texts for the mishnaic tenet. One sage cites the verse, *Distress and grief I will find and I will invoke the name of God* (Psalms 116:3–4). Further in the same psalm we find: *I will raise the cup of salvations and I will invoke the name of God* (Psalms 116:13). The name of the Almighty is invoked in periods of distress and grief as well as in times of salvation.

The Bohusher Rebbe points out a subtle difference between the cited verses. The first quote is taken from two biblical verses – *Distress and grief I will find* (verse 3) *and I will invoke the name of God* (verse 4), while the second quote is a complete verse. When we bless God for good tidings we do so without hesitation. When we are called upon to bless the Almighty in the wake of bad fortune, it is understandable that we pause while we digest the event. A hiatus for consideration and meditation – as indicated by the structure of the biblical verses – is reasonable. Once that stage has passed, however, we are enjoined to acknowledge the Divine will.

Another Hasidic master takes this idea further, not only granting a licence to mull over misfortune, but seeing the gloom as an important and necessary stage in coping. In 1882, a descendant of Reb Zusha – Rabbi Mordekhai Dov Twersky of Hornostaypil (1839–1903) – was travelling, when word arrived that a great fire had ravaged his hometown. His home and his *beit midrash* had gone up in flames, and his precious library with a number of valuable manuscripts had been destroyed. Perhaps most painfully, a manuscript that Rabbi Mordekhai Dov himself had penned on the laws of divorce was lost.

Hearing about the calamity, Rabbi Mordekhai Dov sank into a depression. Suddenly his sad look gave way to a smile and he said to his disciples: "Our sages taught us that we must bless over the bad as we do over the good. Had I been presented with good news that I had just earned a fortune, we would drink a *lehayim* together. Why don't we drink a *lehayim* now?"

The students hastily gathered to drink a *lehayim*. However, one pupil queried: "Master, it is true that we are now fulfilling the directive of our sages to bless God for bad tidings like we bless God for good news. Yet at first you were saddened by the news of the fire. Were you to hear about wealth, would you be sad for even a moment?"

The teacher explained: "We are commanded to bless; we are not commanded to ignore. We should taste the bitterness of the misfortune that has befallen us, for the tribulation has been sent by the Almighty. Similarly, on Pesaḥ we are commanded to chew the bitter herbs and not merely swallow them whole (*B. Pesaḥim* 115b). We must taste the disaster that God has sent and ponder why this is the Divine will. After this stage, as we realise that it is the Almighty's will, we offer a blessing even for the calamity."

Bad things happen in our lives. We are instructed to bless God even in the face of adversity, yet at the same time it is natural, it is legitimate, and perhaps it is even imperative to pause before uttering the blessing. This temporary halt can give us the opportunity to contemplate the blow before acknowledging the Divine hand.

BERAKHOT 54A

Harnessing the evil inclination

AS HUMAN BEINGS we are tempted by the lure of materialistic pleasures. How do these seemingly unholy urges fit into our spiritual worldview? Should they be denounced, shunned, and completely suppressed? Or is there perhaps room to harness them in the service of God?

Our sages expound on the requirements of the biblical verse: *And you shall love God, your Lord, with all your heart, with all your soul and with all your might* (Deuteronomy 6:5). Focusing on the Hebrew word for "your heart" – *levavkha* – the sages note a seemingly superfluous double letter since "your heart" is normally rendered *libkha*. The doubling of the letter *bet*, suggest the sages, indicates that our love for the Almighty must be expressed with two hearts. The heart is seen as the locus of our cravings and aspirations; thus we strive for a relationship with God that stems from both our inclination to do good and our inclination to do evil (*M. Berakhot* 9:5).

How should the evil inclination be used in the service of the Almighty? How are we to express our love for God with the urge to do evil? Various approaches have been suggested. One explanation is that by embracing the drive for good and fulfilling the Divine commandments while at the same time rejecting evil urges to transgress – the Almighty is being served with both inclinations (*Rabbeinu Yona Gerondi*).

Another approach suggests that loving the Almighty with the evil inclination is expressed by retaining fidelity to God, even when we are angry or wish to rebel. Such a state of unrest is the product of the evil inclination; by remaining loyal to God during such moods, we serve the Almighty with both our inclinations (*Maimonides*).

A different line of thought suggests that it is not just via the rejection of the evil inclination or the suppression of its urgings that we can serve God. It is actually possible to use the evil inclination itself in service of the Divine. According to this approach the good inclination refers to attributes considered to be positive, such as mercy and love. The bad inclination refers to attributes considered to be negative, such as cruelty and fear. While mercy and love are undoubtedly preferable to cruelty and fear, there are select times when even these negative attributes are called for. By utilising the appropriate attribute at the right time, in the proper measure, and for a suitable purpose, we serve the Almighty with both inclinations (*Rabbeinu Yona Gerondi*).

The approach which believes the evil inclination itself can be harnessed for good is a central theme in Hasidic thought. In Hasidic tradition the evil urge is viewed as being intrinsically neutral. Left unchecked it tends toward base pleasures; it diverts attention and energy from spiritual achievement. With diligent effort, however, the so-called "evil" urge can be employed for lofty Divine goals. In this manner, we have the opportunity to harness the drive for physical pleasure and use it as a means to achieve worthy spiritual goals. This is the way to serve the Almighty with our evil inclination.

Let us cite one particular example from Hasidic tradition. Rabbi Avraham Ḥayim of Złoczew (d. 1816) relates to the flaw of haughtiness. People might question the efficacy of their prayers and Torah study, wondering: "Who am I that I should merit to pray or to study Torah?" Instead, let them arrogantly think that through their Torah study and prayer they have the power to alter the course of the world. Such "conceit" will encourage them to embark upon the journey of prayer and venture into the depths of Torah. In this way, people serve the Almighty with their arrogance, harnessing this vice to drive themselves to heartfelt prayer and serious Torah study.

This approach is not confined to Hasidic thought. Rabbi Eliyahu Eliezer Dessler (1892–1953) expressed a similar idea in a vignette he shared. Rabbi Dessler was born in Russian Latvia, gained renown while in England, and spent the last years of his life in Israel. He was one of the leading thinkers of the *Musar* movement which emphasised ethics.

Rabbi Dessler remembered that when he was nine years old his father and uncle would piously wake up at midnight on Friday night each week. They would spend nine hours diligently studying together until the time for Shabbat morning prayers arrived.

"I too," recalled Rabbi Dessler, "would get up for a number of hours, and my tutor would study with me." This pious conduct was not limited to the menfolk. Rabbi Dessler recollected: "My righteous mother would also get up, and she would study Midrash and the commentaries of the Ramban and the Malbim on the week's Torah portion." But in the eyes of the budding scholar, his mother's piety was not what captured his youthful attention. He continued: "When my mother got up, it was like a festival for me, because she gave us warm coffee and exquisitely tasty pastries."

Writing many years later, Rabbi Dessler looked back and assessed his own motivations: "While the main purpose of getting up was to study Torah, the baked goods played a significant role in cajoling me to get up enthusiastically." He then quoted his forebear, a founder of the *Musar* movement, Rabbi Yisrael Lipkin (1810–1883) – known as Rabbi Yisrael Salanter after the Lithuanian town Salantai where he received his education. Rabbi Yisrael Salanter relates to our talmudic passage and suggests that this is the meaning of serving the Almighty with the two inclinations – a person should use the desires of the evil inclination to assist in attaining positive results. Rabbi Dessler concluded that it was the enticing pastries that helped him get up and study at such an early hour.

The suggested path is not to suppress desires for physical pleasures. Rather, we are encouraged to direct our urges, channelling them for lofty purposes. While the lure of a tasty pastry may draw us, the challenge is to harness our natural desires for temporal gratification and use them as tools for the pursuit of spiritual growth.

Giants of old

F ROM THE EARLIEST biblical times, giants were part of the landscape (Genesis 4:6). These mighty men, who once struck fear in people's hearts, suffered two great defeats. Their first rout was at the hands of Chedorlaomer, during the war of the four kings against the five kings (Genesis 14:5). In this famous battle, Lot was taken captive – a move that would prove to be fatal for the heretofore triumphant four kings. One person managed to escape and bring the news of Lot's capture to his uncle, Abraham. Abraham quickly entered the fray to rescue his nephew. With his forces, Abraham subdued the four kings, freed Lot, and regained much property that had been plundered.

Who was the refugee who brought the news to Abraham and thus turned the tide of the war? The commentators note that the news bearer is described as *the survivor*. This use of the definite article leads the commentators to attempt to identify the courier. Some suggest that he was a sole survivor from the very battle in which Lot was seized (*Shadal*).

Our sages, however, look further afield for the identity of this news bearer. Who was the ultimate survivor in biblical lore? During the Deluge, all life was being wiped out except for Noah and those on his ark. A midrash relates that the giant Og managed to climb onto one of the ladders on the outside of the ark. As he hung on, he swore to Noah and to his sons that he would be their slave forever. In exchange, Noah drilled a small hole in the ark, and each day he would proffer food to the giant, who thus weathered the storm (*Pirkei DeRabbi Eliezer* 23). Though he was not inside the ark, Og managed to survive the flood and was therefore known as *the survivor* (*B. Nidda* 61a). Thus *the survivor* who brought the news to Abraham was the famous refugee, Og.

One opinion among the sages maintains that Og's motives in reporting to Abraham were selfish. He hoped that Abraham would fall in battle and he could marry the beautiful Sarah (*Devarim Rabba* 1:25). Whatever his motives, Og had now survived not only the flood but the onslaught of the four kings as well.

Og's penchant for survival was shown once more when the fearsome giants were vanquished again, this time by the Ammonites (Deuteronomy 2:20–21). In this context, Og's size is described via the dimensions of his baby cradle. The verse informs us that it was nine cubits long by four cubits wide – at least four and half metres by two metres. Perhaps it was even more – if the cubits used were based not on a normal person's forearms, but on Og's own forearms! The cradle was not made of wood but of iron, so that it could hold this colossal baby's weight (Deuteronomy 3:11).

Maimonides seeks to extrapolate from the size of the cot just how big Baby Og was. He assumes that a person's bed is generally a third longer than his height. Thus Og must have measured six cubits in height. The average height of a person, notes Maimonides, is three cubits. Baby Og was therefore twice the height of an average person. This huge cot was displayed in the capital city, Rabat Benei Ammon, and served as a reminder of victory for the Ammonites who bested the giants (*Ramban*). Meanwhile Og the survivor moved north and settled in Bashan.

Despite Og's endurance, our sages describe the leadup to his eventual downfall. When the Jewish people reached the area of Edre'i on the east bank of the Jordan River, Moses announced: "We camp here tonight, and tomorrow we conquer the city." Early the following morning they set out, but the landscape had changed. Moses looked up and saw Og sitting on the wall of the city with his feet reaching to the ground. Not understanding what he saw, Moses wondered: "What's going on? Did they build another wall overnight?"

The Almighty explained: "Moses, what you see is none other than Og." Moses was frightened. "Do not fear, Moses," the Almighty reassured, "for he will fall before you" (*Devarim Rabba* 1:24).

The Talmud continues the fantastic story. Og saw that the entire camp of Israel measured three square parasangs. "I will uproot a mountain of that size and throw it on the entire camp and kill them all," schemed the giant. Og found such a landform, picked it up and held it aloft planning to bury the Jewish people. The Almighty sent ants to bore holes in the uprooted mountain. It slipped down onto Og's neck. Og desperately tried to brush the mountain off, but his teeth grew, extending downward and locking his head in position. Og's demise was not far off. Moses – no pipsqueak himself – was ten cubits tall. He took an axe with a ten cubit handle, and jumped ten cubits into the air. Moses reached up and, with the axe thirty cubits above the ground, he struck Og in the heel! The blow to the tender "Og's heel" – as perhaps we should call it in our tradition – was sufficient, and the giant came crashing down (*B. Berakhot* 54b).

What remains of this giant? In days of old, people would surely have stared with awe at the size of Og's cradle. This cradle, however, is no more. The Talmud rules that whoever sees the massive rock that Og had planned to use in order to crush the Jewish people, must recite a blessing praising God for miraculous salvation (*B. Berakhot* 54a).

Today, we barely recall Og's tenacious ability to survive. The only memento of his exploits – a rock – is no longer identifiable. Alas, the giants of old who so capture our imagination are but a distant memory, alive today only in Jewish lore.

Perhaps, though, "giants" may be gauged not only by the measurements of their cradle, the height of their heels, or the size of the mountains they uproot. Perhaps there still are "giants" walking among us today…

Our cousins, Ammon and Moab

O UR SAGES ENUMERATE eight places where a commemorative blessing should be recited in recognition of a miracle that occurred there (*B. Berakhot* 54a–b). At each of these places one must give thanks and praise to the Almighty with the blessing: "Blessed are You, O God, our Lord, King of the universe, Who performed miracles for our ancestors in this place."

The Talmud accepts the appropriateness of thanking the Almighty for miraculous salvation, but questions the relevance of the blessing at one particular site – the halite pillar on Mount Sodom near the Dead Sea, known as "Lot's Wife." We are told that the blessing should be made when looking at this pillar of salt, traditionally formed when Lot and his wife fled from Sodom: *His wife looked behind him and she became a pillar of salt* (Genesis 19:26). The Talmud asks why we praise God for the punishment visited upon Sodom, and specifically for the death of Lot's wife; it would seem more appropriate to mourn than to celebrate.

The Talmud concedes that the blessing over the salt pillar is indeed different from the other seven specified sites that merit a blessing. At this location we do not celebrate; we acknowledge the Almighty's judgment and recite the standard text that is recited when bad news is received: "Blessed are You, O God, our Lord, King of the universe, the true Judge" (*M. Berakhot* 9:2). The Talmud, however, is unsatisfied with this answer: If there is only sombre acknowledgment and no thanks or praise in the blessing over Lot's Wife, why is it included in the list of sites where praise is given?

Another source is quoted that solves this problem. In truth, two blessings are recited at this site: one refers to Lot and the other alludes to the fate of his wife. Over the pillar of salt, the blessing recognising Divine judgment is pronounced. At the same site, however, a second blessing of praise is recited: "Blessed are You, O God, our Lord, King of the universe, Who remembers the righteous." This blessing is said after considering how Lot was saved from the destruction of Sodom and its neighbouring cities: *And so it was when God destroyed the cities of the plain, and God remembered Abraham, so He sent Lot from amidst the upheaval, as He overturned the cities where Lot dwelled* (Genesis 19:29). Lot's rescue was thanks to Abraham, so when we see Lot's Wife, we praise God for remembering Abraham and saving his nephew Lot from the destruction.

One commentator notes that the blessing offering thanks at the site of Lot's Wife – "Who remembers the righteous" – is different from the blessing pronounced at the other miracle locations; namely, "Who performed miracles for our ancestors in this place" (*Maharsha*). Indeed, Lot was undeserving of miraculous salvation; the blessing highlights that his escape was thanks to the merit of his uncle, Abraham.

Thus seeing the pillar of salt which Lot's wife turned into evokes mixed emotions and conveys a number of messages. There is a solemn acknowledgment of Divine justice along with a joyous vote of praise; an expression of the Almighty's unrelenting judgment and a realisation of Divine mercy; a memory of the loss of a wife and an acknowledgment of the salvation of an unworthy nephew in the merit of a virtuous uncle. The directive to recite two different blessings was born of these contradictory elements. This duality appears again in the wake of Lot's escape.

Despite losing his wife, Lot's getaway was successful. Together with two daughters, he fled to a desolate cave. Suspecting that the destruction wrought went beyond the confines of the Sodom plain, they thought that they were the last humans on earth. In order to repopulate the world, the older daughter suggested that the two girls get their father drunk and lie with him on consecutive nights. From these incestuous unions two children were born: Moab, meaning "from father," and Ben-Ami, meaning "son of my people." These two children, conceived in sin, would grow into the nations Moab and Ammon (Genesis 19:30–38). Once again our response might be ambivalent. We might admire the daring of the daughters who felt it incumbent to rebuild humanity, yet we are disgusted by the depraved manner in which they set about this task.

Such a duality appears in a different form during the desert years. Balak, the king of Moab, conspired against the Jewish people. First he engaged the services of Balaam to curse them, and later he employed devious methods to seduce them (Numbers 22ff). The nations of Ammon and Moab did not offer bread and water to the Jewish people, who had just left Egypt. As retribution, it was decided that Moabites and Ammonites could never join the congregation of God by marrying Jews (Deuteronomy 23:4–7). Yet, in recognition of our ancient familial ties, the Almighty ruled out an attack against Ammon and Moab as the Jewish people approached the Land of Israel (Deuteronomy 2:9, 19). Moreover, the familial ties would be strengthened with the acceptance of Ruth the Moabite, who merited being the progenitor of the royal Davidic line (*M. Yevamot* 8:3; *B. Yevamot* 76b–77a).

Despite this familial connection to King David, our sages relate how Ammon and Moab were behind the Babylonian decision to attack his capital city, Jerusalem. Ammon and Moab heard the prophets of Israel prophesying the destruction of Jerusalem. They sent a message to Nebuchadnezzar, king of Babylon: "Leave and come!" thus indicating that the time was right for the conquest of the Land of Israel.

Nebuchadnezzar tarried and demurred: "I am afraid, lest they do to me what they did to those who came before me." He was referring to past miracles that the Almighty had performed for the Jewish people.

Ammon and Moab were not to be deterred and they sent a further message: *For the man is not in his house* (Proverbs 7:19), metaphorically indicating that God's protective presence had departed.

Nebuchadnezzar was unconvinced. He responded: "Perhaps He is still near and will come to protect them in a time of need."

He has gone on a distant journey (ibid.), they replied.

"They have righteous people who will pray for mercy and bring Him back," worried Nebuchadnezzar.

Referring to the righteous, Ammon and Moab replied again with a biblical verse: *He has taken the bundle of silver with Him* (ibid.).

"The wicked may repent," the king suggested. Ammon and Moab reassured him that the chance for repentance had passed and it was now time for punishment.

But Nebuchadnezzar still tried to baulk, saying: "It is winter and I cannot come because of the snow and the rain." Ammon and Moab promptly suggested an alternative route.

"If I come, I will have nowhere to stay," the king responded.

"Their tombs are better than your palaces!" Ammon and Moab explained that there was ample place to lodge troops. Nebuchadnezzar eventually acquiesced to their urgings and attacked the capital (*B. Sanhedrin* 96b).

In this passage our cousins are unfavourably labelled "evil neighbours of Jerusalem." Thus the legacy of Lot's descendants – our cousins and neighbours Ammon and Moab – echoes throughout our history and reverberates with duality. On the one hand, they displayed a devious and corrupt capability for facilitating destruction. On the other hand, this dastardly tendency was coupled with a potential for brotherhood and ultimate salvation; for a messianic era of peace and tranquillity. It is this familial tie for which we pine.

Cornerstones of gratitude

PSALM 107 IS a detailed outpouring of thanks to the Almighty for delivering those in distress. Commentators discuss the historical background of this poetic expression of appreciation. The language of the psalm suggests that it was recited at a large gathering after deliverance from tribulations. Many suggest that it refers to the Exodus from Egypt. Hence, in the Sephardic liturgy, this chapter is recited on Pesaḥ. Other commentators suggest that the psalm is depicting King David's ordeals. A third possibility is that it refers to the return to Zion after the destruction of the First Temple and the Babylonian Exile. Finally, others understand the psalm to be foretelling the thanks which we will express at the time of the final redemption. In this vein, the chapter is recited at the opening of the Yom HaAtzma'ut evening prayer service.

The Talmud, however, is less concerned with the historical underpinnings, focusing instead on the contemporary application of this paradigmatic psalm. Thus the sages, referencing the various verses of the psalm, conclude that four categories of people must give thanks once the danger they are experiencing has passed (*B. Berakhot* 54b).

First, seafarers who have safely reached their destination must express their gratitude.

Second, those who have journeyed through a wilderness must show their appreciation with the appropriate blessing, *Birkat HaGomel*. The commentators discuss what type of journey warrants this recitation. Some say that the benediction is mandated only after a dangerous journey through an area fraught with bandits and inhabited by wild animals. Others say that the term "wilderness" is used by the sages only to follow the psalmist's specific usage, but in fact the completion of any journey should be followed by a blessing of appreciation. Jewish law records both opinions, but requires a minimum journey of one *parsa* – less than five kilometres – unless the route is particularly dangerous (*Shulḥan Arukh, Oraḥ Ḥayim* 219:7). The blessing need not be said until after the completion of the journey; thus it is not recited at a way station (*Mishna Berura*).

The third category of people who should recite a benediction of thanks is those who were ill and have recovered. Here too, the authorities are divided on what type of illness warrants the benediction.

The fourth category is those who were incarcerated and subsequently released. According to one authority, only people who were imprisoned and facing the death penalty need recite the blessing (*Magen Avraham*). Others suggest that release from any detention should be followed by the benediction of thanks (*Mishna Berura*).

Is it only in these four scenarios that we must give thanks? Authorities are divided on whether to expand this list to include others who have experienced deliverance. At the very least, it can be suggested that these four cases are prototypes of those who should express their appreciation (*Maharal*). Seafarers represent those who are being attacked by forces greater than they are. Wayfarers are those who find themselves distanced from their comfort zones with no access to means of protection. Sick people need not grapple with an external enemy; they battle illness that is within their own bodies. Prisoners are those whose adversaries are fellow human beings who deny them freedom. Thus the four cases can be seen as broad categories.

Codifiers rule that anyone who has experienced a miraculous delivery should recite the benediction of thanks. In deference to the opinions that the list is a closed inventory, however, the blessing should be recited without using the Almighty's name (*Shulḥan Arukh, Oraḥ Ḥayim* 219:9).

Notably missing from this list are those who were almost endangered (*Maharal*). While in such scenarios it is certainly appropriate to be grateful that no evil befell you, it is nevertheless unnecessary to recite the benediction.

After identifying those who must give thanks, the passage continues to outline the form of and forum for this expression of gratitude. According to one opinion, appreciation is shown by reciting a blessing that concludes with the words "Who bestows beneficial kindness." Many rabbinic authorities record a different text for the benediction: "Who bestows good upon the undeserving, Who bestowed every goodness upon me." Those present then respond: "The One Who bestowed every goodness upon you should continue to bestow every goodness upon you forever" (*Shulḥan Arukh, Oraḥ Ḥayim* 219:2). While most blessings are recited privately, this benediction has a required forum: it must be pronounced in the presence of a quorum of ten.

Both the form of and the forum for giving thanks can be traced back to the psalm. After each section of the psalm detailing a different ordeal, there is a poetic refrain: *And they cried out to God in their trouble; He delivered them from their distresses.... Let them thank God for His kindness, and let them announce His wonderful works to the children of humans.* Those who cry out for the Almighty's assistance are instructed not to forget God's hand when they are delivered. This chorus suggests the two requirements delineated by the sages. *Let them thank God for His kindness* reflects the obligation to express gratitude with the recitation of a blessing; *Let them announce His wonderful works to the children of humans* suggests the requirement that this be done in a public forum.

The psalm ends with a call: *Whoever is wise, let them consider these things, and let them meditate on the kindnesses of God* (Psalms 107:43). Taking this idea one step further, the thirteenth-century commentator Ramban makes a surprising assertion: "The intent of all the commandments is that we believe in the Almighty and we thank God, our Creator."

This – continues Ramban – is the purpose of all creation: "The Almighty God desires naught from these lower worlds except that humans know and appreciate God Who created them."

In this vein, we might say that the purpose of prayer and of gathering in synagogues to pray together is to thank God and to publicly acknowledge and announce the role of the Almighty in our lives.

BERAKHOT 54B–55A

Tarrying at the table

OUR SAGES DECLARE that sitting for extended periods at the dinner table is one of the actions that can lengthen a person's life (*B. Berakhot* 54b–55a). Why do long meals lead to long life?

There is a superficial linguistic link – *stay longer* at the dinner table so you will *stay longer* in this world – but this is hardly a profound connection. The Talmud goes on to offer a more substantive explanation. The longer the meal, the more chance there is that a needy person will knock at the door asking for food. If the meal is still in progress, the hungry visitor can easily be invited to the table. In the merit of feeding the needy, the host may be granted long life.

The Talmud cites a biblical verse to buttress the importance of the dinner table. *The altar, three cubits high and two cubits wide, was of wood and it had corners and its length and its walls were of wood, and he said to me: "This is the table that is before God"* (Ezekiel 41:22). This verse refers to the altar as *the table that is before God*. Our sages explain: as long as the Temple stood, the altar served as the place to atone for sins. Nowadays, with the Temple no longer standing, the dinner table is the locus of atonement.

One Hasidic master – Rabbi Yisrael Hopsztajn (1737–1814), the *maggid* (preacher) of Kozienice – suggests that the dinner table is better than the Temple altar, even though both are effective in achieving atonement. On the Temple altar, sacrifices were offered up and accepted by the Almighty; whereas food which is eaten at the dinner table imparts strength that lasts beyond the meal, enabling those who have eaten to continue studying Torah and serving God.

Returning to the talmudic passage and putting its various parts together, we arrive at the following conclusion: by extending our stay at the dinner table, we increase the likelihood of assisting the needy; by assisting the needy, we atone for our sins; by atoning for our sins, we merit long life. This would seem to be a roundabout way of saying that the reward for assisting the needy is long life. Why phrase this advice in terms of the dinner table? Perhaps this talmudic passage is not just talking about providing food for the hungry.

One contemporary commentator offers a rational explanation for how a lengthy stay at the dinner table is connected to long life. Rabbi Moshe Tzuriel suggests that sitting at the table and enjoying a meal with the needy, or even with other guests or family members, is a gratifying and satisfying experience. This emotional pleasure also translates into physical well-being, which may lead to long life. While Rabbi Tzuriel's explanation may be true, it is difficult to read this explanation into the talmudic text which specifies the opportunity to provide food for the needy.

A different possible approach is to focus on the unique merit of providing assistance to the needy in the form of ready-made food. Elsewhere in the Talmud we are told about a time of serious drought, when the sages approached Abba Ḥilkiya to beseech the Almighty on behalf of the people for much-needed rain (*B. Ta'anit* 23a–b).

Before the emissaries could voice their request, Abba Ḥilkiya turned to his wife and said: "I know that the rabbis have come on account of rain. Let us go to the roof" – out of sight of the delegation – "and pray for mercy. Perhaps the Almighty will be appeased and bring rain, and then we need not take any credit." The couple went up to the roof to pray. Abba Ḥilkiya positioned himself in one corner while his wife stood in the opposite corner, and the two supplicants offered their prayers. It was not long before clouds began to approach – from the direction of the corner of Abba Ḥilkiya's wife – and soon the rain fell.

The couple descended to the rabbinic delegates. "Why have the rabbis come?" asked Abba Ḥilkiya with feigned innocence.

"We have been sent by the rabbis to the master" – referring to Abba Ḥilkiya – "to ask you to pray for rain."

"Blessed is the Omnipresent – there is no need for the prayers of Abba Ḥilkiya," he responded modestly.

The rabbinic messengers were not fooled. "We know that the rains came because of you!" They then asked Abba Ḥilkiya to explain what had transpired. "Why, when the rains came, did they first come from the direction of your wife's corner?"

Abba Ḥilkiya explained: "My wife is often at home. She can offer the needy bread that they can benefit from immediately. I, on the other hand, give the needy coins, which they cannot benefit from immediately" – indeed, the poor still need to go to some effort to turn the money into food in order to satisfy their hunger.

The merit of Abba Ḥilkiya's wife was that the assistance she provided to the needy was immediately helpful; she gave them a finished product and not just raw materials. On account of this merit her prayers were answered first, and God sent life-giving rain to quench the thirst of the people. This may also be the merit of those who lengthen their time at the dinner table in the hope that they will be able to provide the needy with freshly prepared, ready-made food (*Ben Ish Ḥai*).

Perhaps we can suggest an additional positive dimension of sitting at the dinner table with the hope of helping the hungry. As we said above, the longer we sit at the dinner table, the greater the likelihood that a hungry person will knock at our door. Reward is granted not only for providing for the needy and not only for making that provision user-friendly. Long life is granted even for creating the possibility of assisting others. Sitting for a long time at the dinner table is not wasting time, nor is it merely a social event. Every moment spent tarrying at the table is another minute waiting for a hungry person to walk through the door. Just sitting at the table and thereby increasing the likelihood of providing for the hungry – even before that assistance has actually been extended – is a worthy action deserving of the blessing of long life.

Being privy to changes

W E MIGHT EXPECT certain subjects to be beyond the purview of talmudic discussion. Thus we might be surprised to discover that the Talmud offers advice about bathroom conduct; even though it hardly seems appropriate for our hallowed texts to deal with such unsanctified, mundane matters. The sages tell us that there are three things which lengthen a person's life: lengthening one's prayers, spending extended periods of time at the dinner table, and taking one's time in the privy (*B. Berakhot* 54b–55a).

Focusing on the third item, the Talmud queries whether it is really such a good idea to sit for lengthy periods on the toilet. Quoting an early tradition, it notes that according to some, squatting too much in the lavatory can be a cause of haemorrhoids. An explanation for the contradictory sources is offered. Spending significant time in the toilet does have health benefits; it is squatting for lengthy periods that can be harmful. The recommended length of a toilet stay depends on what type of privy is available. If it is necessary to squat then the visit should be kept to a minimum; if there is a place to sit, an unhurried stay may have tangible health benefits that lead to long life.

A story is recounted corroborating the contention that visits to the lavatory are encouraged. A certain noblewoman commented to Rabbi Yehuda ben Ilai about his appearance, saying: "Your radiant countenance resembles that of pig breeders and usurers." The noblewoman was referring to two professions that were not labour-intensive but still rather profitable. Pig breeders and usurers were generally happy with their lot – an easy, comfortable living – and their faces would consequently shine. The woman's intention was to offer the sage a compliment.

Rabbi Yehuda ben Ilai, who was no pig breeder or usurer, protested determinedly: "Faith! Both of these occupations are prohibited to me!" Usury is a biblical prohibition (Leviticus 25:36–37) and raising pigs is proscribed in the Talmud (*B. Bava Kamma* 82b).

Why then did Rabbi Yehuda ben Ilai have such a luminous countenance? He explained: "There are twenty-four privies between my lodgings and the *beit midrash*. When I go from one location to the other, I check myself in all of them to see if I need to use the toilet!"

The talmudic passage seems to maintain that lengthy and frequent toilet visits can produce a shining countenance and may lengthen life.

Reading this passage we are immediately confounded by the apparent contradiction between what the Talmud advises and common practice. Could the Talmud truly be recommending that on our daily journey to work we stop at twenty-four public facilities? Even the suggestion that squatting is worse than sitting is contrary to current medical knowledge.

The Hasidic master Rabbi Nahman of Bratslav (1772–1810) urges people to be diligent and pray early in the morning without delay. He adds a comment about excessive toilet use before the spiritual practices of prayer and studying Torah: "Don't make the mistake of those who are overly particular about cleanliness, spend much time on the matter, and waste most of their Torah and prayer time because of it. Moreover, they actively destroy their bodies and make themselves sick, as is well known. For it is all futility and foolishness, and it is the handiwork of the evil urge which clothes itself in these stringencies. In truth, as long as a person does not really need to go to the toilet, he is permitted to pray."

Dismissing authorities who suggest otherwise, Rabbi Nahman writes: "Pay no attention to the opinions of those who are stringent in this matter, for they have greatly erred. Even if you find in some halakhic work a stringency in this matter, the law does not follow this opinion. Rather, the law accords with the majority of halakhic decisors who are extremely lenient about this matter."

Rabbi Nahman does not relate to our talmudic passage and we are left wondering what he thinks of Rabbi Yehuda ben Ilai's twenty-four toilet stops on the way to the *beit midrash*. Clearly Rabbi Nahman did not advocate such frequent visits to the privy.

In comparison to the Talmud on the one hand and Rabbi Naḥman of Bratslav on the other, the codes advocate a tempered approach to bathroom visits. Maimonides encourages a bathroom visit before and after each meal. The *Shulḥan Arukh* merely urges people to consider whether they need to go to the restroom, and the Rema adds that a person should make a habit of using the facilities in the morning and in the evening.

The halakhist and Hasidic master, Rabbi Ḥayim Elazar Shapira of Munkács (1871–1937), boldly dismisses the issue in his commentary to the *Shulḥan Arukh*. Throughout his writings it is apparent that the Munkatcher Rebbe sees himself as a protector of tradition; for him to question a talmudic dictum or the classic codes is unusual. Even the formula offered by Maimonides of going before and after every meal, if combined with a visit to the restroom upon waking and before going to sleep as advocated by the Rema, would result in a person going to the bathroom eight times a day – which the Munkatcher Rebbe feels is excessive.

He further notes that his father and predecessor in Munkács had already respectfully dismissed this medical advice of Maimonides. As he puts it: "Even though Maimonides is the light of our eyes in Torah matters, the father of wise people and a leading doctor," nevertheless if a person uses the facilities with the frequency recommended by Maimonides, haemorrhoids will result. Accordingly, the Munkatcher Rebbe does not advocate frequent visits to the privy.

How, then, should the talmudic dictum be understood? The Munkatcher Rebbe adopts an approach that has been suggested by others with regard to medical advice in the Talmud and the codes: human physiology has changed since talmudic times. While frequent visits to the lavatory may have been advantageous for the sages, today we should limit our time in the bathroom.

Changes of all types occur over time: changes in nature, in knowledge, in society, in perceptions, in priorities, and many more. The challenge, of course, is to be able to distinguish between changes of different stripes. It takes wisdom to know which changes justify a recalibration of our ever-evolving tradition and which changes we must reject, resolutely guarding the fortress of our heritage.

Burdens of leadership

L EADERSHIP IS AN essential yet perilous undertaking. Our sages count assuming public office among three actions that shorten a person's life. The Talmud adduces a biblical verse for the first two actions that shorten life – refusal to read from the Torah and refusal to lead Grace After Meals. The third life-shortening action – filling a leadership position – has no clear proof text (*B. Berakhot* 55a).

To buttress the claim about the deadly nature of leadership, the passage cites a rabbinic tradition concerning Joseph. The Torah tells us: *And Joseph died and all his brothers and all that generation* (Exodus 1:6). This verse implies that Joseph predeceased his siblings (*Rashi*). Joseph, the second youngest child and six years younger than his oldest brother Reuben, died at the age of 110 (Genesis 50:26). In contrast, all his brothers reached the age of 120. Our sages explain that Joseph's early death was because "*hinhig atzmo berabbanut*," he undertook a position of leadership (*B. Sota* 13b).

Troubled by this assertion, some commentators explain that this is only the lot of leaders who conduct themselves in an authoritarian manner even in private. In public, however, one of the demands of office is to adopt a strong, authoritarian approach (*Rabbeinu Ḥananel*). Manuscripts of the Talmud contain this very distinction between the public realm and the private sphere.

The difference between public and private conduct of leaders is made clear in another talmudic passage. There the ailing Rebbi urges his son Rabban Gamliel to act with authority. The Talmud explains that this is a directive for public behaviour, where a leader should display authority before constituents. In contrast, in private no such airs are necessary (*B. Ketubot* 103b).

However, this distinction is not accepted by all commentators. Other scholars take a different tack. They suggest that the grim fate of leaders is reserved for those who affect exaggerated airs of authority and act in an unnecessarily overbearing manner. This fits with the talmudic use of the causative verb *hinhig* (caused to lead) rather than the simple *nahag* (led). People who impose their authority on the community are punished with premature death. In contrast, people who are invited to play a public role or are thrust into decision-making capacities in no way deserve an untimely end (*Maharsha*).

This approach fits another rabbinic source that attributes Joseph's lost decade to the ten times he heard his brothers call their father "*your servant*" without protesting. Joseph heard this locution five times directly and five more times via his interpreter (Genesis 43:28, 44:24–31; *Pirkei DeRabbi Eliezer* 29). Standing by silently while his own father was referred to by the degrading appellation "*servant*" was an unnecessary assumption of authority by Joseph.

A later commentator identifies other affected airs in Joseph's conduct with his brothers. Following the death of Jacob, Joseph did not invite his brothers to dine with him because of seating issues. When Jacob was alive, he assigned Joseph the best seat, even in the presence of Reuben the oldest brother and Judah the leader of the group. This caused bad feelings between the brothers. After Jacob died, Joseph felt unable to concede his priority seating because of his public position. This excessive concern with his public image was repaid with his early death (*Iyun Yaakov* based on *Bereshit Rabba* 100:8).

Unfortunately, the shortening of leaders' days may be a natural consequence of their lives. Elsewhere in the Talmud we hear another sage, Rabbi Yoḥanan, bemoaning leadership and claiming that it entombs officeholders: "Woe to leadership, for it buries its possessors" (*B. Pesaḥim* 87b). This statement could mean that officeholders become buried in a landslide of public responsibilities and civic duties. Alternatively, in concert with the other talmudic passages we have cited, the officials may be literally buried as their life expectancy is reduced due to their occupation. Once again, in support of this notion, a scriptural source is cited. The prophet Isaiah outlived four kings – Uzziah, Jotham, Ahaz, and Hezekiah – who all reigned while he prophesied (Isaiah 1:1). Other prophets also brought the word of God during the rule of all four kings: Hosea, Amos, and Micah (*Rashi*).

In another passage, the Talmud discusses the reckless prophecy of Eldad and Medad (*B. Sanhedrin* 17a). Different suggestions as to the content of their prophecy are offered by the sages, but Joshua's response is taken from the biblical text: *My master, Moses, stop them* (Numbers 11:28). Joshua cried out in a panic, either because they were predicting the death of Moses or because they were irreverently prophesying before their teacher Moses. The Talmud asks: What was Joshua's intent when he urged Moses to stop them? The sages suggest that Joshua was advocating that they be appointed to public office, for in this role they would naturally cease prophesying. One commentator explains that public office is never a joyful task and the Divine spirit rests only on the contented. If Eldad and Medad were burdened with civic responsibilities and mired in the needs of the community, perforce their uncontrolled prophesy would cease (*Tosafot*).

In this light, commentators have understood the urgings of the Second Temple sage Shemaya to despise public office (*M. Avot* 1:10). Some commentators explain that Shemaya understood that public responsibility is hazardous to the health of the officeholders.

Nevertheless, serving the public is a danger that simply cannot be avoided by all. This is the thrust of another talmudic passage. Following the advice of Rabbi Elazar to remain in the shadows and thus survive, Rabbi Zeira hid in an attempt to avoid being ordained. Others, perhaps perceiving that the burden of leadership was discouraging a worthy candidate from taking office, presented a different, enticing quote in the name of Rabbi Elazar about rising to a position of responsibility – all one's misdeeds are forgiven. Once Rabbi Zeira heard that a person's appointment to public office is coupled with forgiveness for all wrongdoing, he hastily presented himself before his teachers so that he could be ordained and have his sins forgiven (*B. Sanhedrin* 14a).

Leadership may be an ill-fated and even hazardous occupation; something to be wary of and to avoid. Nevertheless, we all know the necessity of guidance and direction. The body cannot function without the mind to guide it, and a community cannot thrive without leaders to direct it. Leadership is certainly a burden. Yet we dare not shy away from it, for strong leadership is crucial to our collective success.

A year that counts

W E ALL NEED Divine compassion. We ask for it in our daily prayers and we hope that God's mercy will accompany our endeavours. The Talmud specifies three things that depend on Divine mercy: a good king, a good year, and a good dream (*B. Berakhot* 55a).

Commentators question the limited scope of this assertion. Certainly, Divine mercy is a prerequisite for the success of a king, for a year of plenty, and for the materialisation of a promising dream. However, isn't everything contingent on the compassion of the Almighty? Isn't every success, every accomplishment, dependent on God's mercy? Why does the Talmud single out these three?

The classic commentator Rashi notes that these items are granted directly by the Almighty and not through the agency of a ministering angel. According to another commentator, this approach serves only to strengthen the question. Compassion is built into God's decision-making process. When the future is dependent on the Almighty, we can be confident that mercy will be a factor. A ministering angel, however, is merely a bureaucrat carrying out the Divine will; a clerk charged with a specific task who has no room for considerations of clemency. Since the Almighty personally oversees the appointment of a ruler, the prosperity of a year, and the materialisation of a dream, it would appear that we need more Divine mercy for all other ventures (*Ben Ish Ḥai*).

Commentators through the ages have sought to explain this talmudic statement. One suggests that success in these three fields is especially dependent on the initial steps. The effectiveness of a sovereign's rule is determined in the crucial early period when a tone is set and a vision conveyed. Even nowadays, a newly elected official is critically assessed after a brief initial period in office. Similarly, if a year does not begin with rains of blessing, the remainder of the year is spent in hope and prayer that extra rains will come; or, in more dire situations, it is spent in dealing with water shortages. Likewise, a dream that begins well is a positive omen for future events.

The Jewish calendar reflects this idea. On Rosh HaShana we start off the new year by crowning the King of kings and beseeching the Almighty for a prosperous year. We try to begin the year on a positive note, and our sages tell us that if the first day of Rosh HaShana is full of holy excitement, the entire year will follow suit. Conversely, a spiritually cold first day of Rosh HaShana forecasts a year bereft of spiritual achievement. Thus a king, a year, and a dream are unique in that they must begin with the Almighty's mercy. Other things are contingent on Divine compassion as well, but their initial stages are less critical (*Maharsha*).

Other commentators take an opposite approach. Even if these three items display promising beginnings, Divine mercy is necessary so that they live up to their potential (*Iyun Yaakov*). Moreover, another commentator suggests that while on Rosh HaShana all matters are decided by God, the success of the king, the prosperity of the year, and the potential of a dream are all subject to further scrutiny and consideration over the course of the year. Hence, these three items specifically call for the Almighty's compassion (*Kedusha UVerakha*).

This is taken a step further by another commentator, who maintains that only these three items demand the Almighty's constant attention – for at any moment they can take a turn for the worse. Despite hopeful starts, these three items can quickly sour. A promising year that begins well can, through inclement weather, easily turn gloomy. A natural disaster can wipe out the prosperity of an entire year. An ominous twist can turn any dream into a nightmare. A fine ruler can easily make a wrong decision that leads to adverse repercussions. How many times have we had leaders who, when they first graced the public stage, appeared so very attractive, only to disappoint as their tenure went on? For such things, continued Divine compassion is necessary so that a propitious start will indeed herald good things to come (*Tzlaḥ*).

The Talmud offers biblical proof texts for the three items that require God's mercy. The need for the Almighty's compassion for a good year is buttressed by the verse: *The land that God, your Lord, constantly seeks out; the eyes of God, your Lord, are on it from the beginning of the year until year's end* (Deuteronomy 11:12). Why does the biblical verse describe the year as spanning from *the beginning of the year (mereshit hashana)*, employing the definite article, until *year's end (aḥarit shana)*, without the definite article?

Rabbi Menaḥem Ben-Zion Sacks, who founded the day school movement in Chicago in the 1930s and served at its helm until the 1970s, asks this question. He explains that at the beginning of the year we look forward expectantly to the coming year. We formulate various plans and make new resolutions to help assure a better year and a better future. We think to ourselves that this year will not be like previous years; our achievements this coming year will surpass all bygone years. This coming year, we say to ourselves, will be *the* year. Alas, as the year wears on, we often realise that the potential of the year will not be fulfilled. As the year draws to a close, we look back with disappointment and perhaps frustration as we admit that what was supposed to be *the* year has turned out to be just another year, with no special achievements, no spiritual attainment. This year too will fade into anonymity, together with other years that have barely left their mark on our lives.

Reading Rabbi Sacks' analysis together with our talmudic passage, we can understand why a good year requires Divine attention. Only through God's compassion can we realise the full potential of the year, ensuring that this year will be *the year*.

BERAKHOT 55A

Appointing leaders

APPOINTING LEADERS IS no simple task; leadership is so often the subject of tension and infighting. At times, significant constituencies brazenly deny a new leader's authority. Perhaps this is the reason that the Talmud tells us that the Almighty personally announces the appointment of a good leader. God announces only three things – hunger, plenty, and a good leader (*B. Berakhot* 55a).

For each of the three listed items a biblical verse is cited. In the case of a worthy leader, the Talmud references the appointment of Bezalel to coordinate the building of the desert Tabernacle (Exodus 31:1–2). From Bezalel's appointment process, the Talmud adduces a guideline for appointing people to positions of authority. Even though the Almighty personally selected Bezalel, further in the biblical account Moses addressed the people and said: *See, God has appointed Bezalel* (Exodus 35:30). The Talmud concludes that even a Divinely ordained leader should not be appointed without first consulting the constituency.

The talmudic passage continues by describing the conversation surrounding Bezalel's appointment. After selecting Bezalel, God turned to Moses, asking: "Is Bezalel acceptable to you?"

Moses replied without hesitation: "Master of the universe, if he is acceptable to You, certainly he is acceptable to me!"

"Nonetheless," responded the Almighty, "go and tell the Jewish people."

Moses proceeded to the people and presented the idea for their endorsement: "Is Bezalel acceptable to you?"

"If he is acceptable to the Holy One and he is acceptable to you, certainly he is acceptable to us!"

Commentators discuss why the public should be consulted in the appointment of leaders, particularly when the appointment carries a Divine stamp of approval. One commentator suggests that endorsement is merely a formality. When the Almighty appoints a leader no second opinion is necessary (*Iyun Yaakov*).

Another commentator explains that the endorsement process is a tactical move. If the community agrees to an appointment, it is more likely to accept the directives of the newly installed leader. Thus, public approval for promotion to a leadership position is almost indispensable if we are to ensure the effectiveness and success of the new appointee (*Anaf Yosef*).

A similar approach cites the need to avoid slighting incumbent leaders; in this case – Moses (*Riaf*). This too is a tactical move aimed at including people who are already in positions of authority, so that they feel part of the process rather than feeling threatened by the new appointment.

According to both these approaches, the Almighty could have appointed Bezalel without regard for the opinion of others; certainly it was the Divine prerogative to do so. Yet God chose not to exercise unlimited authority. Rather, God involved those who were most affected by the decision, in the appointment process.

Some authorities note that when Joshua was appointed as Moses' successor, no similar process of consultation is recorded in the Bible (Numbers 27:15–23). The Gerrer Rebbe, Rabbi Avraham Mordekhai Alter (1866–1948), offers a variety of explanations. Perhaps endorsement by the people is not required in all cases. While this approach may explain Joshua's unilateral promotion, it does not fit the words of our talmudic passage, where consultation is presented as a rule for the generations. Alternatively, the approval of the people for the Almighty's appointment of Bezalel could be understood as tacit authorisation for all future Divinely orchestrated promotions, including Joshua's. Or perhaps the people were consulted, and this stage was not mentioned in the Bible because it was the norm; an accepted part of any appointment. According to this last approach, we must wonder why the codifiers of Jewish law omit this requirement.

In examining this talmudic passage, Chief Rabbi Avraham Yitzḥak HaKohen Kook (1865–1935) discerns a tripartite formula for the appointment of leaders, presenting three criteria that are prerequisites for leaders.

The first and most important requirement is internal holiness – a pure heart and an unpolluted soul. This criterion, the primary attribute that qualifies one for leadership, can be accurately assessed only by the Almighty. It was this Divine appraisal that led to the selection of Bezalel as manager for the Tabernacle project.

The second requirement is penetrating, profound wisdom. This ensures that the leader has the capability to fulfil the duties of the position and to lead the community wisely. This qualification can be assessed by humans, but only by the wisest of people and not by the masses. When the Almighty asked Moses if Bezalel was acceptable to him, God was indicating that Moses had the ability to gauge this second prerequisite. Moses responded by acknowledging the secondary nature of this requirement: "Master of the universe, if he is acceptable to You" – that is, if he fills the first requirement – "certainly he is acceptable to me!"

The third criterion for leadership can be assessed by all. A leader must be respectable, lucid, and charismatic. Thus the Almighty told Moses to inquire of the people whether Bezalel met this requirement. The people's answer reflected the relative import of charisma: once Bezalel satisfied the primary prerequisite and the secondary requirement, the people had no objection to his appointment on account of this third criterion.

Alas, too often the priorities given to leadership qualities are reversed. Too much stock is placed on external appearance, and not enough consideration is given to a potential leader's soul. Virtuous and upstanding leadership must fulfil all three criteria. "This should be the formula for generations," concludes Rabbi Kook, "to know the ideal way to choose a leader." When this occurs, leaders may effectively and successfully lead the people along a constructive, life-giving path.

BERAKHOT 55A–57B

Perchance to dream

A FEW SIGNIFICANT PAGES of Talmud are devoted to the subject of dreams, their import and interpretation (*B. Berakhot* 55a–57b). A perusal of these pages reveals a variety of approaches as to how dreams should be viewed.

The first approach views dreams as accurate harbingers of future events. In this spirit, the Talmud details the meaning of various objects and images seen in dreams: a well, river, bird, pot, reed, gourd, various animals or famous people, and so on.

A second approach suggests that the portentous value of dreams lies solely in their interpretation. A dream that has yet to be interpreted, suggests one sage, "is like a letter that has not been read." It foreshadows neither good nor bad. How a dream is understood is of prime import. Furthermore, great care should be taken in responding to dreams; for the response definitively, and at times harshly, dictates the effect of the dream. As one sage opines: "All dreams follow the mouth."

Interpretation may truly be potent. One sage describes how he took his dream to twenty-four different dream interpreters in Jerusalem. Each offered a different explanation, and all the interpretations were realised! For this reason, after having an ominous dream, one sage would recite the biblical verse: *Dreams speak lies* (Zechariah 10:2). That same sage, after a positive dream, would recite the same verse, albeit with a different intonation: "But do *Dreams speak lies*? Is it not written *In a dream I will speak to him* (Numbers 12:6)?"

The Talmud offers methods for ameliorating bad dreams or ensuring that a neutral dream turns into a fortuitous omen. "One who has a dream which distresses him should have it remedied in the presence of three people." The Talmud then details the texts to be said as part of this ritual.

Alternatively, if one has a dream but is unsure whether it signifies good tidings or bad news, the prescription is to stand before the *kohanim* as they intone the priestly blessing. During the recitation, the dreamer should recite a supplication beseeching the Almighty that the dream becomes a positive omen. This short prayer should be concluded as the *kohanim* finish their blessing, such that the congregational *amen* affirms the dreamer's supplication in addition to the priestly blessing.

A third talmudic approach to dreams suggests that they are a mixed bag. No dream fully reflects reality; each dream contains an element of truth, yet that truth is intermingled with fanciful images. "Just as it is impossible to have wheat without chaff, so too it is impossible to have a dream without some senseless parts." A dream, therefore, is not an accurate herald of the future. "A positive dream will not be fulfilled in its entirety, nor will a negative dream be fulfilled in its entirety."

Even Joseph's dream in which the sun and the moon and eleven stars bowed down to him contained an inaccurate aspect (Genesis 37:9). The sun and the moon represented Joseph's parents, while the eleven stars signified his brothers. Joseph's dream would indeed be fulfilled decades later when his father and brothers bowed to him. Yet at the time of the dream, Joseph's mother Rachel was no longer alive. The complete realisation of Joseph's dream – his entire family bowing down to him – was therefore impossible. Sifting through a dream to weed out the imaginary and the bizarre while retaining the kernel of truth is the artistry of dream interpreters.

A variation on this mixed-bag approach suggests that not all dreams herald the future; certain dreams may be dismissed out of hand. If a person dreams while fasting, he can attribute the dream to his empty stomach and not view it as a portent of the future (*Arukh*). On the other hand, one sage enumerates three types of powerful dreams: a dream in the morning before waking, a dream about friends, and a dream interpreted within a dream. To this list some add a dream that is repeated.

A final talmudic approach maintains that dreams have no predictive value. Dreams merely provide a window into the subconscious and have nothing to do with the future. "A person is shown nothing but the product of his own thoughts." Thus one sage points out that imagination-defying scenes, images that are beyond the pale of reality, are not seen in dreams: "Know that a person is never shown a palm tree of gold or an elephant entering the eye of a needle." Such impressions are not contemplated while awake and hence will not appear in dreams.

The power of suggestion can also induce dreams. The Talmud relates that the Roman Emperor once turned to a sage and commented: "You say that your people are exceedingly wise. Tell me, what will I see in my dream tonight?" The sage replied: "You will see the Persians pressing you into service of their king, and they will seize you and force you to pasture pigs with a staff of gold." The Roman Emperor pondered this worrisome image for the entire day, and at night actually saw it in his dream.

According to this last approach: Do dreams have a higher purpose, or are they merely images, thoughts, and feelings that should be ignored? This need not be a case of either/or. Maimonides suggests that while a fast after an ominous dream would not necessarily affect the future, such a fast should nevertheless be part of returning to the Almighty and recanting one's previous misdeeds. The Bulgarian scholar Rabbi Eliezer Papo (1785–1828) writes in his ethical treatise both that "It is good not to be concerned about dreams" *and* that dreams can have value. In a similar vein, Rabbi Samson Raphael Hirsch (1808–1888) notes both that our sages doubt the veracity of dreams *and* that a dream can be a tool in the hands of the Almighty to implant ideas in our hearts that can awaken us to walk a Divine path.

Admittedly, it is a challenge to ignore dreams and at the same time to use them for inspirational lessons for life.

Windows into our inner world

THE LENGTHY TALMUDIC discussion dealing with different dreams and their interpretation includes some fascinating but disturbing examples. One such passage describes how a renowned heretic shared his dreams with Rabbi Yishmael. The sage then proceeded to interpret each of the images. The seemingly innocent dreams that the heretic shared with the sage were consistently interpreted as alluding to depraved sins (*B. Berakhot* 56b).

The heretic reported his first dream: "I saw myself pouring oil into olives."

Rabbi Yishmael didn't address the heretic directly, but offered his interpretation: "This man has defiled his mother."

"I dreamed that I plucked a star," continued the heretic.

"You have stolen from a Jew," explained Rabbi Yishmael, for the Jewish people are compared to stars (Genesis 15:5).

The heretic went on to share the other images that he had seen: "I dreamed that I swallowed a star."

"You have sold a Jew and consumed the proceeds from the sale."

Despite the damning interpretations, the heretic persisted: "I dreamed that my eyes were kissing one another."

Again Rabbi Yishmael avoided responding directly, but commented: "He has defiled his sister."

"I dreamed that I kissed the moon."

"He has defiled a married Jewish woman."

The heretic continued: "I dreamed that I was walking in the shade of a myrtle." Understanding that the myrtle signified a wedding canopy, Rabbi Yishmael explained: "He has defiled a betrothed girl." When the heretic described the image as inverted, Rabbi Yishmael understood that the intercourse had been unnatural.

The heretic now turned to birds that appeared in his dreams. "I saw ravens repeatedly landing on my bed."

"Your wife has had liaisons with many men."

Ravens were not the only bird that landed on the bed of the heretic: "I saw pigeons repeatedly landing on my bed."

"You have defiled many women," explained Rabbi Yishmael.

"I dreamed that I took two doves and then they flew away."

"You have married two women and then dismissed them without properly giving them a bill of divorce."

"I dreamed that I have been shelling eggs."

"You have been stripping the dead of their possessions."

Suddenly the heretic demurred: "You have been right about all the dreams, except for the last vision; I am not guilty of stripping the dead of their clothes!"

The heretic, however, was quickly exposed, for at that moment he was accosted by a woman who shouted: "This cloak which you are wearing belonged to so-and-so who is dead. You have stripped it from him!"

The heretic's dreams sounded harmless enough, yet they were interpreted in the worst possible light. Though the Talmud tells us that the interpretations were accurate, we may wonder whether prima facie, Rabbi Yishmael's assessment was fair. A plausible reading might suggest that the harsh interpretations were tailor-made for the dreamer based on his known record. Had another dreamer, a person of different moral fibre, related the same visions to Rabbi Yishmael, it is likely that he would have offered less condemnatory interpretations.

This approach is buttressed by another set of dream interpretations, this time apparently for a rabbinic protagonist. In this case the situation is reversed. Using homiletic devices, lewd dreams were understood to allude to Torah themes, and visions of illicit relationships were explained in terms of love for tradition (*B. Berakhot* 57a).

Thus the Talmud says that if one dreamed that he had intercourse with his mother, he may expect to obtain understanding. If one dreamed he had intercourse with a betrothed woman, he may expect to obtain knowledge of Torah. If one dreamed he had intercourse with his sister, he may expect to obtain wisdom. If one dreamed that he had intercourse with a married woman, he is guaranteed a portion in the World to Come. The Talmud adds an important caveat. This last interpretation is valid only if the dreamer does not know the woman and did not think about her in the evening before falling asleep.

The contrast is of course disconcerting. Every possible sin is read into the apparently innocuous dreams of the heretic, while the indelicate dreams of the student of Torah are understood to herald an increase in knowledge, wisdom, and understanding. Is the Talmud merely providing excuses for the embarrassing dreams of the rabbis?

Perhaps the central message is that every dream must be understood as reflecting the dreamer's inner world. They are formed by the context and environment of the dreamer. If this world is a world of Torah, even dreams that appear erotic at first blush, truly reflect Torah.

Dreams can therefore be considered a language. To foreigners the dream dialect sounds nonsensical. Even when a foreign language is translated, those who cannot comprehend the original may raise an eyebrow and wonder whether the translation is accurate; whether it really represents the meaning of the string of noises that reach the ear. Each language has its own conventions. Intonation can drastically change meaning. In some languages pronunciation is key to understanding words; in other languages the meaning is dependent on the context. The Talmud tells us that in the dream dialect, it is the personal background of the dreamer that is critical for comprehending the dream vernacular. Thus, when assessing a dream the identity of the dreamer is paramount.

While to some this may sound like apologetics, it is nevertheless possible that our sages are not merely cleaning up embarrassing, erotic dreams. The Talmud appears to be presenting an approach to dreams in general. Dreams are symbols that reflect our inner world. If our inner world is one of Torah, then our dreams bespeak Torah; if our inner world is one of licentious behaviour, then even seeing an innocent image of kissing the moon is a reflection of a corrupt lifestyle.

The talmudic passage should be read as more than a Rosetta Stone for understanding different dreams; dreams should be seen as a window into our inner world.

We might, therefore, ask ourselves a salient question: What are we communicating about ourselves in the dialect of dreams?

Visions of peace

O UR SAGES TELL us that a dream featuring a river, a bird, or a cooking pot is an indicator of peace (*B. Berakhot* 56b). How do these particular items symbolise peace?

A bird – specifically the white dove – is an international peace symbol. Following the great deluge, Noah wanted to know whether the land was once again inhabitable. He sent birds out as his reconnaissance unit (Genesis 8). The dove returned to Noah with an olive branch in its beak, indicating that the Almighty's wrath had subsided and plant life had once again begun to bloom. The image of the dove carrying an olive branch has become a symbol of the hope for peace.

In Jewish tradition, water is a powerful symbol with multiple layers of metaphoric meaning. The Torah is compared to water, while those bereft of Torah are considered thirsty and urged to drink from the waters of our tradition. A Jewish king is crowned by pouring the holy anointing oil over his head. This ceremony is conducted next to a spring of water, symbolically indicating that the sovereign's rule shall continue just as water continues to bubble forth from the spring (*B. Horayot* 12a; *B. Keritot* 5b). Water is a life-giving force. Perhaps it is for this reason that a vision of a river serves as a herald of peace.

What about a pot? How is a piece of kitchenware an omen for peace? An oft-quoted explanation is cited in the name of Rabbi Mordekhai Bannet (1753–1829), the rabbi of Nikolsburg in Moravia (today

Mikulov in the Czech Republic). Rabbi Bannet explains that there are no two greater enemies than fire and water; there is no way that the two can work together or even coexist. The only way that fire and water can join forces is when a pot serves as an intermediary. Only with the help of the mediating pot can the fire be used to heat the water. Since the pot makes peace between the fire and water, a vision of a pot is a portent of peace.

Alas, the pot has limitations as a peacemaker. The tale is told of two rival factions who late one Saturday night knocked at the Jerusalem door of the renowned talmudist, Rabbi Dov Berish Weidenfeld (1881–1965), originally rabbi in Trzebinia, Poland. Rabbi Weidenfeld recounted that as soon as he saw his visitors, he understood why they had come to him. They hoped – in the words of Rabbi Mordekhai Bannet – that he would act as the pot, the intermediary who would bring about peace between warring factions.

"Before they could say anything," related Rabbi Weidenfeld, "I told them that I was prepared to speak with them, but that they should be aware that I was unwilling to discuss the ongoing dispute or to hear even one word about the two opposing groups. When they understood that I was serious, they excused themselves and left my house."

Rabbi Weidenfeld explained why he was unwilling to serve as the pot mediator. "The words of Rabbi Mordekhai Bannet are true only if the fire is a good fire. If the fire does little more than create smoke and soot, then the pot merely gets dirty and the contents of the pot are never cooked. This was the case here. The burning fire was nothing more than smoke and soot. If I had tried to act as a mediator, not only would I not have succeeded in achieving peace, but I was liable to become sullied myself with the mudslinging of their fight."

Rabbi Weidenfeld concluded: "In this case there was no real disagreement between the rabbinic leaders of the factions; the fight was between their followers."

Let us return to our talmudic passage. Rabbi Yosef Neḥemia Kornitzer, who served as the rabbi of Kraków, Poland, during the inter-war period, suggests that the three items listed in the Talmud as symbols of peace suggest three ways that peace can be achieved.

The first route to peace is to flee from any form of disagreement. At the first indication of tension, a fight can be avoided by flight. This is the way of the bird, which hastily takes flight at the slightest rustling of leaves. The bird is therefore a symbol of peace, for it flies away at even a distant hint of impending danger.

The second path to peace is the mediation of the pot. It serves as an intermediary between opposing forces – fire and water. The fire seeks to consume completely, and the water seeks to extinguish the flames. Only through a medium can a harmonious outcome be achieved. The fire burns and the food is cooked thanks to the pot, which channels the heat to the water to cook the food, while at the same time ensuring a safe distance between opposing forces.

The third avenue to peace is flexibility and the ability to adapt to all situations. Fights often develop when people stubbornly refuse to compromise. Being willing to cooperate, to make concessions, and to forgo what is rightfully yours can go a long way toward ensuring peace. This is the way of the river. As it winds its way through the landscape, it gushes forth when the conditions allow and trickles through when necessary. If it encounters a rocky outcrop it merely circumvents it, seeking the path of least resistance.

Peace, therefore, can be achieved by being like a bird and fleeing from a fight, by being like a pot and serving as a mediator between opposing forces, or by being like a river and flexibly adapting to every situation.

Whatever the path, visions of peace continue to animate our dreams.

Reedy dreams

As we have seen, the significance of dreams is a subject of dispute amongst our sages. One opinion suggests that the outcome of a dream is contingent on the choice of biblical verse to be recited upon awakening from it (*B. Berakhot* 56b).

The Talmud provides examples of this principle. Let us say one has dreamed of a *kaneh*, a reed or stalk. The sages tell us that upon waking from such a vision, the following biblical verse should be recited without delay: *[Even] a cracked reed he will not break* (Isaiah 42:3). In this verse Isaiah describes how the messianic king will be so gentle that he will not even break a cracked reed. That verse should be recited before a more negative reed-related verse comes to mind: *Behold, you have relied upon the support of this cracked reed* (Isaiah 36:6). Here the same prophet castigates King Hezekiah for his reliance upon an alliance with Egypt, the so-called support of a cracked reed. The verse continues: *If a person leans upon it, it will enter his hand and pierce it.*

This approach is an extension of the opinion stated twice in our tractate that if someone awakens and a biblical verse "falls into his mouth," it truly contains an element of prophecy (*B. Berakhot* 55b, 57b). Thus the recitation of the appropriate verse that mentions a reed influences how the dream will materialise.

The Talmud proceeds to present a different approach. The outcome of a dream featuring a reed is not conditional on the biblical verse recited immediately upon waking. Rather, a reed seen in a dream is a positive omen for wisdom, as it is written: *Acquire wisdom* (Proverbs 4:5). The Hebrew word for "acquire" is *keneh*, which is made up of the letters *kuf, nun, heh*, the very same letters which form the Hebrew word for reed – *kaneh*.

From here the Talmud continues to the case of one who sees more than one reed in a dream. Such a vision is a premonition for understanding. This too is based on the linguistic link between the Hebrew words for "reed" and "acquire," since the verse says: *And with all your acquisitions* – implying the plural – *acquire understanding* (Proverbs 4:7).

The Talmud here doesn't mention what is arguably the most famous dream that features a *kaneh* – Pharaoh's second dream (Genesis 41). On that fateful night Pharaoh dreamt that seven thin cows devoured seven plump cows and then showed no outward signs of their hearty meal. Pharaoh awoke with a start but then returned to sleep and had a second vision. In this second dream he saw seven heads of grain on one *kaneh*, with every kernel well-formed and plump. Without warning, seven other heads of grain appeared on the stalk, but these heads were shrivelled and withered by the east wind. The thin heads proceeded to swallow up the seven plump, well-rounded heads of grain. The vision was so vivid that only when Pharaoh awoke did he realise that he had been dreaming.

Pharaoh turned to his magicians but they could not offer a meaningful interpretation that satisfied him. Following the butler's suggestion, Joseph was released from the prison pit, cleaned up, and brought before Pharaoh. Upon hearing the dreams Joseph explained that the seven healthy heads of grain, just like the seven fat cows of the first dream, indicated seven years of plenty. The seven gaunt, ugly cows of the first dream and the seven withered heads of grain on the same stalk in the second vision warned of seven lean years of hunger.

Joseph continued to explain the sequence of approaching events. The coming seven years would be years of prosperity throughout the land of Egypt. The following seven years would be so harsh that all the affluence of the first seven years will be forgotten. The memory of the good years would be erased.

At this point, Joseph had completed his appointed task; the dreams had been successfully interpreted. Surprisingly, Joseph continued, offering advice to the ruler of Egypt: *Now, Pharaoh should find an intelligent and wise person, and appoint him over all of the land of Egypt* (verse 33). Joseph continued with details of this nationwide programme that would save Egypt from total destruction.

Where did Joseph get the right – or rather the audacity – to offer advice to the ruler of mighty Egypt, urging him to implement a national seven-year programme of collection and storage? Only the previous day Joseph was languishing in an Egyptian prison with little hope for salvation. When his hour arrived, perhaps he should have prudently kept to the task of interpreting Pharaoh's dreams, rather than taking the risk of proffering advice on Egyptian national policy.

One Hasidic master, Rabbi Shalom Rokeaḥ of Belz (1779–1855), explains Joseph's conduct by referencing our talmudic passage about having a dream with a *kaneh*. In Pharaoh's second dream, as we recall, he saw a *kaneh* with seven heads of grain. Joseph understood that the stalk was divinely forecasting something connected to wisdom. The multiple heads on the stalk may have also indicated understanding. Joseph's suggestion to appoint a wise person to oversee the collection and storing of surplus grain during the seven years of plenty was not gratuitous advice from a gaolbird to a sovereign of a powerful nation, but an intrinsic part of the dream interpretation.

Joseph was also conscious of how his interpretation could affect the outcome of the dream. He did not want the qualities of understanding and wisdom to be bestowed on Pharaoh. He therefore boldly suggested appointing another person who would be an understanding and wise leader. As we know, Joseph himself was to be that person.

Our sages indicate that dreams may have many layers of meaning. An object seen in a dream may have hidden significance on numerous planes. Moreover, what we say when trying to interpret a dream may have a decisive influence on its outcome.

Empty pomegranates

POMEGRANATES ARE ONE of the seven species with which the Land of Israel is blessed (Deuteronomy 8:8). It is no wonder they played a prominent place in Jewish ritual art from ancient times. Images of pomegranates were woven into the hem of the robe worn by the *Kohen Gadol* (Exodus 28:33–34). In the Temple constructed by King Solomon, images of pomegranates adorned the capitals of the two pillars known as *Yakhin* and *Boaz* which stood at the entrance (1 Kings 7:13–22). Pomegranates were also depicted on coins of ancient Judea. This tradition was revived in modern-day Israel when the two-shekel coin entered circulation on Ḥanukka 2007. This new coin features a pomegranate as well as a double cornucopia, that is, a double horn of plenty. It was modelled after a coin struck by Yoḥanan Hyrkanus, the Hasmonean king and *Kohen Gadol* in the second century before the Common Era.

It is unsurprising, therefore, that our sages consider seeing pomegranates in a dream to be a fortuitous omen. The Talmud tells us that the significance depends on the size and condition of the dream fruit. If the pomegranates are small, the dream indicates that the dreamer's business will be fruitful like a pomegranate. If the pomegranates are large, the business will not only be fruitful, but will expand and grow. If the pomegranates are split, there are two possible meanings. Dreamers who are Torah scholars may anticipate attaining further Torah knowledge. Dreamers who are not well versed in Torah can expect to have the opportunity to fulfil more of the Almighty's commandments (*B. Berakhot* 57a).

Of all fruit, why is the pomegranate a symbol of succeeding in business, expanding Torah knowledge, or increasing *mitzva* fulfilment? A pomegranate's many seeds represent fertility, the capacity to reproduce and grow; the size of the fruit suggests the extent of this potential. On Rosh HaShana there is a widespread custom to partake of a pomegranate and to say: "May it be Your will that our merits increase as [the seeds of] a pomegranate." Thus we evoke the fertile potential of the pomegranate.

The talmudic passage concludes the pomegranate discussion by expounding on a biblical verse: *Like a section of pomegranate are your temples* (Song of Songs 4:3, 6:7). This curious, poetic simile appears twice in Scripture, and our sages use it to teach a lesson. They homiletically interpret the unusual word used for "temples," *rakateikh*, as implying the word for "empty," *reik*: "Even those who are empty are as full of *mitzvot* as a pomegranate [is full of seeds]." While the number of actual seeds of a pomegranate varies with each individual fruit, the pomegranate is said to contain 613 seeds corresponding to the 613 commandments.

This adage – "Even the empty are filled with *mitzvot* like a pomegranate" – appears numerous times in talmudic literature. In one version the proverb is extended to include not just empty people, but even the sinners among the Jews. According to another reference, the city of Tiberias was called Rakat as well, for even the empty ones (*reikanim*) of that city were filled with *mitzvot* like a pomegranate (*B. Eruvin* 19a; *B. Megilla* 6a; *B. Ḥagiga* 27a; *B. Sanhedrin* 37a).

The commentators ponder the upshot of this oft-quoted passage. If empty people – and perhaps even sinners – are so full of *mitzvot*, why are they still called empty?

The Hasidic master Rabbi Yaakov Leiner of Radzyń (1828–1878) understands that such empty people are filled only by one *mitzva* – the merit of giving donations and offering assistance. While this *mitzva* can be fulfilled in countless ways, those who perform it may nevertheless be empty of other merits.

Another commentator, Rabbi Yosef Ḥayim of Baghdad (1834–1909), also attempts to explain why such people are nonetheless called empty. First he suggests that if one measures their intentions they appear to be filled with *mitzvot*. Alas, when it comes to action they are sorely lacking. On account of their inaction, they are still considered empty.

Rabbi Yosef Ḥayim offers a second suggestion which focuses on the purity with which empty people perform *mitzvot*. While such people are filled with merits from performing untold *mitzvot*, their performance is faulty. They fulfil the Divine commandments while concurrently deriving mundane pleasure. There is a mix of the good and the bad, just like in the pomegranate where the seed and the surrounding pulp are fused. Despite being full of *mitzvot*, such people are sadly empty of pure actions done solely for the sake of God with no pulp attached.

One of the twentieth-century leaders of the Ponevezh Yeshiva in Bnei Brak, Rabbi Dovid Povarsky (1902–1999), suggests that the key to understanding why such apparently full people are still termed "empty" lies in the comparison to the pomegranate. He notes that most fruits are filled inside, not just the pomegranate. Other fruits, such as an apple, are composed of a single homogeneous substance. The pomegranate, however, is made up of many separate pieces. While some people are indeed filled with many small, individual merits, their entire being has not coalesced into one entity. Their lives as a whole cannot be said to be meritorious and filled with good deeds.

Without discounting the ideas expressed in these explanations, it would appear that they miss the thrust of the sages' message, or as least go against the grain of the talmudic dictum. Our sages are urging us to view these people as filled with merits, despite their initial empty appearance. The commentators, however, appear to be intent on declaring the opposite, as if to say that despite being filled with *mitzvot*, these people are still essentially empty in some significant way.

Perhaps we should adopt the more positive, straightforward reading of the statement. Even people who, relatively speaking, are deemed "empty" are still full of good. This may lead us to a further connection between the pomegranate and Rosh HaShana. As we usher in a new year, we beseech the Almighty to view us as filled with merits like a pomegranate. God should focus not on our emptiness but on the myriad of *mitzvot* we have performed, and on our fruitful potential.

A taste of the future

O UR SAGES TELL us that certain objects or experiences are but a pale reflection of other far stronger or more intense ones. The Talmud provides a list of five items, each of which can be considered one-sixtieth of another experience (*B. Berakhot* 57b).

The first item on the list is fire. We are told that fire is one-sixtieth of the scalding Gehenna, the purging fires to which sinners are subject in the afterlife. This gives a sense of the harshness of Gehenna: if earthly fire burns us, what would the fires of Gehenna do to us?

The second item is honey. The Talmud says that honey is one-sixtieth of manna, that magical desert food with which the Jewish people were nourished during their forty years of wandering in the desert. Indeed, when the Bible attempts to describe this mysterious bread from the sky, it uses honey as a reference point: *And the House of Israel called it manna; it was like coriander seed, white, and it tasted like tzapiḥit –* a biblical word whose meaning we do not know, perhaps something like a wafer – *in honey* (Exodus 16:31).

The talmudic list continues, noting that Shabbat is one-sixtieth of the World to Come. In the Shabbat liturgy, this special day is often referred to as resembling the coveted World to Come. Conversely, in Grace After Meals, the World to Come is referred to as a time that is entirely Shabbat.

Moving on to a less cheerful example, our sages tell us that sleep is one-sixtieth of death. The sleepy state of semi-consciousness is likened to deathly unconsciousness. In this vein, we thank the Almighty for returning our rejuvenated soul when we wake up in the morning. Moreover, waking up is compared to the revival of the dead.

The list is rounded off with dreams, which are considered one-sixtieth of prophecy.

Each of the five listed items is given in the same proportion; that is, they represent one-sixtieth of something else. That is a ratio of 1:59. What is the significance of this ratio?

In his commentary to the Torah, Rabbi Uziel Meizlish (1744–1785) relates to one of the items in the talmudic list just cited. Rabbi Meizlish was a student of the famed Rabbi Dov Ber (d. 1772), the *maggid* (preacher) of Mezrich (Międzyrzec Korecki) and the Hasidic master responsible for the spread of Hasidism throughout Eastern Europe. Rabbi Meizlish explains that on Shabbat a person can perceive what his portion will be in the World to Come. By taking note of his own excitement and spiritual awakening on Shabbat, and multiplying this feeling by a factor of sixty, a person can assess the spiritual delight he will experience.

Alas, what if a person feels no holy awakening on Shabbat, if he is bereft of all spirituality on this day set aside for the spirit? If his feelings score a zero on the spirituality scale, then multiplying this zero by sixty... leaves, alas, zero. Such a person may sense that he is undeserving of the pleasure of the World to Come. To counter this, Rabbi Meizlish urges people, even if they do not naturally feel the sanctity of Shabbat, to do their utmost to sensitise themselves to it, and to perceive the unique quality of this special day. If a person succeeds in connecting to the spirituality of Shabbat, he will be privileged to experience it sixty-fold in the future.

Thus Rabbi Meizlish explains how the proportion cited by the talmudic sages – at least regarding the relationship between Shabbat and the World to Come – can have bearing on our lives and can be used to further spiritual goals. The Hasidic teacher does not, however, explain the significance of the specific proportion given by the Talmud.

In the following generation of Hasidic leaders, Rabbi Ḥayim Tirer of Czernowitz (c. 1770–1815), who moved to Safed toward the end of his life, relates specifically to the one-sixtieth proportion. He notes that Shabbat contains a fraction of the taste of the World to Come, but only a miniscule fraction. In Jewish law a taste is no longer discernible when a mixture has sixty parts to one. This statutory benchmark has far-reaching implications. For instance, if milk accidentally falls into a pot of meat soup, the question arises as to whether the soup can still be eaten or must be discarded because it is a forbidden admixture of meat and milk. The answer to this question depends on the ratio of milk to soup. If there are at least sixty parts meat soup to the one part milk, the effect of the milk is nullified and the soup may still be eaten. Similarly, Rabbi Ḥayim of Czernowitz explains that if Shabbat were less than one-sixtieth of the World to Come, it would be nullified by the overpowering taste of this material world. The 1:59 ratio ensures that once a week we can enjoy a discernible taste of the World to Come.

Perhaps we can continue the line of thought of Rabbi Ḥayim of Czernowitz and explain the flip side. What if the ratio between Shabbat and the World to Come had been lower – say 1:50 or 1:40? If this were the case, then the taste of the World to Come on Shabbat would be palpable to all. The Shabbat experience would be so akin to the World to Come that each week we would effectively leave the temporal realm and the overpowering experience of the World to Come would envelop us each Friday eve. Instead, the 1:59 ratio ensures that we can taste the World to Come without becoming overwhelmed.

Once a week we savour the flavour of Shabbat. For connoisseurs, a faint hint of the World to Come is detectable by the palate. It is not an intense flavour that boldly announces itself. Rather it is a faint aroma, a delicate taste which accompanies Shabbat. It is a flavour that bespeaks another world to those sensitive enough to discern it.

BERAKHOT 57B

Bless you

THE TALMUD OFFERS a list of six things that are propitious signs when experienced by the ill: sneezing, perspiration, loose bowel movements, seminal discharges, sleep, and dreaming (*B. Berakhot* 57b).

What is so encouraging about these physical, almost uncontrollable actions? Let us look at the simple sneeze, a mere twitch of the nose that results in a reflex action from the lungs.

To explain the significance of the sneeze, we can begin by exploring its history, as that history has been transmitted in our tradition. Our sages tell us that originally there was no such thing as sickness in the world. When people's sojourn in this world was over and the time for their demise arrived, wherever they were and without prior warning they would sneeze. The force of the exhalation would expel their inner soul and they would die. Just as the Almighty granted life by blowing a soul into an earthly body, a sneeze would expel that godly life-force, sending it back to its Maker and returning the body to its previous state as a clod of earth (*Pirkei DeRabbi Eliezer* 52).

Our forefather Jacob turned to the Almighty and requested: "Master of the universe, don't take my soul from me before I have the opportunity to give final instructions and guidance to my children and to my household." God acquiesced to his request. Jacob is the first biblical personality described as falling ill before dying. As Jacob lay on his deathbed, he called his grandchildren and then his children to be blessed before he died (Genesis 48–49). Our sages describe the astonishment of Jacob's contemporaries, as they had heretofore never encountered a sick person on his deathbed.

In a parallel source, a different explanation of Jacob's request is offered. The opportunity for the sneezer to prepare for death by offering parting blessings is not the focus of the request. Rather, Jacob had seen how children often quarrel after a parent's demise. The opportunity to offer parting words allows the parent to clarify final wishes and to try to prevent arguments between children. This was a particularly understandable concern for Jacob, given the family history (*Yalkut Shimoni*, Psalms 874).

Let us return to the history of the sneeze. Since sneezing was seen as an exhalation of the life force, it was perceived as rather ominous: a sign of imminent death. Conversely, sneezing without dropping dead became a sign of continued life. In this light we can understand the biblical passage in which Elisha revives the son of the Shunamite woman, and he awakens with seven sneezes before opening his eyes (II Kings 2:35).

With this background we can also understand the grandiose statement of one of the talmudic sages. Speaking as a habitual sneezer, he declared that the following tradition was equal to all the rest of his learning. It is a good omen when one sneezes during prayer; for just as the sneezer feels relief in this world after sneezing, so too the sneezer shall feel relief in supernal worlds after praying (*B. Berakhot* 24b; *Rashi*).

The aggadic account of the history of the sneeze concludes with a practical instruction. In light of the original nature of sneezing as deadly, upon hearing someone else sneeze we should respond with the blessing: "Life!"

While blessing someone with good health after a sneeze is a courteous and considerate response, some sages are against the practice. Two reservations about such a blessing are voiced in the talmudic literature (*T. Shabbat* 7:3). As mentioned above, calling out "Bless you!" after a person sneezes can disrupt Torah study, and therefore the royal household of Rabban Gamliel avoided the practice (*B. Berakhot* 53a). It is unclear how widespread this custom was. Even so, outside the *beit midrash* this reservation does not appear to apply, and a blessing following a sneeze is acceptable.

A second concern is that offering a blessing after a sneeze is reminiscent of pagan practices and as such should be avoided. We have much evidence that offering a blessing after a sneeze was a prevalent practice in ancient times among non-Jews. The Greeks, for instance, assigned much importance to the sneeze, telling tales of how the sneezes of their deities foretold events or served as omens. It is understandable that some of our sages are concerned that saying "Bless you!" after a sneeze is perilously close to endorsing pagan beliefs.

Despite these concerns, later codifiers do recommend offering the sneezer a short blessing. As one authority outlines, the appropriate blessing for a sneeze is "Health." The sneezer should respond by first saying: "You should be blessed," and then offering a short prayer in the form of a biblical verse: *I yearn for Your salvation, God* (Genesis 49:18; see *Maharshal*).

Another talmudic passage warns against blessing oneself after sneezing during a meal, lest the sneezer-blesser choke on the food (*Y. Berakhot* 10d). From this passage it emerges that it is acceptable for people to offer themselves blessings after sneezing, as long as it is not while eating.

Let us return to the aggadic explanation of the origins and development of the sneeze. It is not uncommon for ancient traditions to offer metaphysical accounts for natural phenomena. These narratives do not aim to offer historical explanations of the phenomena of the natural world. Indeed, a critical scientific eye would quickly dismiss such explanations as fairytale nonsense. Rather, the goal of such narratives is to frame our reality in a meaningful manner. These accounts, therefore, tell the story of the beliefs and aspirations of those who retell the story, carefully passing traditions from one generation to the next. As such, these narratives can – and should – be mined for meaning by all those who hold the narrative sacred. This endeavour seeks to reveal the truth; albeit not the historical or scientific truth. This buried treasure is the story of our identity; it is our collective memory, it reflects who we are.

While a sneeze is a reflexive response to an irritation in the nose, an involuntary expulsion of air from the lungs, it is also an opportunity for us to bless one another and to thank the Almighty privately for the soul which resides within us. This soul cannot be merely expelled like a dusty irritant. It is an integral part of our being.

BERAKHOT 57B

Cucumber delicacies

THE BEAUTY OF aggada – the non-legal portions of our rabbinic tradition – is the timeless relevance that is encapsulated in the stories, parables, aphorisms, and tales. Of course, this is also the challenge of aggada: mining difficult passages and plumbing their depths to find the lessons contained therein. Yet aggada may be read with another agenda. Not only is it a commentary on our existence, journeys, and challenges, it is also a reflection of the times of the authors. A careful reading of aggadic passages can yield clues as to the reality in which our sages lived. From the words of our sages we can learn, for instance, which products were available in their times.

The Talmud lists ten actions that lead a formerly sick person to have a relapse which leaves the person in worse condition than before. The ten actions are: shaving, bathing, eating the meat of an ox, fatty meats, roasted meat, poultry, a roasted egg, cress, milk, or cheese (*B. Berakhot* 57b).

The passage goes on to suggest two further items that may be added to this list. There are those who say that nuts have the same effect, and there are those who say that *kishuim* fall into this category as well.

Kishuim are plants apparently from the Cucurbitaceae plant family such as zucchini, squash, or cucumber. To prove the properties of the last item, the Talmud explains the etymology of the word: Why are they called *kishuim*? Because they are as *kashim* (hard) on the body as swords. The Hebrew word for the vegetable indicates its harmful properties.

The Talmud, however, is unconvinced. It cites a tradition that describes the dinner tables of two important people, Antoninus and Rebbi. We are told that neither radish, nor horseradish, nor *kishuim* were ever missing from their tables in summer or winter. How then, the Talmud asks, could *kishuim* be so harmful? The Talmud explains that there is a difference between large *kishuim*, which can be harmful, and small *kishuim*, which can be helpful. It was the latter that were always to be found at the tables of Rebbi and Antoninus.

Who were these two people, and what was so special about the food that was always to be found on their tables? Rebbi is the well-known sage Rabbi Yehuda the Prince, who served as leader of the Jewish community in Judea during the Roman occupation toward the end of the second century of the Common Era. His fame rests principally on his monumental work in redacting the Mishna.

The identity of Antoninus is somewhat less clear. Some have identified him as the Roman Emperor Marcus Aurelius Antoninus Augustus, who reigned during the years 161–180 CE (*Dorot HaRishonim*). Alternatively, Antoninus was a local Roman official who befriended Rebbi, studied Torah with him, and was sympathetic to Jewish causes. Elsewhere in the Talmud we are told of the close relationship between Antoninus and Rebbi (*B. Avoda Zara* 19b).

Commentators discuss why the Talmud points out that radish, horseradish, and *kishuim* were always on the tables of Antoninus and Rebbi. According to one explanation, the status of these two privileged individuals dictated that they often hosted guests. At the lavish feasts in their homes the vegetables were necessary to assist in digesting the plentiful food served. The constant presence of vegetables suggests that elaborate meals were being served. As such, the vegetables are indicators of the wealth of Rebbi and Antoninus (*Tosafot*).

An alternative approach focuses on the Talmud's observation that the vegetables were at their tables regardless of the season of the year. Only the wealthy could ensure that seasonal vegetables be available at their tables all year round (*Maharsha*). According to this approach we have a glimpse of the table of the other sages. For most people, vegetables were seasonal and would not be served the year round. The wealthy, however, could afford to have such vegetables, either grown under greenhouse conditions or brought from afar.

This analysis is supported by a different passage that relates to the wealth of Solomon (*Tanḥuma, Yitro* 7). Commenting on the verse *He made everything beautiful in its time* (Ecclesiastes 3:11), the sages note that had anyone but King Solomon said this verse about the Almighty, we would laugh and comment: "How do you know what is beautiful in its time and what is not beautiful?" King Solomon, however, could make such a definitive statement since he never had anything missing from his table.

The passage continues by describing the wealth of King Solomon as reflected by what was served at his table. Even ice – or perhaps some early form of ice cream – during the hot summer month of Tammuz could be found at King Solomon's table; even *melaspamon* was served in the month of Nissan, at the end of winter. We don't know what a *melaspamon* is, but other versions of the passage use the word *melafefon* – the modern word for cucumber. According to one authority, a *melaspamon* is a cross between an apple and a melon (*Yalkut Shimoni*).

Be this delicacy what it may, the items served by Solomon all share a common feature – they are seasonal. Only the wealthy could obtain such foods when they were out of season. It is not hard to imagine how difficult it would be to procure ice cream or sorbet during the scorching summer months without modern methods of refrigeration.

The conclusions about the meals of our sages can – and should – be corroborated by contemporaneous sources. Nevertheless, it is nice to hear the sages telling us themselves about their world. Perhaps more importantly, glimpses of the world of our sages remind us that they were not merely mythical figures; our sages lived within a specific reality just as we do today.

Blessing of the masses

THE TALMUD RECORDS the appropriate blessing to be recited upon seeing a multitude of Jews: "Blessed are You, God, our Lord, King of the universe, the sage of secrets" (*B. Berakhot* 58a). This benediction gives expression to the Almighty's knowledge of the secret thoughts of every single individual in the crowd despite each person's individuality. Our sages say that just as their faces are different to each other, so too their thoughts are different to each other.

The Talmud defines a multitude of Jews as an assembly of at least 600,000 people. The commentators explain that the number 600,000 represents all possible types of people. Despite the diversity of people's minds, thoughts, opinions, and personalities, the Almighty knows the secrets of them all. When we see such a throng of people it is appropriate to recall God's infinite awareness. That is the thrust of the mandated benediction (*Ramban*).

Other commentators offer a different explanation for the blessing. The presence of so many people ensures that cumulatively there will be great brainpower present. Yet there are still some ideas that are beyond the human ken; concepts and views to which only the Almighty is privy.

The blessing over the multitude was instituted in recognition of God's unlimited capability and knowledge as opposed to the finite capabilities of humans and their limited knowledge (*Meiri*).

The Talmud reports how one sage, Ben Zoma, was situated on a step of the Temple Mount. From this vantage point he could see crowds of people ascending to Jerusalem for the thrice-yearly festival pilgrimage. When confronted with this sight, he dutifully recited the required blessing over a multitude. Ben Zoma was then moved to say an additional blessing: "Blessed are You, God, our Lord, King of the universe, Who created all these to serve me."

The Talmud goes on to explain the reasoning behind this additional blessing. It is a variation of an idea that Ben Zoma was wont to say: "How much effort did Adam, the first human, exert before he had bread to eat! He ploughed, he sowed, he reaped, he gathered stalks, he threshed the stalks, he winnowed the chaff from the grain, he separated the waste from the grain, he ground the grain into flour, he sifted the flour, he kneaded the flour into dough, and he baked it. After all that, he ate the bread. But as for me," – said Ben Zoma – "I wake up in the morning and I find all this already prepared before me."

Ben Zoma continued: "How much effort did Adam exert before he had clothing to wear! He sheared the wool, he cleaned it, he disentangled it, he spun it into threads, and he wove the threads. After all that, he had a garment to wear. But as for me, I wake up in the morning and I find all this already prepared for me."

"Indeed," concluded Ben Zoma, "All tradespeople diligently come to the entrance of my home, and I wake up in the morning and find them all before me."

Let us return to Ben Zoma's startling blessing: "Who created all these to serve me." While Ben Zoma may have been a prominent sage, it hardly behooves him to suggest that he is the centre of the world. Moreover, the Talmud describes Ben Zoma as someone with Mosaic qualities, to the extent that like Moses he deserved to have the Divine Presence rest upon him. The only reason Ben Zoma did not actually have such a connection with the Almighty was that the generation in which he lived was undeserving (*B. Sanhedrin* 11a). Moses is described in the Bible as the most humble human being alive (Numbers 12:3). This makes comparing the apparently haughty Ben Zoma to the humble Moses all the more bizarre!

Despite his seemingly nondescript name, Ben Zoma – meaning the son of Zoma – and his lack of rabbinic title, he is described as someone who was totally devoted to the service of the Almighty. Ben Zoma was so staunch in his commitment to God and Torah study that he was never able to commit to marriage (*B. Kiddushin* 49b; *Rashi*). His scholarly accomplishments were lauded by his colleagues. Ben Zoma was recognised as one who had intimate knowledge of the esoteric Torah (*Bereshit Rabba* 2:4). He was also one of the four sages who entered the mystical realm known as *Pardes* (*B. Ḥagiga* 14b).

Seeking to understand Ben Zoma's declaration, the commentators grapple with the image of an accomplished and respected sage suggesting that the whole world was created for his own personal benefit.

The most popular explanation suggests that his words should be read as an expression of appreciation, not haughtiness. Moreover, Ben Zoma acknowledged that leaders are only as good as their followers. As mentioned, the reason he did not reach the spiritual heights that Moses had attained was because the generation was undeserving. Seeing the masses stream to the Temple, Ben Zoma nonetheless recognised that his achievements were thanks to the people.

In a similar vein, one contemporary commentator, Rabbi Moshe Tzuriel, suggests that Ben Zoma's declaration should not be read as showing conceit. Rather, Ben Zoma's words should be understood as an expression of appreciation for the contributions of the people to his life. Rabbi Tzuriel expands on the importance of acknowledging what others have done for us, going so far as to call this trait a fundamental of Judaism. Ben Zoma, according to Rabbi Tzuriel, was a positive example of someone who thanked others for their part in his life.

Thus when Ben Zoma saw masses of people and recited the appropriate benediction over a multitude, he added an extra blessing acknowledging how so many people contributed to his own survival, well-being, and achievements. Instead of focusing on what he did not achieve, Ben Zoma unreservedly acknowledged the contribution of those around him to what he did achieve, and he publicly expressed gratitude for their efforts.

Often we are quick to blame others for our failures. Ben Zoma reminds us that we should be more conscientious in crediting others for our achievements.

Gracious guests

As we have just discussed, the Talmud records how Ben Zoma unreservedly expressed gratitude for the efforts of others (*B. Berakhot* 58a). Thus when Ben Zoma looked down from his vantage point on the Temple Mount and saw masses of people ascending to Jerusalem, he recited the appropriate blessing over a multitude, and added an extra blessing acknowledging how so many people contributed to his own survival and well-being.

With this idea of wholehearted appreciation setting the tone, Ben Zoma compares the attitudes of two types of guests. A good guest who is offered food by his host after he has rested from his journey says sincerely: "My host went to so much trouble for me! He has placed so much meat before me. He has served so much wine to me. He has brought me so many rolls. And he went to all this trouble for my sake!"

An ungrateful guest who is offered the same refreshments in the same manner might view the matter entirely differently. He may pettily think: "What trouble did the host go to for me? I ate one piece of bread. I ate one piece of meat. I drank one cup of wine. All the trouble that this host went to was for his own benefit. He took [all the food] for his own wife and for his own children!"

The difference is apparent, and can be seen clearly by looking at the focus of each guest's assessment. The good guest takes note of the efforts of the host, while the bad guest notices only what he actually received.

The talmudic passage continues by offering scriptural allusions to the two types of guests. Regarding the good guest, the following verse is evoked: *Remember, so that you will aggrandise his work that people shall see* (Job 36:24). This verse exhorts people to acknowledge publicly the efforts made on their behalf. For the bad guest a different verse is cited: *Therefore people fear him, he does not see any of the wise-hearted* (Job 37:24) – the guest fails to appreciate the benevolence that the wise-hearted host has bestowed upon him.

In truth these biblical verses can be read as referring to God's providential role in giving sustenance to humans. Following this line of thought, one commentator suggests that the "guests" described by Ben Zoma are metaphors for human beings who are temporary residents in this world, just as travellers are temporary residents in the place where they stop off during their journeys. During our stopover in this physical world, all our material needs are provided for by a most gracious host – the Almighty (*Maharsha*). The question remains whether we will be good guests who are appreciative of what we have, or bad guests who are unable to acknowledge what we have been given.

One of the Hasidic masters, Rabbi Zvi Elimelekh Shapira of Dynów (1783–1841), offers a different metaphoric understanding of Ben Zoma's guests. When Shabbat coincides with a festival or with Rosh Hodesh – the first day of a new month, which is considered a minor festival – the central blessing of the additional *Amida* prayer is changed. Normally it is dedicated to commemorating Shabbat, but for a festival or Rosh Hodesh it is replaced by a benediction for the festival or Rosh Hodesh. Only a passing mention of Shabbat is retained from the original formula. Rabbi Zvi Elimelekh finds this practice surprising: Isn't the holiness of Shabbat greater than that of the festivals, and certainly than that of Rosh Hodesh? How could such a breach of the honour of Shabbat be allowed?

Using Ben Zoma's idea of the conduct of hosts and guests, Rabbi Zvi Elimelekh presents an explanation. The festivals were all instituted to commemorate events in our people's history – Pesaḥ recalls the Exodus, Shavuot the giving of the Torah, and Sukkot the protective cocoon provided by the Almighty during the desert years. Even the commemoration of the new month dates back to the lead-up to the Exodus from

Egypt, when we were enjoined to mark Rosh Ḥodesh and to keep a calendar. Not so the weekly Shabbat, which is independent of the Jewish calendar and dates back to creation. Since the beginning of time, each seventh day has been sanctified as the day of rest.

Rabbi Zvi Elimelekh suggests that in a sense, on the seventh day of the week, Shabbat is like a host. Occasionally a festival or Rosh Ḥodesh comes to visit the Shabbat host at her seventh-day home. When this occurs, Shabbat graciously makes way for the festival – whether it is one of the major festive celebrations or for the more minor Rosh Ḥodesh commemoration. Shabbat then offers the festival guest pride of place in the centre of the *Amida* prayer. As a good guest, the festival in turn graciously acknowledges the Shabbat host who has welcomed the guest into her domain.

Rabbi Zvi Elimelekh continues by citing another talmudic passage from our tractate that deals with host-guest relationships. Our sages tell us that while the host should be the first to break bread, it is the guest who should be honoured with leading the recitation of Grace After Meals. The host breaks the bread so that generous servings will be offered to the guests. Were the guest to dish out the rations, the guest would undoubtedly allocate more modest portions. But at the end of the meal, the guest leads the recitation of Grace After Meals so that he may include an extra blessing for the generous host (*B. Berakhot* 46a).

In a similar vein, the Shabbat host honours the festival guest with the *Amida*'s special blessing that acknowledges the uniqueness of the day. Like a good guest, the festival adds an extra mention of the Shabbat host in that benediction, even referring to the Shabbat host in the conclusion of the blessing before mentioning the festival guest.

As hosts we aspire to be like Shabbat, who so generously welcomes the festival guests into her domain; as guests we hope to appropriately acknowledge the kindness of our hosts, heaping blessings on their heads. Moreover, whether in our capacity as guests at someone else's table or as sojourners in the Almighty's world, Ben Zoma urges us to focus on the positive. We should acknowledge the generous goodwill of our host and view all that is benevolently offered us in the most positive light.

It was Greek to me

ONE OF THE themes of Ḥanukka is the triumph of Jewish tradition over Hellenistic culture and Greek thought. Nevertheless, the Talmud recognises the legitimacy of non-Jewish wisdom (*B. Berakhot* 58a). Moreover, our sages prescribe a blessing that is to be recited upon encountering a wise gentile, a blessing that is not unlike the blessing to be recited over a Jewish sage:

"One who sees a wise person of Israel should say: 'Blessed is the One Who apportioned from His wisdom to those who fear Him.' One who sees a wise gentile should say: 'Blessed is the One Who gave of His wisdom to His creations.'"

Though there is a slight difference in the wording of the two benedictions, the essence of the blessings is the same. A wise person – Jew or gentile – should be recognised as such, and thanks should be given to the Almighty for providing the world with such wise people. In another talmudic passage we are told: "Whoever says a wise word – even if that person is from the nations of the world – is called a wise person" (*B. Megilla* 16a). Thus our tradition acknowledges that wisdom is not uniquely Jewish.

At the same time, our sages see a significant difference between Jewish knowledge and gentile knowledge. "If a person says to you: 'There is wisdom among the gentiles' – you should believe it. If a person says to you: 'There is Torah among the gentiles' – you should not believe it" (*Eikha Rabba* 2:13). Torah is a uniquely Jewish branch of learning which bespeaks our special spiritual connection with the Almighty. As such, it is a province of study that is fully realised in a Jewish context. Torah study is more than an intellectual pursuit; it is an enterprise that reflects our identity. Perhaps we could even say that if gentiles were to study the texts of our tradition, they would attain wisdom but not Torah.

Recognising the existence of wisdom among gentiles is not to say that we should make a point of learning from these sources of knowledge. Our sages urge us to immerse ourselves in the primary objective – the study of Torah – and not divert our attention to external wisdom. Thus we are advised: "Don't say 'I have studied Jewish wisdom, now I will study the wisdom of the nations of the world.' ...You are not licensed to leave Jewish wisdom" (*Sifra, Aharei Mot* 13:11). This should not be read as a dismissal of non-Jewish wisdom. It does, however, show a clear preference for the pursuit of our own sources of knowledge. It appears that substantively there is nothing wrong with gentile wisdom. Its only drawback is that it is not our beloved Torah.

One rabbinic source, however, records a ban against teaching youths Greek. This ban dates back to the second century before the Common Era (*M. Sota* 9:14). The Talmud provides the historical context of this prohibition (*B. Sota* 49b). During the Hasmonean period, the two sons of King Alexander Yannai – Hyrkanus and Aristobulus – fought each other for the crown of Judea. During the battle each side sought to enlist the assistance of the Roman general Pompey. He eventually assisted one side in besieging the coveted Jerusalem. During this siege a daily black market ritual took place. The faction inside the wall would lower coins from the Temple treasury in a pouch. In exchange, the faction outside would hoist lambs back over the wall, for daily communal sacrifices.

An old man within the city walls, who was familiar with Greek wisdom, communicated surreptitiously with the Roman besiegers in a code known only to the Greco-Roman aristocracy. He told them: "As long as those within the walls are engaged in the Temple service, they will not be delivered into your hands."

Taking stock of this intelligence information, the besiegers did not send over lambs the next day. Instead, in an attempt to foil the Divine protection granted to the besieged Jerusalemites, they hoisted up a pig. As the swine was lifted against its will, it stuck its hoofs into the wall. The entire Land of Israel shook. At that time it was declared: "Cursed be the person who raises pigs, and cursed be the person who teaches his son Greek wisdom!" The siege ended when the Romans entered the capital and took control of Judea.

Though the Talmud describes a specific historical episode, it would appear that the aversion to Greek stemmed from fear of disloyalty to Judaism. The old man, who was presumably Jewish, expressed disdain for Jewish rituals and saw nothing wrong with abetting the enemy to bring about the downfall of Jerusalem.

Further in the passage we are left with a different impression. We are told that the *nasi* Rabban Gamliel had a thousand youths in his household. Five hundred of them studied Torah, while five hundred studied Greek wisdom. It would appear that there were two legitimate tracks of study of equal standing, at least numerically and perhaps even ideologically.

This unexpected testimony is explained as an exception to the rule. Since the *nasi*'s family was responsible for dealing with the Roman authorities, it was granted special licence to instruct its children in Greek language and wisdom. In this vein we can understand the exclamation of Rebbi, who was also from the family of the *nasi*: "In the Land of Israel, why use Syriac? Either use the holy tongue or Greek!" Thus it appears that the licence to study Greek was granted for utilitarian purposes and was restricted to those whose station and occupation might require a familiarity with the language. The norm, however, was to avoid instructing youths in Greek.

As we have seen, the rejection of Greek was not only connected to concerns about loyalty. Our sages discouraged the study of foreign wisdom for reasons that highlight how they perceived Torah study (*B. Menahot* 99b; *Y. Pe'ah* 15c). An eager student once asked his relative, the astute Rabbi Yishmael: "May I, who have completed the entire Torah, be permitted to study Greek?"

The sage responded: "We are enjoined to immerse ourselves in Torah study both by day and by night (see Joshua 1:8). Go find a time that is neither day nor night, and then you can study Greek!"

While later authorities discuss the possibility of non-Torah-related studies, the Talmud seems to eschew foreign wisdom. A utilitarian need is acknowledged, yet this dispensation is limited to those who will need to interact with gentiles. Study of foreign culture carries the danger of misplaced loyalty, though it would appear that this is not the primary reason for its rejection by the sages. The study of non-Jewish subjects is rejected chiefly because it is a distraction from the holy pursuit of Torah.

BERAKHOT 58A

In the presence of the King

IN *FIDDLER ON THE ROOF*, Leibish asks the rabbi of the Russian shtetl Anatevka: "Is there a proper blessing...for the tsar?" The rabbi could have quoted the talmudic passage which gives the wording for this very benediction: "Blessed are You, God, our Lord, King of the universe, Who gave of His glory to His creations" (*B. Berakhot* 58a).

Which gentile leaders qualify for this blessing? Is it limited to kings and queens, or do other heads of state qualify as well? Some sovereigns are figureheads who exercise no real power over the people. Should the blessing be recited upon seeing them? What about local rulers or judges? Over the ages, commentators and halakhic authorities have discussed the conditions for reciting this blessing.

Perhaps the blessing should be said only over leaders who have the authority to mete out capital punishment. This definition would include judges in some localities, but would exclude many monarchs and rulers today. Perhaps the blessing should be recited only over leaders whose edicts cannot be altered by a higher authority. This too might qualify judges who serve in the highest court of the land, but might leave out the heads of many states, whose orders are subject to judicial review.

While serving as rabbi of the Carpathian town of Munkács, Rabbi Ḥayim Elazar Shapira (1871–1937) considered the conditions for the blessing over sovereigns. The heir presumptive of the Austro-Hungarian Empire – presumably Archduke Franz Ferdinand – had travelled to the region, and a rabbinic delegation which met with him pronounced the full text of the prescribed blessing, invoking the Almighty's name. Rabbi Shapira, however, wondered whether this was the appropriate course. Perhaps the Almighty's name should not have been used. After all, Franz Ferdinand's uncle, Emperor Franz Joseph, was still the ruling monarch. As long as the Emperor lived, the Archduke did not have the authority either to sentence a subject to death or to pardon the condemned. The heir presumptive might one day fill this role, but at the moment he was not vested with such authority.

Rabbi Shapira merely expressed his doubts without ruling on the matter. As we now know, Archduke Franz Ferdinand was assassinated on June 28, 1914 and never became ruler; that role fell to Charles, the last monarch of the Habsburg dynasty.

Beyond defining the halakhic conditions for when the blessing should be said, the Talmud also offers some advice. A person should always make an effort to run to meet kings – and not only kings of Israel but even kings of other nations. This suggestion is codified in Jewish law (*Shulḥan Arukh, Oraḥ Ḥayim* 224:9). The Talmud explains why it is valuable to see a gentile ruler. If one proves deserving, he will be able to contrast the glory of the messianic king in the end of days with the glory of gentile kings in our day.

The passage continues with the story of the blind sage Rav Sheshet, who joined everyone in going to greet the king. Seeing Rav Sheshet, a certain troublemaker sneered: "Whole pitchers go to the river; where do broken ones go?" A broken pitcher is of no use when water is to be drawn, taunted the troublemaker. What is the point of those who cannot see the glory of the king's retinue taking part in a royal procession?

Rav Sheshet was not perturbed. He blithely responded: "Come and see that I know more about the king's procession than you do."

As Rav Sheshet stood next to his adversary, a troop marched past and the crowd cheered. "The king has come," declared the agitator.

"Not yet," replied Rav Sheshet calmly.

A second regiment passed by, and again the troublemaker suggested to Rav Sheshet that the monarch was present. Rav Sheshet was unmoved: "The king has still not come."

A third troop arrived and the crowd grew silent. This was the cue Rav Sheshet had been waiting for. "Now the king is certainly coming," he pronounced.

The troublemaker was impressed with Rav Sheshet's perception. He queried: "How did you know this?"

"Earthly royalty is a reflection of heavenly royalty," began Rav Sheshet, "and regarding heavenly royalty it is written: *And behold God was passing, and a great powerful wind, smashing mountains and breaking rocks, went before God, yet God was not in the wind. And after the wind came an earthquake, yet God was not in the earthquake. And after the earthquake came a fire, yet God was not in the fire. After the fire came a silent, thin sound* (1 Kings 19:11–12)." It was in the silence that the prophet Elijah perceived the Almighty's presence, and it was the silence that led Rav Sheshet to conclude that the king had arrived.

Rav Sheshet proceeded to pronounce the mandated blessing, at which the troublemaker was surprised and asked: "You recite a blessing over someone you cannot even see!?" In this sense the blessing over a sovereign is unique among blessings pronounced over visible phenomena: This blessing alone may be recited even when the object – in this case the sovereign – is hidden from view. The blessing over sovereigns is pronounced over the intangible splendour and glory of the royal retinue; perception of the phenomenon therefore suffices (*Sha'arei Teshuva*).

Based on Rav Sheshet's story we can suggest a further reason to take advantage of opportunities to see rulers. Since human sovereigns reflect the heavenly Sovereign, by observing earthly kings we can begin to perceive how one must act in the presence of the King of kings. When a visiting head of state arrives, roads are blocked off, traffic comes to a halt, and the flow of life is disrupted. The leader's entourage is given priority. A temporal ruler's reign is perforce limited, by human mortality as well as by the vagaries of politics. There may well be outside forces with the power to appoint and dismiss rulers.

If a temporary leader is accorded so much respect, we can extrapolate as to how much respect we should give to the everlasting Ruler of rulers. If we display awe in the presence of a human sovereign, how much more so should we display awe in the presence of the Sovereign of sovereigns.

A fatal glare

CAN YOU IMAGINE a taunted sage glaring at an opponent and the opponent miraculously turning into a heap of bones? The Talmud relates three such cases, the first of which appears in our tractate (*B. Berakhot* 58a).

As we just recounted, the blind sage Rav Sheshet went to witness a king's procession. A certain troublemaker taunted the sage by saying that there is no point in the blind coming to see a royal procession. Rav Sheshet demonstrated his ability to participate in the procession and even to distinguish between the king's retinue passing by and the presence of the sovereign himself. The Talmud relates two versions of this irreverent agitator's fate. According to one version the blind Rav Sheshet glowered at him – the Hebrew reads *natan bo einav*, literally "gave him his eyes" – and he became a heap of bones.

The second reference to the talmudic glare of death appears in the famous story of Rabbi Shimon ben Yoḥai (*B. Shabbat* 33b–34a). Rabbi Shimon ben Yoḥai was sentenced to death by the Romans, after he made disparaging remarks about the authorities. Forced to flee, he first hid in the *beit midrash*. When that hiding place became unsafe, he fled to a cave. With only his son for company, Rabbi Shimon ben Yoḥai subsisted for years on water, carobs, and Torah study.

When the danger passed and Rabbi Shimon ben Yoḥai was able to return to civilisation, he chanced upon the very person whose words had brought about the Roman decree that had forced him into hiding. Meeting this person in the marketplace, Rabbi Shimon ben Yoḥai exclaimed: "Is this one still alive?" Rabbi Shimon ben Yoḥai glared at this wretched fellow and he became a heap of bones.

In the third such incident related in the Talmud, Rabbi Yoḥanan taught that the Almighty will one day take precious stones and pearls that measure thirty cubits by thirty cubits, and from these colossal rocks will cut openings of ten cubits by twenty cubits. God will then place them at the gates of Jerusalem. One of the students present scoffed at this fanciful suggestion: "Nowadays we cannot find precious stones and pearls that are even the size of an egg or of a small dove; can stones of such immense proportions ever be found?!"

Time passed. That student was aboard a ship when he saw ministering angels hewing stones, just as described by his teacher Rabbi Yoḥanan. He turned to the angels: "Whom are these for?" The angels' response confirmed Rabbi Yoḥanan's teaching.

The student returned to his teacher and declared: "My master, lecture! You are worthy to lecture, for just as you described, so I saw!"

Rabbi Yoḥanan was unimpressed by his disciple's enthusiasm. He retorted: "You empty person! Had you not seen it yourself, would you not have believed it? You are one who mocks the words of the sages." Rabbi Yoḥanan glared at the student and the student became a pile of bones (*B. Bava Batra* 75a; *B. Sanhedrin* 100a).

As we read these three accounts, it seems rather strange that the venerable sages should wantonly cause the death of their opponents. Moreover, if the sages were so powerful that they could cause death with one fatal glare, surely they could have inspired repentance with a sympathetic look in the direction of their antagonists.

This puzzle leads some Hasidic masters to suggest alternative explanations for the deathly glare of the talmudic sages. In truth the phrase "he became a heap of bones" calls out for explanation since there are many ways to describe the moment of death. The Talmud normally uses the phrase "his soul rested" when describing death. What then is the meaning of the glare of death that turns a person into a pile of bones?

Rabbi Naḥman of Bratslav (1772–1810) offers an interesting approach. The Talmud states that the sage turns a sinner into a *gal atzamot*, a pile of bones. He explains that when people sin they cannot see the extent of the damage that their actions cause. The *tzaddik*, the righteous person with a pure soul, is able to perceive the harm wrought. When a person sins, the *tzaddik* does not look at the sinner, rather he gives his own eyes to the sinner – *noten bo einav* (translated above as "glared at") – so that the sinner himself can appreciate the destruction he has caused. Once the sinner takes in what he has done, the damage is revealed (*gal*) before him. In disgust at his own actions, the sinner closes (*otzem*) his eyes so that he will not have to look upon his own foul handiwork. Rabbi Naḥman concludes: "And there is no greater punishment than this, when a person perceives the damage he has wrought."

A later Hasidic master – Rabbi Yehoshua Heschel Rabinowitz of Monasterzyska (1860–1938), who was born in Zińków and died in New York – offers an interpretation closer to the original meaning of the phrase. He notes that the fatal talmudic glare is mentioned in cases where the antagonist sneered at the sages. Such mockery comes from haughtiness, for the evildoer is belittling the greatness of our talmudic heroes, and assumes that he knows more than the venerable sage he is mocking.

When the sage "gives his eyes" to the misguided offender, he shows him the extent of his mistaken ways. At that moment the sinner's conceit bursts, as he realises how worthless he is. In his own eyes, the self-important antagonist suddenly feels no more than a pile of bones. Such is the extent of the realisation of his erroneous course.

Indeed, there are moments when we feel so downcast because of our own mistakes; when we feel so worthless because of the damage that we have caused; when we feel like nothing more than a heap of dry bones lacking all vitality. Fortunately, we have the opportunity to revive ourselves and to tackle the lifelong challenge of becoming more than mortal flesh subject to decay. We can re-embark upon the quest to fulfil our tremendous God-given potential as human beings.

BERAKHOT 58A

The ability of the disabled

THE TALMUD PRESENTS countless examples of sages who had physical deformities or disabilities. As we have seen, the blindness of Rav Sheshet is the subject of one passage (*B. Berakhot* 58a). Rav Sheshet's blindness did not impede his intellectual capabilities. Indeed when Rav Sheshet and his colleague Rav Ḥisda met, Rav Ḥisda's lips would quiver at the thought of the vast bank of knowledge at Rav Sheshet's disposal (*B. Eruvin* 67a).

Rav Sheshet was not the only blind talmudic sage. Rav Yosef, who is referred to as a veritable Sinai – a repository of all Torah knowledge – was also blind (*B. Berakhot* 64a; *B. Horayot* 14a; *B. Kiddushin* 31a; *B. Bava Kamma* 87a; *B. Bava Metzia* 116b). There were other blind sages whose blessings were sought or whose spiritual greatness was recognised (*B. Ḥagiga* 5b; *B. Gittin* 68b; *Y. Ḥagiga* 1:8; *Y. Pe'ah* 8:8). Indeed our forefather Isaac was visually impaired and yet was still able to bestow Divine blessings (Genesis 27).

Blindness was only one of the physical challenges faced by some of our sages. Others had to contend with different physical disabilities or abnormalities. Rabbi Zeira was short and had a problem with his leg; he was known to all by the nickname "the small man of the singed thighs" (*B. Bava Metzia* 85a). Rabbi Yoḥanan's bushy eyebrows were like curtains before his eyes; he needed to brush the hair aside with a silver fork when he wanted to see what was happening around him (*B. Bava Kamma* 117a; *B. Ta'anit* 9a and *Rashi*). Other sages had other deformities (*Y. Ta'anit* 4:1; *Y. Megilla* 4:8). One sage, Naḥum Ish Gam Zu, was blind in both eyes, and missing both hands and both feet (*B. Ta'anit* 21a). The great heights reached by these sages, and the significant contributions that they made to Jewish tradition, are indeed inspiring.

The numerous talmudic examples, however, appear to be at odds with a passage in the Zohar. Commenting on the biblical requirement for *kohanim* serving in the Temple to be without physical blemish (Leviticus 21:16–24), the Zohar derives a broader principle about who can become a conduit for sanctity. Holiness does not rest on someone who is blind, broken, or blemished. Thus, for instance, even excessively bushy eyebrows disqualify a *kohen* from Temple service (*B. Bekhorot* 43a). Similarly, when describing the prerequisites for receiving prophecy, Maimonides mentions that the potential prophet must be *shalem begufo*, physically flawless. The position expressed in the Zohar and supported by the rules for *kohanim* and prophets seems to contradict the talmudic reality described above.

The Munkatcher Rebbe, Rabbi Ḥayim Elazar Shapira (1871–1937), was deeply troubled by this contradiction. After collecting the talmudic examples of disfigured sages, the Munkatcher Rebbe sought an explanation for the contradiction between the Talmud and the Zohar. Granted, the blind and the lame could not serve as *kohanim*, but did this formal Temple limitation perforce mean that they could not reach great spiritual heights?

One suggestion that the Munkatcher Rebbe entertains distinguishes between the two sources. The Zohar refers only to congenital disabilities; people born blind, for instance, cannot attain the loftiest spiritual heights. Citing esoteric sources, the Munkatcher Rebbe notes that a congenital disability may be a reflection of a blemished soul which does not have the same spiritual potential as an untarnished soul. People who develop disabilities later in life, however, are not spiritually limited; hence the numerous talmudic exemplars.

This distinction fits well with the stories of our forefathers. Isaac became blind only in his old age, and Jacob began limping only after his encounter with a mysterious assailant (Genesis 32:31). Alas, this proposed distinction is not hinted at in the Talmud or Zohar. Who says that all the talmudic sages who had disabilities were not born thus? The Talmud describes how some of the sages acquired their disabilities, but it never suggests that all disabled sages were born without deformity.

Moreover, according to some sources from Jewish mystical tradition, even a disability acquired later in life is a reflection of a spiritual defect. Could this mean that our talmudic heroes and even our forefathers developed spiritual defects?

Ultimately the Munkatcher Rebbe rejects this distinction. Clearly troubled by the contradiction between the talmudic exemplars and the statement of the Zohar, he returns to the question repeatedly without finding an explanation that he deems satisfactory. He eventually leaves the paradox unresolved and concludes that it would be a *mitzva* to explain this problematic passage in the Zohar.

For many of us, the Zohar's statement may be troubling, even without the background of the numerous talmudic sages with disabilities. Can spiritual potential really be dependent on physical characteristics?

Wouldn't it be more appropriate to suggest that irrespective of physical defects, spiritual heights can be reached by all?

Perhaps the Zohar reflects a theoretical position that is superseded by the practical reality described in the Talmud. The Zohar voices a position based on a certain measure of logic. We might think that the Almighty's messengers in the temporal world must be without blemish – spiritual or physical. An esteemed and honourable messenger lends credibility to the message; an unsightly messenger may detract from the status of the message or may not be as effective in delivering it. In this vein, the Zohar declares that holiness rests only on the unblemished. The reality – as orchestrated by the Almighty – is very different from the theory. A Divine message can be effectively carried by the blind and the lame, the blemished and the broken. Thankfully, we have many examples in the talmudic literature that clearly demonstrate the ability of all to reach spiritual and intellectual heights. Thus the Zohar's theoretical position is sidelined.

The sum of the talmudic evidence is clear: physical limitations need not entail spiritual or intellectual limitations. Those with physical deformities or disabilities can certainly contribute to the perpetuation and evolution of our hallowed tradition.

BERAKHOT 58B

Sigh of sadness

OUR SAGES MANDATE a variety of blessings that should be recited upon seeing various natural phenomena or human-made structures. Among the lesser-known blessings are the benedictions recited over houses of Israel in various states. Thus, upon seeing houses of Israel that stand in all their glory – meaning that the local community is under no threat – we pronounce: "Blessed are You, God, our Lord, King of the universe, Who establishes the boundary of the widow" (*B. Berakhot* 58b).

The commentators note that this blessing must belong to the Second Temple era. Prior to this period, when the First Temple stood, Israel could hardly be called a widow (*Rashi*). In this sense, the blessing recognises the Almighty's hand in re-establishing the former glory of Israel.

What types of houses mandate this blessing? Some authorities maintain that the blessing is recited specifically over synagogues (*Rif*). Others maintain that the blessing is not limited to synagogues, but that it may be relevant only to houses in the Land of Israel (*Rashi*). Halakha follows the former opinion and the blessing is recited only over synagogues (*Mishna Berura* 224:14). In deference to the latter opinion, however, when the blessing is recited outside of the Land of Israel, the Almighty's name is not invoked (*Peri Megadim*).

The Talmud continues with the blessing that should be recited upon encountering houses of Israel that are in a ruined state: "Blessed are You, God, our Lord, King of the universe, the true Judge." This is the same blessing that is mandated for other sorrowful events, such as receiving bad news (*M. Berakhot* 9:2).

The Talmud goes on to speak of an exchange between two sages as they passed a ruined house. Ulla and Rav Ḥisda were walking along the road when they chanced upon the house formerly occupied by Rav Ḥana bar Ḥanilai. As they passed the entrance, Rav Ḥisda let out a long sigh. Ulla turned to his colleague and asked: "Why do you sigh?"

Ulla explained his question by quoting a talmudic tradition: "Rav has said that a sigh breaks half a person's body, as it says: *And you, O mortal, sigh! With a shattering of the loins and with bitterness, sigh before their eyes* (Ezekiel 21:11)." The loins are at the centre of a person's body, and as the sigh shatters them half the body is broken.

Ulla continued citing talmudic sources to buttress his surprise at Rav Ḥisda's sigh: "Rabbi Yoḥanan went even further, saying that a sigh breaks a person's entire body, as it says: *It will be when they say to you, 'Why are you sighing?' And you will say, 'Because of the tidings that are coming.' And every heart will melt and all hands will hang limp and all spirit will be dulled and all knees will turn to water; it is approaching and it will be – declares the Lord God* (ibid., v. 12)." In context the verse is describing the people's reaction when they hear of the fall of

Jerusalem. Rabbi Yoḥanan explains that it is the act of sighing – not the bad news – that breaks the person.

According to one commentator, Rav and Rabbi Yoḥanan are not arguing about the possible damage of a sigh, but describing two types of sighs. Rav is referring to a sigh due to physical pain; such a sigh breaks half the body. Rabbi Yoḥanan is referring to a sigh born of physical pain and emotional grief; such a sigh breaks the entire body (*Ben Ish Ḥai*). Whatever the exact damage caused by a sigh, both opinions agree that it is a reaction that can cause physical harm. Ulla therefore asked Rav Ḥisda why he was engaging in this dangerous practice.

Rav Ḥisda responded: "How can I not sigh! In this very house there were sixty bakers during the day and sixty bakers during the night, and they would bake bread for whoever needed. And Rav Ḥana bar Ḥanilai, the master of the house, never removed his hand from his money purse because he was worried that if he were approached by a poor person of noble background, in the brief time that it would take him to locate his purse, the poor person's embarrassment at his reduced circumstances would overcome him and he would leave. In addition, the house had four gates open in all four directions. Anyone who entered hungry left satisfied."

Rav Ḥisda continued to describe the abundant generosity that was characteristic in this house: "And in years of famine" – when even people who were not accustomed to taking charity were forced to do so – "they would throw wheat and barley outside the house so that anyone who was embarrassed to take during the day could come and take at night." Rav Ḥisda concluded: "Now that this house has turned into a heap of rubble should I not sigh?!"

Ulla sought to soothe his colleague, once again quoting Rabbi Yoḥanan: "From the day the Temple was destroyed, a Divine decree was passed against the houses of the righteous, stating that they too will be destroyed, as it says: *It is in my ears that God, Master of legions, said: 'To be sure, many houses will be desolate; great and splendid ones will be without occupants'* (Isaiah 5:9)."

"Rabbi Yoḥanan also said," continued Ulla, "that in the future the Holy One, blessed be He, will restore them to their inhabited state, as it says: *A song of ascents. Those who trust in God are like Mount Zion, that does not falter but abides forever* (Psalms 125:1). Just as the Almighty will restore Mount Zion to its inhabited state in the future, so too the Almighty will restore the houses of the righteous to their inhabited state in the future."

Alas, Rav Ḥisda was not to be consoled. Realising that any further attempt to comfort his colleague was futile, Ulla ended the exchange by saying: "It is enough for a servant to be like his master." The houses of God's servants, namely the Jewish people, cannot be expected to remain standing in all their glory while the Almighty's own house, the Temple, lies in ruins.

Strangely, in the entire conversation the blessing over ruined houses was not recited. Could it be that the Talmud felt it was superfluous to state the obvious – that our venerable sages pronounced the appropriate blessing? Or perhaps the Talmud is suggesting that while the benediction is mandated by law, the goal of the recitation should not be overlooked.

We should truly be moved by the desolate places of our people. If we feel this sincerely and deeply, then when we chance upon houses of Israel that stand in all their glory – be it beautiful synagogues or homes built on what was once a bleak landscape – we will genuinely feel the joy of a heritage raised from the dust of ruins and gloriously rebuilt.

BERAKHOT 58B

Nice to see you

IT IS ALWAYS nice to see friends whom you have not seen for a while. After an extended separation, the joy of catching up with old acquaintances is palpable. Our sages acknowledge this feeling by mandating a benediction for the occasion. If you haven't seen your friend for thirty days, the *Sheheḥeyanu* blessing is appropriate: "Blessed are You, God, our Lord, King of the universe, Who has kept us alive, sustained us, and brought us to this time" (*B. Berakhot* 58b).

This blessing is generally recited at festivals and upon other joyful seasonal events, such as tasting a new fruit. It is also mandated for moments of personal joy, for instance upon the acquisition of significant new possessions. In this spirit, seeing a friend after a lapse of thirty days warrants the recital of the benediction.

Commentators note that this blessing is not pronounced for just any acquaintance; it is only seeing a good friend that justifies a benediction (*Tosafot*). Codifiers go even further, mandating the blessing only for truly beloved friends whom we are genuinely happy to see (*Shulḥan Arukh, Oraḥ Ḥayim* 225:1). A further limitation is noted: if one had previously received regards from the person or a letter saying that the friend is alive and well, then one need not recite the blessing upon meeting face to face (*Mishna Berura*). Common practice, however, takes this even further. The *Sheheḥeyanu* benediction upon seeing people is generally not said at all (*Rema, Oraḥ Ḥayim* 223:1). The blessing in this context, it appears, has fallen into disuse. It is difficult to explain this halakhic development.

How should we understand the trend of the post-talmudic commentators to limit the recitation of this benediction, and how are we to comprehend the subsequent cessation of its recital?

The Hasidic master and halakhic authority Rabbi Ḥayim Elazar Shapira of Munkács (1871–1937) tackles this question. First, he comments on the narrowing of the conditions for when the blessing should be said. If we pronounced the blessing over every friend that we have not met in the last thirty days, imagine the situation on market days, when everyone gathers to sell their wares. Particularly considering the requirement to love our fellows, if we truly treat everyone as our friend we would need to recite the benediction endlessly. This scenario made it necessary to limit the cases where the blessing is required.

The Munkatcher Rebbe does not explain what the problem is with needing to recite the blessing repeatedly. We can surmise that this might disrupt the flow of commerce on market day. More importantly, the *Sheheḥeyanu* blessing is designed to reflect excitement and joy; ceaseless recitation would blunt its force. In talmudic times apparently this benediction was appropriate; with changing realities, however, conditions for its recitation needed to be adjusted.

The narrowing of the conditions for the benediction over friends still does not explain why it is never pronounced today. Here too, the Munkatcher Rebbe offers an explanation which reflects his understanding of modern times. He bemoans our exilic existence which entails a spiritual exile as well as a physical exile from our Land. The spiritual exile is expressed in many ways, including the lack of brotherly love between people and the jealousy with which we suspiciously view one another. The Munkatcher Rebbe sadly points to insincerity and two-facedness – which he terms "politics" – as a staple of the times. Given this lamentable situation, requiring a sincere *Sheheheyanu* is simply not realistic nowadays.

Furthermore, given the general lack of sincerity, if people were allowed to recite the blessing they would give it lip service, pretending that they were happy to see their so-called friends while suppressing their inner malice. The benediction would then be recited in vain. To avoid this infraction of the law against misusing God's name, the *Sheheheyanu* blessing over friends is not said.

Nevertheless, the joy over seeing a good friend is still tangible, and it is not a simple thing to disregard or brush aside the talmudic dictate. Taking this into account, the Munkatcher Rebbe goes on to suggest that a less formal expression of joy – albeit without the official benediction – may fulfil the talmudic requirement. An example would be saying something like "Thank God, it's good to see you." One could argue, of course, that any less formal replacement does not properly discharge the original blessing obligation. In general, blessings may be said in any language, but it appears that an exact translation, rather than a paraphrase, is necessary.

Despite acknowledging and discussing how the recitation of *Sheheheyanu* has fallen into disuse, the Munkatcher Rebbe did have the opportunity to recite the benediction. In 1930 he travelled from his home in Mukačevo, Czechoslovakia, to visit the Land of Israel. When he met the venerable Rabbi Shlomo Eliezer Alfandari (1820?–1930) – a meeting the Munkatcher Rebbe had been pining for – he recited the *Sheheheyanu* blessing.

Today, we do not say the *Sheheheyanu* blessing when seeing friends whom we have not seen for some time. Despite the strange situation of a talmudic blessing that has fallen into disuse, it is still nice to express our happiness upon seeing a friend by thanking the Almighty for the joyful moment.

A lot can happen in a year

AFTER EXTENDED PERIODS of separation from friends, the Talmud mandates appropriate blessings. As mentioned, if one has not seen a friend for thirty days, the *Sheheḥeyanu* blessing is recited: "Blessed are You, God, our Lord, King of the universe, Who has kept us alive, sustained us, and brought us to this time." If a full twelve months have passed since seeing this friend, a different blessing is called for: "Blessed are You, God, our Lord, King of the universe, Who resurrects the dead" (*B. Berakhot* 58b).

It sounds somewhat strange to recite the blessing over the revival of the dead just because one has not seen a friend for a year. An extended absence is hardly akin to the finality of death, nor does a touching reunion rank with the miracle of resurrection of the dead.

One early Hasidic master, Rabbi Pinḥas of Koretz (1726–1791), explains the blessing in mystical terms. The joy of two people meeting creates an angel. This angel has a life expectancy of one year. If within this period the two meet again, the angel receives a new lease on life. Alas, after a twelve-month separation between friends, the angel is no more. When friends meet again after a yearlong absence, the angel is resurrected. The blessing is pronounced over the miraculous revival of their joint angel. Hence, the benediction over resurrecting the dead – in this case a dead angel – is appropriate.

The Talmud offers a different explanation for why a blessing over the revival of the dead is appropriate after a yearlong separation. The heart does not forget the deceased until twelve months have gone by.

Twelve months is the amount of time that it takes for a person to forget, or at least to stop thinking actively about, a friend. In this sense twelve months of disengagement may be brought about by death or merely by separation, but the result is the same: the memory of the person recedes from the foreground to the recesses of the heart.

The Talmud adds a biblical proof text for the analogy between death and extended separation: *I have become forgotten as the dead from the heart; I have become like a lost vessel* (Psalms 31:13). With time, the heart can forget a live person, just as the memory of the deceased fades with the passage of time.

The quoted verse adds a third element – *a lost vessel*. The Mishna discusses the laws of returning lost items. The basic requirement is that a found item must be returned to its rightful owner. The problem, of course, lies in locating the owner. The sages declare that if the object has an identifying mark, the finder must publicly announce that an item has been found. The rightful owner is invited to come forward and claim the object after demonstrating ownership by describing the identifying mark.

To what extent must the finder announce the find? The Mishna offers two opinions. The first opinion requires announcing the find such that local people have been properly notified. At that point the finder is considered to have made a reasonable effort to alert the owner and to have provided ample opportunity for the owner to reclaim the lost item. The second opinion requires an announcement that is more far-reaching. The find must be announced in Jerusalem at each of the three festivals – Pesaḥ, Shavuot, and Sukkot – and for an additional week as well. There was a special place in Jerusalem set aside for this purpose. A large stone served as the official location for announcing lost objects. This site was known as *even hato'en*, the stone of claims (*M. Bava Metzia* 2:6; *B. Bava Metzia* 28b).

What was the logic of this thrice-yearly Jerusalem requirement? Unlike the pilgrimage itself, the Bible does not mention a need to make the journey to Jerusalem to return lost articles. As we all know, people do not lose objects just in their own locales; thus there is a need to announce the find to a broader audience. The tri-annual festival pilgrimage to Jerusalem provided the perfect forum to notify as many people as possible.

But why three festivals and a week; wouldn't an announcement at one of the festivals suffice? After all, the announcement at one festival would serve to notify the public about the item. Individuals could then return home and check whether they had lost such an item. If they had indeed lost the item, they would need to wait for the next festival to claim ownership. It would seem from this that announcements at two festivals should be adequate; what is the need for the third announcement?

According to some commentators, the additional festival served as a precaution, lest someone missed one of the three annual pilgrimages. The extra week made it possible for the owner of the lost object to spend three days travelling home, take a quick look to see if he indeed lost the object in question, and, if he had, to spend three more days on the return journey to Jerusalem. Upon his arrival he could then claim the object.

Another explanation of the three festivals and the week brings us back to the twelve months it takes to forget (*Rashi*). If a person lost an object on the day after Shavuot, for instance, the finder would post an announcement on Sukkot, Pesaḥ, and Shavuot of the following year. With the extra week, a full twelve months would have passed. The finder could then safely assume that the owner had forgotten about the item, for an absence of twelve months dulls the memory. Thus the third element in the proof text: the psalmist is telling us that just as people are forgotten after twelve months, so too are lost vessels.

The twelve-month rule can assist us in understanding another law connected to comforting those who lost relatives (*B. Mo'ed Katan* 21b). The Talmud criticises people who offer comfort to mourners after more than twelve months have passed since the death. A parable is offered to illustrate the point. Imagine that a person broke his leg, which in time thankfully healed. When this person chances upon a doctor, the doctor says to him: "Come to my office. I will break your leg again and then cure it, so you can see how fine my remedies are." This suggestion is of course foolish; such a course has no value for the poor chap who broke his leg and has fortunately recovered. Let the doctor show off his prowess elsewhere, not by re-opening old wounds.

Comforting someone more than twelve months after a death is, in effect, re-opening an old wound. Twelve months gives the mourner a chance to recover. It is during this period that the damage to the heart slowly heals, as the memory of the loved one recedes. The comforter may well have consoling words to tender, but evoking the pain of losing a loved one just for the sake of being able to offer words of comfort is foolish and unkind. Twelve months is not just a calendar year; it is a long time. It is time enough to forget.

Beauty is in the eye of the beholder

HOW SHOULD WE react when we see someone or something beautiful? Should we stare and gawk? Should we feast our eyes or avert them? The Talmud says that one who sees beautiful creatures or beautiful trees should acknowledge the Almighty by reciting the following blessing: "Blessed are You, God, our Lord, King of the universe, Who has this in His world" (*B. Berakhot* 58b).

What type of beautiful creatures warrant such a benediction? Commentators explain that seeing beautiful animals or beautiful people, whether they are Jews or not, justifies the recitation of the blessing (*Shulḥan Arukh, Oraḥ Ḥayim* 225:10). Furthermore, the blessing can be recited over males or females, though the Talmud dislikes the idea of one gender feasting its eyes on the other (*B. Avoda Zara* 20a–b; *Mishna Berura*).

Over what aspect of the experience is the blessing recited? Some commentators explain that the benediction is pronounced over the sensory pleasure of beholding beauty. Much as blessings are recited over scents and tastes, so too it is appropriate to pronounce a blessing over sights. Saying a blessing thus reframes the sensory experience in a manner that acknowledges the hand of God (*Ra'avad*).

Other commentators highlight not the pleasure but the novelty. Even if there is no particular enjoyment in seeing the object, the fact that one has never before seen such a beautiful object justifies acknowledging the Almighty's role in creation (*Meiri*).

How often can this blessing be recited? If someone lives with a beautiful person, should they recite the blessing daily? Monthly? Yearly? According to one prevalent opinion, the blessing can be said only once over a particular subject. Once the benediction has been pronounced over a certain beautiful person, for instance, it cannot ever be recited again over that same person (*Shulḥan Arukh*). Others maintain that the blessing may be recited once every thirty days (*Meiri*).

Alas, this blessing has largely fallen into disuse, and on the rare occasions when it is recited it is said without the Almighty's name. Why don't we say this blessing nowadays? One codifier in the early nineteenth century suggests that in modern times we are exposed to such a gamut of incredible images that we have become desensitised to wonderful scenes, pictures, and spectacles. Thus a blessing is no longer warranted (*Ḥayei Adam*). If this could be said in the early nineteenth century, it is all the more true in our day and age when technology has brought spectacular images into our homes.

Another reason offered for the neglect of this blessing is that it was instituted for only the most exquisite sights, such as a person of extraordinary beauty or an exceptionally beautiful tree (*Maimonides*). Since it is so difficult to judge which sight is rare enough to warrant the blessing, it is not said (*Mishna Berura*).

A third possible explanation highlights the subjectivity of beauty, which makes the qualifications for this blessing too blurred. The trend of halakha – and, for that matter, of law generally – is to seek more precise definitions. If a rule's stipulations are undefined when the rule is instituted, over time they tend to become more precisely delineated. Without such precision, the rule – in this case the rule that beauty warrants a blessing – may fall into disuse.

The subjectivity of beauty brings to mind another talmudic passage (*B. Ketubot* 16b–17a). The sages discuss what should be said in the presence of a bride as we dance before her. According to the School of Shammai we praise the bride as she is. We focus on whatever actual qualities the bride has in the realms of beauty, status, and character without exaggerating or misstating them. The School of Hillel takes a different tack. We always say that the bride is beautiful and charming, irrespective of her actual appearance.

The School of Shammai is surprised by the School of Hillel's suggestion, and asks: "If she is lame or blind, do we say about her that she is a beautiful and charming bride? Doesn't the Torah say: *Distance yourself from falsehood* (Exodus 23:7)?"

The School of Hillel responds: "What then is your opinion if someone made a bad purchase in the market? Should one praise the purchase or denigrate it? Naturally one would praise it!" What type of answer is this? The School of Shammai would surely respond to the School of Hillel by saying: "Indeed! Don't tell a lie. Evaluate the purchase on its real merits."

The School of Hillel is not advocating lying. It is merely a proponent of a different concept of truth. The School of Shammai speaks on behalf of objective truth and facts that are not subject to opinion or personal tastes. In that vein we praise the bride, using societal norms as yardsticks for assessing her qualities. The School of Hillel promotes a subjective truth: the beauty of the bride is in the eyes of the groom. Similarly, the value of the purchase should not be measured by absolutes, but through the subjective eyes of the purchaser.

Elsewhere our sages describe how twice a year – on *Tu B'av* (the fifteenth of Av) and Yom Kippur – the daughters of Jerusalem would all wear simple white clothing and go dance in the vineyards. Young men who were looking for a match would come to this event, and the young women would encourage them not just to look at external beauty, but to consider a variety of virtues (*M. Ta'anit* 4:8). While the young women would encourage the young men to look at objective facts, the choice as to which values should be deemed paramount – beauty, family background, or piety – would be the subjective choice of the suitor.

At times we are drawn by external beauty. While this may be a natural reaction, it is folly to just follow such externalities. Real beauty is something far deeper, but it is not buried so far beneath the skin that a grand mining expedition must be organised to excavate it. As our relationships develop, as we reveal the godliness within people, we expose the beauty within. Beauty is in the eye of the beholder – the one who beholds the inner worth of the other. It is this beauty that we seek; it is this beauty for which we bless the Almighty.

Wisdom of the other

THE BABYLONIAN SAGE Rav Ketina was once walking along the road (B. *Berakhot* 59a). When he passed the door of a necromancer, a powerful tremor shook the earth. Rav Ketina called out to the necromancer, who communicated with the dead using the bones of a corpse: "Does the bone necromancer know what is causing this rumbling?"

Without hesitation, the necromancer called back: "Ketina, Ketina, why shouldn't I know? When the Holy One, blessed be He, remembers His children who endure in misery amid the nations of the world, He sheds two tears that fall into the Mediterranean Sea. The sound of these teardrops is heard from one end of the world to the other. And this is what we perceive as an earthquake."

Rav Ketina responded harshly: "The bone necromancer is a fraud and his words are lies. For if his explanation was founded in reality, there should have been two earthquakes – one for each teardrop!"

Surprisingly, the Talmud comments that it was not as Rav Ketina had claimed. Indeed there had been two earthquakes, and the necromancer's explanation did fit the facts. Rav Ketina's stark rejection of the necromancer was, therefore, rooted elsewhere. Evidently he did not want to give credit to a practitioner of a craft that is foreign to our tradition and forbidden by Torah law (Leviticus 19:31, 20:6, 27; Deuteronomy 18:9–14).

Rav Ketina offered his own explanation for the earthquake, and cited a scriptural verse in support: God claps His hands, and the earth shakes as a result. The talmudic passage goes on to present three other possible explanations, each with a biblical proof text: God emits a sigh, God kicks the sky, or God thrusts His legs under the throne of glory.

Hai Gaon (939–1038) and many commentators in his wake offer a sweeping qualification of this entire exchange: "This passage is aggada. With regard to it and anything like it, the sages said, 'We do not rely on the words of aggada.'" Hai Gaon continues that God cannot be compared to any physical being; hence we cannot refer to the Almighty's tears, hands, sighs, or legs. Any talmudic passage that contravenes this principle must not be read in a literal sense. Rather, such passages should be interpreted strictly as metaphor.

Hai Gaon's relegation of anthropomorphism – biblical and rabbinic – to the world of symbolism, metaphor, and allegory is an approach that has been widely accepted in Jewish thought for centuries, and has been codified as a principle of our faith. Though the approach may have been a response to probing questions from Karaites or Muslims, and later from Christians, it is an attitude of our tradition that continues to hold sway to this day.

Rav Ketina's encounter with the necromancer certainly does not suggest any uneasiness with anthropomorphism, and hence Hai Gaon's insistence that the passage be reinterpreted. Even with the repudiation of its literalness, the tale remains part of Jewish tradition, and thus motivates us to search for relevance and meaning. One possible avenue is to explore the relationship to the necromancer as "the other."

As noted, Rav Ketina's objection was not based on the thrust or content of the necromancer's words. Viewing human experience and natural phenomena as a cause-and-effect relationship with the Almighty is not a concept foreign to rabbinic thought. Rav Ketina's objection was to the necromancer himself. As the Talmud comments, Rav Ketina was concerned that others would mistakenly follow the bone sorcerer. Consequently, Rav Ketina sought to contradict anything the necromancer said, refusing to accord him even minimum respect in public.

This raises the question of how much room our tradition has for the intellectual contribution of the other. Rav Ketina's message is that the necromancer has no place. Does this apply to others whose source of knowledge is outside our tradition? Or is the objection limited to those who ply trades that are anathema to our heritage?

From other statements in rabbinic literature, it would appear that the contributions of the other are to be recognised and even appreciated. Commenting on the description of Haman's cronies first as *his intimate friends* and later in the verse as *his wise men* (Esther 6:13), the Talmud notes that whoever says something wise – even if he is from the nations of the world – is acknowledged as a wise person (*B. Megilla* 16a).

As mentioned earlier, the sages distinguish between two types of knowledge: Torah and wisdom. Wisdom is the province of all – Jew and gentile alike. There is no reason to claim that Jews alone can possess wisdom. Torah, on the other hand, is the heritage unique to the Jewish people (*Eikha Rabba* 2:13). Here too we see that wisdom can be found in the other.

What then is the difference between the necromancer and other wise people? It appears that the source of the knowledge is at the root of the issue. The necromancer employs the deceased for information gathering. This method is forbidden by the Torah, possibly because it seeks to create a pathway to knowledge that circumvents the Almighty. In contrast, the wise person seeks truth using the Divine faculty of wisdom. While there is no guarantee that the wise person will credit or even acknowledge God in his achievement of wisdom, at least he does not intentionally bypass the Divine.

In our quest for knowledge and wisdom, there are many sources available to us. Limiting ourselves to our own family – whether it is immediate family or even extended family – narrows the scope of opportunity. The inevitable result of such a course is missed information that would have otherwise enriched our existence. Yet, uncritically drawing on all sources can result in wisdom that is of dubious origin and whose veracity is doubtful. We do well to consider carefully what we imbibe as we seek to quench our insatiable thirst for knowledge.

The sun's new cycle

ONCE EVERY TWENTY-EIGHT years, on a Wednesday, we perform a rare ritual. The source for the ritual is a passage in the Talmud that records a tradition about blessings over astronomical events. "One who sees the sun at the beginning of its cycle, the moon in its mightiness, the planets in their orbits, or the signs of the zodiac in their order should say: 'Blessed are You, God, our Lord, King of the universe, Who creates the natural world'" (*B. Berakhot* 59b).

Of the four astronomical events mentioned in the source, only one is commonly commemorated, that is "the sun at the beginning of its cycle." While the codifiers explain the other astronomical events – when the moon, the five planets visible to the naked eye, or the constellations of the zodiac align in prescribed ways – it is not customary to recite the blessing over these events. Perhaps this is because the calculations can be made only by skilled astronomers; they are beyond the ability of most people (*Maimonides; Yad Ephraim; Mishna Berura*). However, the blessing over "the sun at the beginning of its cycle" is recited. "The beginning of its cycle" means the time that the sun returns to the position in the heavens which it occupied when it was first created.

The Talmud inquires: "When is it that the sun is at the beginning of its cycle?" The sage Abbaye responds: "Every twenty-eight years the cycle begins again." Abbaye is referring to a major solar cycle. In truth, the sun is in its original position relative to Earth once a year. The blessing, however, is prescribed for when the sun is in its original relative position, on the same day and at the same hour as its original placement at the time of the creation of the universe.

The sun was created and placed in the heavens on the fourth day of creation (Genesis 1:14–19), so the blessing is always recited on the fourth day of the week – Wednesday. Elsewhere in the Talmud there is a disagreement as to whether the world was created at the beginning of

spring or at the beginning of autumn (*B. Rosh HaShana* 11a). Our talmudic passage adopts the approach that the world was created at the
beginning of spring, in the month of Nissan.

Abbaye goes further, detailing the exact hour of the event – and
hence, of the ritual: "When *Tekufat Nissan* falls in the hour of Saturn, on the evening of Tuesday which is the night before Wednesday."
Nissan is the month when spring begins. *Tekufat Nissan* refers to the
vernal equinox – the twenty-four-hour period when the day and night
are equally long. On this day sunset is at 6 p.m. and dawn is at 6 a.m.;
there are twelve hours of darkness and twelve hours of daylight.

The vernal equinox is an annual occurrence, yet for the blessing
it must occur on a particular day of the week, at a particular time. That is
the meaning of "the hour of Saturn." Our sages referred to seven celestial
bodies – Saturn, Jupiter, Mars, the Sun, Venus, Mercury, and the Moon. Each
body is said to "serve" for one hour starting at the beginning of the week
in a continuous cycle. "The hour of Saturn" refers to the day of the week
that begins with Saturn "serving," which is Tuesday evening. The reference
to "Saturn serving" is an astrological phenomenon, not an astronomical
calculation, since the orbit of Saturn around the sun is actually calculated
at twenty-nine years and 167 days. Thus the vernal equinox must fall at the
beginning of the fourth day of the week, that is, at 6 p.m. on Tuesday.

The "hour of Saturn" happens every week on Tuesday evening. The
sun can be found in its original relative position once a year, and the vernal
equinox is also an annual occurrence. Nevertheless, these events coincide
only once in twenty-eight years, and that is when the blessing is recited.

The sun, however, is not visible in all places at 6 p.m. on Tuesday.
Therefore the following morning – Wednesday morning – we go outside to
look at the sun and recite the blessing. Even if the sun is hidden by clouds,
as long as its rays shine forth, the blessing may be said. Ideally we recite the
blessing early in the morning, but if it is so cloudy that the rays of the sun
cannot be discerned, we wait until midday in the hope that we will still see
the sun. If by midday the sun has still not appeared, we recite the blessing
without God's name … and wait twenty-eight years for the next opportunity.

It is customary to perform this rare ritual with a group of people,
for it is considered a greater honour for the Almighty when *mitzvot* are
performed *en masse*.

This event is referred to as *Birkat HaHama*, the blessing of the sun. The Talmud prescribes a lone short blessing for the ritual; the same blessing that is recited upon seeing other natural phenomena. Nevertheless, in recent generations passages have been added to the ritual, presumably to add to the atmosphere and to acknowledge the rarity of the event.

On Wednesday, April 8, 1981, 4 Nissan 5741, as a young schoolboy in Melbourne, I remember that the entire school went outside and stood in front of the synagogue. Together we recited *Birkat HaHama*. I did not know what an equinox was and certainly had never heard of the "the hour of Saturn." Our teachers simply explained that the sun had returned to the very same point it had been when it was first created, and that we were gathered together to acknowledge that God had created the world.

On Wednesday, April 8, 2009, the eve of Passover 5769 – after waking up our children while it was still dark, standing on the balcony of our house, together with our fledgling community in Zur Hadassa – we recited the benediction together.

Looking around at those gathered, we wondered whether we would once again have this rare experience when it rolls around again on Wednesday, April 8, 2037, 23 Nissan 5797.... Perhaps even again on Wednesday, April 8, 2065, 2 Nissan 5825.

...Maybe the youngest people in attendance were dreaming of Wednesday April 8, 2093, 14 Nissan 5853.

BERAKHOT 59B

The gift of giving

THE MISHNA TELLS us that if someone builds a new home or purchases new items, the *Sheheheyanu* blessing should be recited. The text is: "Blessed are You, God, our Lord, King of the universe, Who has kept us alive (*sheheheyanu*), sustained us, and brought us to this time" (*M. Berakhot* 9:3).

The Talmud records a dispute regarding which type of new clothing warrants the *Sheheḥeyanu* blessing (*B. Berakhot* 59b). One opinion maintains that the blessing is recited only when the recipient does not already own a garment of the type just purchased. Thus the purchase of a first suit would justify the *Sheheḥeyanu* blessing, but a second suit would not. Another opinion disagrees, saying that even if the owner already has a suit, the acquisition of a new suit warrants a *Sheheḥeyanu*. One commentator explains that this dispute refers to inherited items; newly purchased items always call for the recitation of the *Sheheḥeyanu* blessing (*Rashi*). In the Jerusalem Talmud, the term "new" is further clarified: the garment need not be brand new. *Sheheḥeyanu* is recited even if the clothes were previously worn, as long as they are new to the buyer, that is, subjectively new (*Y. Berakhot* 91a).

After clarifying this aspect of the blessing over new clothes, the Jerusalem Talmud introduces an additional factor. The *Sheheḥeyanu* blessing is recited only over clothes that were purchased. If the new garments were received as a gift, a different blessing is called for – the *HaTov VeHaMetiv* blessing. The text is: "Blessed are You, God, our Lord, King of the universe, Who is good and Who confers good (*Hatov VeHaMetiv*)."

The Babylonian Talmud records no such distinction between the purchase of new clothes and the receipt of new clothes as a gift. Moreover, the *HaTov VeHaMetiv* blessing is limited by the Babylonian Talmud to situations in which there are at least two beneficiaries. Thus, for instance, a new wine brought to the table warrants the *HaTov VeHaMetiv* blessing only if it is to be drunk together with other people.

One commentator seeks to explain the position of the Jerusalem Talmud in light of the *HaTov VeHaMetiv* conditions delineated in the Babylonian Talmud. *HaTov VeHaMetiv* is indeed only recited when two people benefit, but the giving of a gift of new clothes may benefit two people. For instance, if the recipient is poverty stricken, then the giver is thankful for being fortunate to be in a position to assist the needy (*Rosh*).

One later commentator references a talmudic passage that supports the idea that a giver of a gift can be a beneficiary as well. The halakhic act of betrothal normally involves a man giving a woman something of monetary value – most commonly today a ring. The Talmud cites a case in which a woman gives money to a man and says: "Take this money and I will become betrothed to you." The Talmud states that if the man accepts the money and declares that she should be betrothed, the act is halakhically valid.

Under normal circumstances, if the woman is not the recipient but the active party in the transaction, the law does not recognise this deed as an act of betrothal (*B. Kiddushin* 5b). Why is this case different? The Talmud explains that we are talking about a specific scenario: The male is a distinguished person, and the woman is indeed the recipient in that she accrues benefit from her gift being accepted by such an important person. With the benefit that she receives, she commits herself to become betrothed. Thus we have a second example in which the giver is also the beneficiary (*B. Kiddushin* 7a; *Ma'adanei Yom Tov*).

Perhaps this idea – that the one who gives is actually the one who benefits – can be expanded beyond the two examples just cited. Whenever we give gifts, the recipient is not the only beneficiary. Any giver – regardless of wealth or social status – gains as well. On a simple level, the giver has the satisfaction that the gift proffered was accepted. More significantly, the giver is filled with a sense of delight that the gift has brought someone else happiness. The giver has selected the particular present for the particular person, and brought a smile to someone's face. Thus a gift granted is a joyous occasion for both the recipient and the giver. This is reflected in the halakhic position that the *HaTov VeHaMetiv* blessing should be recited upon receiving clothes from another.

There are of course those who find it difficult to accept gifts from others. For such people, the biblical verse *He that hates gifts shall live* (Proverbs 15:27) has become almost a principle of faith. Perhaps it comes from an over-developed sense of independence that bars any thought of accepting from another. Without addressing the psychological needs of such people, we can gain some insight from the rule that *HaTov VeHaMetiv* is recited over the gift of new clothes. When we accept gifts, it is not only we as recipients who benefit. We are also allowing the giver to extend a hand of friendship, to become part of our lives. Thus accepting a gift is also a form of giving.

In *Fiddler on the Roof*, the silver screen version of Sholem
Aleichem's "Tevye the Milkman," Tevye proffers a hearty piece of cheese
to Perchik. They banter over it:

"Have a piece."

"I have no money and I'm not a beggar."

"Ah, take it. It's a blessing for me to give."

"Very well, for your sake."

Perchik takes the gift and quickly devours it in a manner suggesting that he may not have eaten for some time. Tevye understands
that Perchik cannot accept a gift; the political principles of the student
revolutionary from Kiev preclude the idea of begging for food. While
Tevye does not quote – or for that matter misquote in his inimitable
and irresistible manner – the talmudic position advocating the *HaTov
VeHaMetiv* blessing, he nevertheless makes the same point. Indeed, we
should be grateful if we are in a position to give to people. To paraphrase
Tevye, it is a blessing for us to give.

BERAKHOT 59B–60A

New acquisitions

AS WE JUST discussed, if someone builds a new home or purchases
new items, the *Sheheheyanu* blessing is recited (*M. Berakhot* 9:3).
Over what type of new items should the benediction be pronounced?
A new spoon? A new dinner set? A new bicycle? What about used,
second-hand goods? Do they call for a *Sheheheyanu* blessing? Our sages
here employ the term "*kelim*" for items that warrant a *Sheheheyanu*. It is a
word that carries a variety of meanings; it can refer to utensils, containers,
or perhaps clothing.

To arrive at a list of items that justify pronouncing the blessing,
we must first explore the reason for saying it. Is the blessing a function
of the cost of the new acquisition? Perhaps the benediction depends

on the subjective value of the item to the owner. Maybe the blessing is not dependent on the specific person acquiring the article, but rather is an acknowledgment of a new utensil made available for human use.

Halakhic authorities explain that the *Sheheḥeyanu* is a personal expression of joy. Indeed, the wording of the blessing focuses on the subjective viewpoint of the reciter of the benediction: "Who has kept us alive, sustained us, and brought us to this time." Thus *Sheheḥeyanu* would seem to be dependent upon individual feelings of happiness. Cost of the item is not the major consideration. Unadulterated pleasure over the new acquisition is the defining factor in considering whether the blessing should be pronounced. The list of items that warrant a *Sheheḥeyanu*, therefore, would include clothing, utensils, books, and for that matter any item that causes a person to feel joy and happiness (*Radbaz*).

Some medieval commentators therefore rule that the acquisition of an everyday item – such as a new undershirt – does not warrant a *Sheheḥeyanu*, for a person does not get excited over the acquisition of undergarments. The purchase must be a significant one to call for a *Sheheḥeyanu*. For example, buying fancy new clothes would call for a *Sheheḥeyanu* recitation (*Tosafot*). Other commentators disagree. They focus on the subjective benchmarks for the blessing. Since *Sheheḥeyanu* is dependent on the person's feelings, if the person is overjoyed at new underwear – as a person of little means might be – then the benediction should be recited (*Rosh*).

One halakhist, reflecting the reality of his time period, adds that buying a new horse or a new milk cow justifies a *Sheheḥeyanu*. The reason that people were previously not accustomed to recite the blessing in these cases, he explains, was that they were pessimistically afraid that the animal would die in the imminent future before they could derive any benefit from the new acquisition (*Eshel Avraham Buczacz*). Along these lines, the great halakhist Rabbi Moshe Feinstein (1895–1986) is of the opinion that the blessing should be pronounced when purchasing a new car.

The Talmud rules that even if the person purchasing the new item has a similar one already in his possession, the blessing may nevertheless be recited provided the acquisition of the new asset brings joy

(*B. Berakhot* 59a–60b). Moreover, the "new" utensils need not be brand new; even used items that bring joy to their new owner warrant the benediction (*Y. Berakhot* 14a). Similarly, a house need not be built from scratch to justify the blessing; even a renovation to an existing house, making the structure more spacious or comfortable, would deserve a *Sheheheyanu* (*Eshel Avraham Buczacz*). Once again we see that the criteria for the blessing are subjective, dependent on the outlook of the person acquiring the new item.

Codifiers discuss whether shoes are sufficiently important to warrant the blessing. Some say that shoes are like any other garment – if their acquisition provides significant joy they justify the benediction. Others suggest that shoes never reach the status to warrant a *Sheheheyanu* (*Shulhan Arukh* and *Rema, Orah Hayim* 223:6).

At what point should *Sheheheyanu* be recited – upon the acquisition or the first use? Since the blessing is an expression of heartfelt joy the question is this: At what point does a person feel a surge of happiness over the new possession? Halakhic authorities point out that the feeling of delight is first felt upon acquisition of the new item, even if its use is delayed to a later time. Just knowing that we have a new possession at our disposal can lead us to a sense of contentment. Thus the blessing should be recited upon acquiring the new item; there is no need to wait until it is actually used.

Strangely, common practice is to treat *Sheheheyanu* over new items as optional, and many do not recite it on occasions clearly mandated by our sages (*Rema, Orah Hayim* 223:1). This may be because the blessing is perceived as being relevant primarily to seasonal events, as implied by the wording of the blessing: "Who has kept us alive, sustained us, and brought us to this time." Reciting *Sheheheyanu* over non-seasonal occurrences, such as new clothes, is seen as a secondary application and one that can be overlooked (*Mishna Berura*). Some codifiers object to this trend of neglecting *Sheheheyanu* over non-seasonal occasions, and note that this application of the blessing was instituted by our sages and included in the Talmud, and therefore should not be ignored (*Magen Avraham*).

Indeed, it is a shame to disregard the blessing, for reciting this benediction affords us the opportunity to acknowledge the Almighty's hand in our individual good fortune. We thank God for keeping us alive, for sustaining us, and for bringing us to a time when we can enjoy the quality of life that new acquisitions bring us.

On leniencies

LET US NOW explore another facet of the *Sheheḥeyanu* blessing recited on new clothes. The Talmud here cites a parallel source that records a dispute in a case where someone is acquiring a second item (*B. Berakhot* 60a). Rabbi Meir holds that a purchaser may recite the blessing over new clothes, provided he does not already have a similar garment. A second suit, for instance, would not justify a *Sheheḥeyanu* recitation. Rabbi Yehuda argues that a new garment always calls for a *Sheheḥeyanu*.

In the ensuing talmudic discussion it is suggested that there is a further point of disagreement between the two sages. Rabbi Meir would not require the recitation of the *Sheheḥeyanu* blessing if the purchaser bought the item, returned it, and then once again bought it. Rabbi Yehuda, however, would mandate the blessing even though the purchaser has previously owned that very item, because it is once again considered new and hence *Sheheḥeyanu* must be said.

Rabbi Yehuda's position is clear. *Sheheḥeyanu* is said over any purchase. Rabbi Meir has narrower standards for his *Sheheḥeyanu* requirement. Only if the purchaser does not own a similar garment and only if he has never previously owned this specific garment, must he recite the blessing.

The Talmud wonders why only the similar garment stipulation is mentioned in early sources, whereas the "bought-and-returned-and-bought" condition is not explicitly stated. The Talmud explains that this is to emphasise the leniency of Rabbi Meir's position. Not requiring a blessing over "bought-and-returned-and-bought" is under-standable since the joy of the new garment is already past. Rabbi Meir goes further with his lenient ruling: even if the garment is truly brand new, yet the purchaser owns a similar garment, he need not recite the blessing. The Talmud explains its choice to detail only one case, with a pithy but enduring statement: "The power of permissibility is preferable."

Elsewhere in the Talmud this principle appears as an accepted rule of talmudic discourse. It is preferable to relate how sweeping the permissive ruling is rather than how sweeping the restrictive ruling is (*B. Beitza* 2b). In that case, Rashi explains the logic of the preference for a permissive ruling. To rule stringently is always easier, for prohibiting something permitted does not cause obvious damage. It is far bolder to rule leni-ently, for this reflects confidence in one's understanding of the matter at hand. For this reason, it is preferable to relate how sweeping the per-missive view is.

While the original talmudic statement – "The power of permis-sibility is preferable" – appears to refer solely to talmudic discourse, many authorities understand this statement as reflecting an ideal in normative halakha as well: We prefer *kula*, leniency, and avoid *ḥumra*, stringency.

Without referencing the talmudic dictum preferring lenient rulings, one medieval authority sees the avoidance of *ḥumra* as a principle of halakhic decision making. In the context of adjudicat-ing whether an animal that has been ritually slaughtered is fit for eat-ing, the thirteenth-century Provençal commentator Rabbi Menaḥem Meiri (1249–1315) writes: "Anytime a decision is required and a scholar may easily permit the matter without dispute, a scholar who is reliable should not try to be overly pious and seek out stringencies; rather he should be concerned about the finances of Israel." Declar-ing the animal non-kosher would involve a financial loss; concern for the financial well-being of the community is a valid justification for avoiding a *ḥumra*.

Despite this preference for permissive rulings, we often find halakhists – whether in response to direct questions or in their written works – declaring: "As for one who is stringent, a blessing should come to him." This statement often appears when the halakhist is unable or unwilling to make a clear choice between normative alternatives. Consequently, the halakhist chooses the path of maximum position compliance. Alas, this statement also lauds the choice to be stringent, and in our culture this pronouncement says less about the stature and confidence of the halakhist and more about the practitioner who chooses to adopt or ignore a particular *ḥumra*.

In a harsh passage, the great transmitter of kabbalistic lore Rabbi Ḥayim Vital (1542–1620) uses kabbalistic teachings to explain the trend towards *ḥumra*. He writes: "Since they despise the Tree of Life" – a reference to the esoteric Torah – "the Holy One, blessed be He, does not assist them. They falter in the details of the Tree of Knowing Good and Evil" – a reference to the revealed Torah – "and they turn it to evil, defile the pure, prohibit the permitted, and make non-kosher what is kosher." Rabbi Ḥayim Vital is suggesting that neglect of the esoteric Torah results in a lack of Divine assistance and consequently the need for *ḥumra* since the actual law is not known. *Ḥumra* therefore is an evil born of mistaken priorities. It can be combated only by studying the hidden Torah and thereby meriting Divine guidance in legal decision making.

In relating to this talmudic passage, Chief Rabbi Avraham Yitzḥak HaKohen Kook (1865–1935) presents a different position. Following the tradition he received from his teachers, Rabbi Kook proposes that it is nearly always preferable to avoid the path of *ḥumra*. According to Rabbi Kook, *ḥumra* is the ideal in limited circumstances only: "In this generation of ours, when – because of our numerous sins – the honour of Torah has been degraded to dust, there is more need to adopt stringencies and other regulations aimed at safeguarding the honour of Torah, as opposed to all other stringencies in the world."

Leaving aside the question of whether Rabbi Kook's analysis of his times is relevant to our generation, the underlying logic of his position is clear. *Ḥumra* is a situation-specific tool to be employed sparingly; it is an approach which may be useful in bolstering specific areas of law that are widely neglected. It is not a panacea for questionable halakhic competence or indecisiveness, and it is certainly not a way of life. Each *ḥumra* must be carefully examined and evaluated in order to determine if it is truly necessary and appropriate to the generation's needs.

Unrelenting faith

THE MISHNA TEACHES that prayerful requests should only address the future; beseeching the Almighty concerning something that has already occurred is considered a prayer in vain and should be avoided (*M. Berakhot* 9:3).

Two examples of such prayers in vain are presented. In one case, someone's wife is pregnant and he asks the Almighty to ensure that the baby be of a certain gender. This prayer is considered to be in vain, for the foetus' sex has already been determined and cannot be naturally changed. In the other case, someone is travelling along the road and hears screaming in the city, and he responds by praying: "May it be [Your] will that this [screaming] is not taking place within my house." This too is a prayer in vain, for the crying out has already happened – perhaps in the traveller's home, perhaps elsewhere.

What then should a traveller do as he approaches his hometown and hears despairing cries? One medieval commentator offers two possible options. First, the traveller can rephrase his prayer in terms of the future: "If the calamity is in my home, please save my household from danger." Alternatively, he should have faith in the Almighty and assume that the cries are not coming from his home (*Meiri*).

This second approach – a somewhat difficult task in the face of real cries – is exemplified by a story recounted in the Talmud (*B. Berakhot* 60a). Hillel the Elder was on the road. As he approached his hometown he heard the sound of screaming in the city. With conviction and almost blasé certainty, he declared: "I am confident that this [screaming] is not [coming from] within my home." The Talmud cites a biblical verse to explain Hillel's confidence: *Of evil tidings he will have no fear; his heart is firm, confident in God* (Psalms 112:7).

How could Hillel have been so confident? Surely Hillel's home was not immune to tragedy! The Baghdadi scholar Rabbi Yosef Hayim (1834–1909) explains that our talmudic passage is testifying to the supreme, almost unparalleled faith of Hillel. He was so sure that God would not allow tragedy to befall his household that he was willing to publicly assert: "I am confident that this screaming is not coming from within my home."

According to Rabbi Yosef Hayim, Hillel's supreme trust in the Almighty is demonstrated in another talmudic vignette as well. The Talmud relates how the two sages Hillel and Shammai would prepare for Shabbat. Whenever Shammai would chance upon a choice piece of meat he would set it aside for the Shabbat meal. If he found a better cut the next day, he would eat the first and save the second for Shabbat. Thus he would continue throughout the week until he had the choicest cut of meat for Shabbat. Hillel, on the other hand, was far less focused on the Shabbat meal. Each day Hillel would eat whatever he was fortunate to acquire, thanking the Almighty each day (*B. Beitza* 16a). Rabbi Yosef Hayim explains that here too Hillel's conduct was guided by his absolute trust in God, that come Shabbat he would have a hearty meal befitting the holy day.

Rabbi Yosef Hayim explains the common denominator of these two exempla of Hillel's faith. Even people who have strong faith in the Almighty are generally hesitant to declare their faith openly. Believers may choose not to express themselves in the confident terms voiced by Hillel, lest God decide otherwise. This would leave them red-faced with their public statements ringing in their ears, embarrassed before all those who heard their declaration. "Where is your prophetic vision now?" the scoffers might taunt the one who had faith in the Almighty.

Hillel, however, was of a different calibre. He did not fear the public reaction; he declared his unwavering faith without hesitation. According to this explanation, Hillel was a paragon of trust in the Almighty, setting a standard that is beyond the grasp of most.

An alternative explanation comes from Hasidic circles. Rabbi Itamar Wohlgelerenter of Kónskowola (d. 1831) explains that Hillel's confidence was the result of his intimate understanding of the nature of his family. Hillel had taught his family that no matter what happened, they need never cry out in anguish and despair, since everything is orchestrated by the Divine. Even calamity should be accepted with equanimity and love for the Almighty. Tragedy could befall the household of Hillel, yet he was confident that his family would react to the misfortune without crying out; without indicating a loss of faith in God.

Rabbi Itamar of Kónskowola connects Hillel's confidence in his household to the verse: *And you shall rejoice in all the good which God your Lord has given to you and to your household* (Deuteronomy 26:11). Rejoicing in what the Almighty has given is not merely the province of the individual; it is a challenge for the entire household.

According to this reading, the verse cited in the talmudic passage – *Of evil tidings he will have no fear; his heart is firm, confident in God* (Psalms 112:7) – is not limited to the fortitude of Hillel's heart; rather it refers to the collective heart of Hillel's household.

Appreciating the Almighty in the face of adversity on a personal level is undoubtedly a laudable achievement. Surely we may aspire to such a lofty level. Inculcating such a feeling in the members of our household is even more impressive. The talmudic passage does not only tell us about Hillel's own unshakeable faith in God. We are privy to information about Hillel's family and about his success in transmitting his ideals to the members of his household.

The talmudic passage may therefore also be alluding to the challenge that community leaders and activists must tackle. When we turn our attention towards public needs with the noble goal of making a contribution to our society, how do we ensure that we do not simultaneously turn away from our own household? Disseminating lofty ideals must not come at the expense of those nearest and dearest to us. We must strive to instil those very ideals in our family as well.

Fear factor

WE ALL HAVE moments when we experience fear. It may manifest itself as an uncomfortable tingling deep inside us, or it may hit us in waves. Our sages relate to the causes of fear, of what we should be fearful, and how we should treat fear (*B. Berakhot* 60a).

A student was following Rabbi Yishmael ben Rabbi Yose in the marketplace of Zion. The sage noticed that the disciple was anxious. He turned to the student, saying: "You are a sinner!" Buttressing his accusation with a biblical verse, Rabbi Yishmael continued: "For it is written: *Sinners were afraid in Zion* (Isaiah 33:14)."

The student was quick to defend himself. "Is it not written: *Praiseworthy is the person who is always fearful* (Proverbs 28:14)?"

The sage dismissed this source, explaining that fear is commendable only in the context of Torah matters. If people are constantly wary of forgetting their Torah learning, they will carefully, continuously, and conscientiously review the material (*Rashi*). In that case fear serves as a catalyst for better Torah study and is therefore laudable. Perpetual fear in other contexts, however, is not a virtue.

Continuing with the theme of fear, the Talmud adds a second vignette that highlights the dangers of fear. Yehuda bar Natan, who was following Rav Hamnuna, emitted a deep sigh. Hearing the sigh, Rav Hamnuna commented: "That person wants suffering brought upon himself, for it is written: *For my sigh ushers in my bread, my moan pours forth like water because I feared a fright and it has overtaken me, that which I dreaded has come upon me* (Job 3:24–25)." A sigh, as a sign of fear, can herald suffering. Fear's tendency to weaken people (*B. Gittin* 70a) may explain its ability to be a harbinger of suffering.

The same defence was offered and dismissed: "But it is written: *Praiseworthy is the person who is always fearful?*"

"This verse is written concerning words of Torah."

What brings about fear? The sages enumerate various actions that precipitate fear if the people undertaking them do not subsequently wash their hands. People who eat the herb cress experience fear for thirty days without knowing why they are afraid. Likewise blood-letting from the shoulder without washing the hands instils anxiety for seven days. A haircut causes fear for three days, and paring nails for one day (*B. Pesaḥim* 111b–112a; *Rashbam*).

In another passage, our sages explain that fear can be perceived even when the cause is invisible to the human eye (*B. Megilla* 3a; *B. Sanhedrin* 93b–94a). The Bible recounts: *I, Daniel, alone saw the vision; and the people who were with me did not see the vision, yet a great fear fell upon them and they fled into hiding* (Daniel 10:7). The Talmud asks: Since these people did not see the vision, why were they afraid? The sages explain that even though the people did not see the vision with their own eyes, their guardian angels did perceive the vision and thus precipitated their fear. One sage, Ravina, derives a general rule from this biblical account. If one becomes frightened for no apparent reason, that person's guardian angel must have perceived something that justifies the fear.

Our sages offer a remedy for one who is confronted by unexplained fear: Read *Shema*. This Torah passage has the power to eliminate evil spirits (*B. Berakhot* 5a). If the anxious person is standing in an unclean place where it is inappropriate to study Torah, he should jump four cubits, thus leaving the space where the fear was sensed. If this is impossible, the Talmud offers an incantation that provides strength in the face of unseen danger: "The goat of the slaughterhouse is fatter than I." The incantation is suggesting that the invisible cause of the fear should focus its attention on goats and leave the fearful person alone.

Elsewhere in the Talmud, our sages offer another method for combating fear. Rabbi Yehuda was wont to say that there are ten powerful creations found in the world, yet there is something that can disable each of them. A solid mountain can be cut by iron; hard iron can be softened by fire; fiery flames can be extinguished by water; mighty water can be absorbed by clouds; strong clouds can be scattered by wind; persistent winds cannot fell a human body; an able person can be broken by fear; formidable fear can be dispelled by wine; the effect of potent wine is dissipated by sleep. Death is the most powerful force created, yet even death can be overcome by giving charity, as it says: *And charity will save from death* (Proverbs 10:2). A stiff drink, therefore, is a remedy for fear (*B. Bava Batra* 10a).

Hasidic masters offer a different perspective on fear. They suggest that true and worthy fear should be reserved for the Almighty. All other things that we fear should only remind us of how we should feel in the presence of God (*Me'or Einayim*).

One of the early Hasidic masters, Rabbi Meshulam Feivish of Zbaraz (1740–1795), demonstrates this idea with an insightful parable. Imagine that an angry king sends one of his most fearsome soldiers to arrest one of his subjects. If the citizen is foolish, upon seeing the frightening soldier he tries to appease the messenger with gifts and endearing words. A wise subject, however, understands that such attempts are futile. He tells himself: "The soldier is merely acting on the king's orders. I should hurry to present my case before the king." Another Hasidic master, Rabbi Zvi Elimelekh Shapira of Dynów (1783–1841), goes even further, stating that it is a disgrace for a righteous person to be fearful of anything but the Almighty.

If a person experiences fear, the Hasidic masters recommend recalling that all fear is misguided…except for fear of God. Fear of anything else should be viewed as a reminder or a prompt for the only appropriate fear: Fear of God.

Justice and a good lawyer

THE MISHNA RELATES to the prayers appropriate for wayfarers entering and departing a city. It presents two opinions as to the number of prayers which should be said in such a case (*M. Berakhot* 9:4).

According to the first opinion, a traveller should recite two prayers – one upon entering a city and one upon departing. A second opinion suggests that four prayers should be said – two upon arrival and two upon departure.

The Mishna does not give the text of these prayers, merely stating their basic thrust. One should give thanks for protection afforded in the past, and ask for protection from dangers in the future.

The Talmud quotes an early source that offers a possible text of the four prayers mentioned in the Mishna (*B. Berakhot* 60a). The traveller entering the city should pray: "May it be Your will, God my Lord, that You bring me into this city in peace." Once the traveller has entered the city safely, he should offer a second prayer, this time a prayer of thanksgiving: "I thank You, God my Lord, for having brought me into this city in peace."

The traveller preparing to leave the city should turn to the Almighty and pray: "May it be Your will, God my Lord and the Lord of my forebears, that You bring me out of this city in peace." After he has left the city, he should express his appreciation and anticipate the next leg of his journey: "I thank You, God my Lord, for having brought me out of this city in peace. Just as You have brought me out in peace, so should You lead me in peace, uphold me in peace, and guide my footsteps towards peace. May You save me from the hand of every enemy and ambush along the way." This prayer is similar, but not identical, to the well-known text of *Tefillat HaDerekh*, the Wayfarers' Prayer that is recited when embarking upon a journey. *Tefillat HaDerekh* is first mentioned earlier in our tractate (*B. Berakhot* 29b–30a).

Does every entry and exit from a city necessitate such prayers? Are we really so fearful of the dangers of a new place that whenever we arrive and depart we need to pray about it? The Talmud discusses these questions. One opinion maintains that the prayers are relevant only in a city where they do not "judge and execute," meaning a place where execution is carried out without due legal process. This is clearly an unsafe environment, for there is no recourse to a court of law where mistakes can be remedied and injustices rectified. Entering such a place justifies a call to God for Divine protection. Likewise, safe deliverance from this place is most certainly a reason to thank the Almighty.

The focus of the talmudic passage is the importance of the existence of a legal system with courts that mete out appropriate punishments for those who commit crimes. If the city has a just legal system, the prayers are not mandated.

One commentator explains that where a legal system is in place, the onus is on the traveller not to commit a capital crime. In the event that he has already committed such a crime, he is better off not entering the city and placing himself in a life-threatening situation. In both cases – where he has committed a crime or where he is about to commit one – the traveller should not beseech God for assistance (*Rashi*).

The Talmud also offers a different approach. Even in a city where they do "judge and execute," the prayers are still warranted, lest the traveller be falsely accused of some heinous crime. Were this to happen he would need someone to speak on his behalf. If no such person were to come forward to argue for the innocence of the traveller, the court system would be of little use to him. Therefore, even a city governed by law can be dangerous, and praying for the Almighty's assistance is warranted.

The sum of the two opinions is that there are two concerns that travellers should keep in mind as they enter a city: whether the city has a just legal system and whether there are people there who would step forward to advocate on behalf of the accused.

In this light, a legal system is viewed as a boon rather than a burden. Perhaps that is one of the reasons that our tradition celebrates an annual Day of Judgment – that is, Rosh HaShana. A just system of law provides security, stability, and a measure of safety.

Knowing the dangers of lawlessness can help us understand the seven Noahide laws which, according to our tradition, address all of humanity. Six of these laws instruct against certain actions or conduct, while one is a positive command. The first six Noahide laws are the prohibition of idolatry, the prohibition of murder, the prohibition of theft, the prohibition of sexual promiscuity, the prohibition of blaspheming the Almighty's name, and the prohibition against eating flesh taken from an animal while it is still alive. The seventh law is different from the others in that it does not involve refraining from certain conduct; rather, it requires an active course. This last Noahide law mandates a just legal system with an effective judiciary, where wrongs can be redressed fairly by a court of law (*T. Avoda Zara* 8:4; *B. Sanhedrin* 56a).

What about the importance of having someone to lobby on our behalf? Where else in our tradition do we find this concept? Here we turn to the liturgy of the High Holy Days. In the Ashkenazic rite there is a pertinent line worth quoting: "When there is no advocate to intercede on our behalf against the Accuser who reports our transgressions, You [God] speak for Jacob and invoke the merit of the observance of the statutes and law. Vindicate us in judgment, O King of judgment." If we have no advocate, we turn to the Almighty, the Judge of judges, to argue the case on our behalf.

Dangers of bathing

OUR SAGES PRESCRIBE prayers for all types of situations. Thus the Talmud relates that someone who enters a public bathhouse should say: "May it be Your will, God my Lord, that You spare me from this [danger] and from its like. May no matter of ruin or iniquity befall me. If a matter of ruin or iniquity should befall me, then let my death atone for all my sins" (*B. Berakhot* 60a).

What was so dangerous about bathhouses? Roman bathhouses had a hot room, the *caldarium*, which was built on pillars. The area below the *caldarium*, called the *hypocaust*, was connected to a furnace and heated the floor of the *caldarium*. If the floor of the *caldarium* was to collapse, the bathers would fall into the *hypocaust* and die. This was a real danger, as is apparent from the continuation of the talmudic passage.

Rabbi Abahu entered a public bathhouse and the floor beneath him gave way. Fortunately for Rabbi Abahu and the other bathers, a miracle happened. Instead of falling into the *hypocaust* below, he was left standing on one of the pillars. From that perch, Rabbi Abahu managed to save 101 men with his one arm. One commentator explains that Rabbi Abahu did not literally hold onto 101 people with one hand. Rather he held onto one or two people who each held onto one or two people and so on, thus forming a human chain (*Rashi*).

Bathhouses were truly hazardous places; unless, that is, you were fortunate enough to take your bath in the same place as Rabbi Abahu. Thus the Talmud adds that when leaving this unsafe site, a prayer of thanksgiving is called for: "I thank You, God my Lord, for having spared me from the fire."

The Talmud cites one sage, Abbaye, as objecting to the wording of the prayer upon entering the bathhouse. Asking the Almighty to spare us from peril is appropriate, but the last line – "If a matter of ruin or iniquity should befall me, then let my death atone for all my sins" – invites danger. A person facing a dangerous situation should avoid speaking of impending disaster. In the words of the Talmud: "One should not open his mouth to Satan" – that is, one need not give Satan any ideas.

Abbaye objects to another prayer for the same reason. Earlier, our tractate reports a prayer which is recited by mourners as they acknowledge the righteousness of the Almighty's judgment: "Master of the universe, I have sinned greatly before You, and You have not exacted from me one thousandth [of what I deserve]. May it be Your will, God our Lord, that You seal our breaches and the breaches of all Your people, the House of Israel, in mercy." This formula too gives Satan material to work with and therefore should be avoided (*B. Berakhot* 19a; *B. Ketubot* 8b).

One commentator explains that Satan serves as the prosecutor in the heavenly court. By our mentioning the possibility of death, Satan the prosecutor has the opportunity to say: "See, the accused himself admits that he is worthy of the punishment of death!" (*Maharsha*).

The Talmud continues with a biblical paradigm of the folly of giving the heavenly prosecutor the chance to open his mouth. The Jewish people lamented: *Had not God the Lord of hosts left us a remnant, we would have been like Sodom and Gomorrah* (Isaiah 1:9). The people felt that they would have been justly wiped out like those two cities that were infamous for debauchery; were it not, that is, for the mercy of the

Almighty. Alas, the mention of these nefarious cities and the admission that the Jews might have deserved such harsh punishment spurred Isaiah to respond in kind: *Hear the word of God, O chieftains of Sodom, listen to the law of our Lord, O people of Gomorrah* (ibid., v. 10).

Other biblical passages seem to support this idea, encouraging us to use caution in our choice of words. Thus in the generation after the Great Deluge, the people hatched a plan: *Let us build for ourselves a city and a tower such that its top should reach the heavens; and we will make for ourselves a name, lest we be scattered across the face of the entire earth* (Genesis 11:4). The very fear that they voiced became part of the punishment when the Almighty foiled their plot: *And He scattered them from there across the face of the entire earth* (ibid., v. 8).

Following the Exodus from Egypt, the fledgling Jewish nation stood at the banks of the Reed Sea with the Egyptians hot in pursuit. They turned to Moses and wailed: *Because there were no graves in Egypt, have you taken us to die in the desert?!* (Exodus 14:11). Alas, so it was to be. The generation that had merited freedom was destined to wander and eventually die in the desert (Numbers 14:35).

The concern about giving Satan a chance to prosecute in the heavenly tribunal has led to a slew of euphemisms in our tradition. It is one of the reasons that diseases are often mentioned in hushed tones or by code words rather than by their real name.

Perhaps the most fascinating aspect of the injunction against providing an opportunity for Satan the prosecutor to open his mouth is that the injunction is recorded in codes of Jewish law (*Rema, Yoreh De'ah* 376:2). According to one halakhic authority, this is the very reason for the custom for those who are fortunate enough to have living parents to refrain from reciting the Mourner's *Kaddish* (*Yad Ephraim*).

On a more upbeat note, the Safed kabbalist Rabbi Eliyahu di Vidas (died c. 1579–1585), in the introduction to his ethical work entitled *Reshit Ḥokhma* (The Beginning of Wisdom), explains that this is the meaning of the verse: *Who is the person who desires life and loves days, that he may see good in them? Guard your tongue from evil and your lips from speaking falsehood* (Psalms 34:13–14). Guarding our tongue – and not opening our mouth to Satan – is the key to a long and meaningful life.

What doctors can do

SHORT PRAYERS OF supplication and thanksgiving traditionally accompany our every step. The Talmud suggests a prayer for some-one who goes to a blood-letter for curative purposes: "May it be Your will, God my Lord, that this therapy should serve me as a remedy. You should heal me, for You are God the faithful healer, and it is Your remedy that is genuine" (*B. Berakhot* 60a).

Before beginning the medical procedure, the patient turns to the Almighty and beseeches Divine assistance. The suggested prayer con-cludes by bemoaning the supposed need for medical experts instead of turning directly to the Almighty: "It is not the place of people to seek medical treatment, but they have accustomed themselves to do so."

This expression of lament is dismissed by another talmudic sage on the basis of a biblical verse. The Torah discusses a case in which two people quarrel and one strikes the other, causing injury. Among other payments, the aggressor must pay for the medical expenses of the victim. From this we derive that permission is granted to physicians to provide medical treatment. Thus there is no place to regret the use of doctors.

According to the commentators, this is a clear rejection of the approach that we should rely entirely on God to provide healing and should have no part ourselves in the healing process (*Rashi*). Further-more, even though the biblical source deals with a wound inflicted by humans, we do not say that only such an injury may be treated by doctors. Medical attention may be sought even for ailments that have no traceable human cause (*Tosafot*).

The commentators discuss the nature of this licence granted to physicians. According to one approach, the role of physicians is a neces-sary evil. In an ideal world – states Ramban, who was both a scholar and a physician – we would turn to God alone for remedies. It is solely due to our lowly spiritual state that doctors are an essential part of our lives.

An alternate approach states that once permission is granted to doctors to provide medical care, it becomes a holy obligation and is classified as a *mitzva*. This line is espoused by Maimonides, himself a sought-after physician. This position is adopted by many codifiers, who further state that physicians who decline to provide treatment are in effect spilling blood. Doctors are enjoined to go to extreme lengths to heal the sick. What are the boundaries of this right and obligation? First, only qualified physicians may provide care. Second, indemnity for causing damage during treatment is granted only to officially licensed doctors. Moreover, the right to provide treatment is granted to the most qualified physician present; other doctors must defer to a more capable colleague (*Shulḥan Arukh, Yoreh De'ah* 336:1).

A story is related about a sick person who came to the Hasidic master and legal authority, Rabbi Menaḥem Mendel Schneersohn of Lubavitch (1789–1866), known by the title of his multi-volume halakhic work *Tzemaḥ Tzedek*. The ailing visitor reported to the Hasidic master that the doctors had told him that there was no hope for his recovery. The Tzemaḥ Tzedek replied: "According to our sages, the biblical verse teaches that physicians have the right to heal. Where physicians are unable to provide a remedy, they are like any other person and have no special authority or licence to state an opinion!"

A later, colourful Hasidic master reacted in a similar fashion. Rabbi Ḥayim Shmuel of Chęciny (1843–1916) was an ardent lover of the Land of Israel. He had a penchant for clocks, and the twenty-four clocks in his house were all set to the time in the Holy Land. On Shabbat and before prayers, he spoke Hebrew exclusively. Whenever he heard someone speaking negatively about the Land of Israel he would admonish that person for repeating the sin of the spies, who offered an unfavourable report about the Land to the Jewish people.

Rabbi Ḥayim Shmuel was once visited by a sick disciple, who told him that the doctors had despaired of curing him. He responded: "Physicians have the right to heal, but not – heaven forfend – to cause the sick to give up hope!"

Let us return to the talmudic passage. A prayer of thanksgiving is prescribed for someone who was sick but recovered: "Blessed are You, God our Lord, King of the world, Who heals for free." According to another version of the passage, the blessing should end with the words "Who heals the living" (*Rabbeinu Ḥananel*). A third, popular variation prefers the words "Who heals the sick" (*Bahag*).

While health obviously is a physical desideratum, one Hasidic master puts a spiritual spin on it as well. Rabbi Avraham Ḥayim of Złoczew (d. 1816) was a scion of a well-known rabbinic family, a student of the famous early Hasidic masters, and a forebear of later halakhic greats. This pious leader comments on our passage in his work, a work which is primarily a compilation of the Hasidic thoughts he received from his teachers.

While the doctor has the right to heal the ailing, the sick themselves are obligated to do all in their power to ensure and restore their good health. Indeed there is a biblical directive, echoed later in the prophets, to look after ourselves conscientiously (Deuteronomy 4:15; Joshua 23:11). When the body is weak, the soul suffers as well and our service of the Almighty is hindered.

Perhaps we could add that the word which is used in these verses to refer to the physical body is *nefesh* – a term employed in later texts to refer to the soul. In order to guard our *nefesh*, we are enjoined to turn to physicians and seek remedies for our physical ailments. Only with a fit body can we embark upon spiritual pursuits and thus maximise the vast potential of the *nefesh*.

Accompanying angels

THE TALMUD PRESCRIBES an unexpected statement to be made before entering the restroom: "Be ennobled, O noble ones, holy ones, servants of the Supreme One. Render honour to the God of Israel. Disengage yourselves from me until after I enter, do what I will, and then return to you" (*B. Berakhot* 60b). This is a request that the angels who accompany us leave, while we momentarily attend to our bodily functions.

As we have seen, Abbaye objects to certain formulae of entry and exit prayers. Here too he voices an objection. One should not tell the angels to leave, lest they leave and not return. This concern leads Abbaye to suggest an alternative text to be recited before entering the restroom: "Guard me, guard me; aid me, aid me; assist me, assist me. Wait for me, wait for me while I enter and exit, for such is the way of people."

What is the charge of these accompanying angels who seem to have a penchant for flightiness and desertion? In this passage their function is not clear, yet elsewhere in the Talmud we are told of their task. The sages inform us that anyone who suffers along with the community when it is faced with tribulations will be privileged to witness the community's consolation. The Talmud notes that a person may wonder: Who will testify that I did not share in the community's anguish? Four possibilities are entertained. First, the beams and stones of a person's house may attest to acts committed away from the public eye. Second, a person's own soul may bear witness against him. Third, the two ministering angels who escort a person may testify to his actions. Fourth, perhaps the person's own limbs will testify about actions they performed (*B. Ta'anit* 11a). From this talmudic passage it is apparent that the accompanying angels watch over our every move and are prepared to offer testimony before the heavenly court should the need arise.

From another talmudic passage, it appears that the angels do not always stand by silently and merely watch (*B. Shabbat* 119b). At the end of the Friday night service, we recite a passage beginning with the word *VaYekhulu* – the biblical verses which describe how creation was completed and how the Almighty rested on the seventh day and blessed it (Genesis 2:1–3). Our sages tell us that whoever prays on Friday night and recites *VaYekhulu* is blessed by his two ministering angels. They place their hands on his head and quote the following biblical verse: *And your iniquity will depart and your sin will be atoned* (Isaiah 6:7).

That may not be all the angels say. The passage continues by quoting an earlier source which states that two ministering angels – a

good angel and a bad angel – escort a person home from the synagogue on Friday night. When they enter the home, if they find the
Shabbat candles lit, the table set, and the bed made, the good angel
says: "May it be the will [of God] that it should be this way next
Shabbat." Hearing this blessing, the bad angel has no choice but to
answer *amen*. If they enter the home but it is not prepared for the
holy Shabbat, the evil angel says: "May it be the will [of God] that
it should be this way next Shabbat." This time the good angel has no
choice but to answer *amen*.

These descriptions of the activities of the accompanying angels
may not seem so positive. Do we really want someone looking over our
shoulder every moment, watching our every move, commenting on the
condition of our homes, and giving us privacy in the privy only after we
urge them to leave for a moment? Why would Abbaye be so concerned
about the angels deserting us after we go into the bathroom? Mightn't
we be glad to dispense with their prying eyes?

Perhaps the explanation for Abbaye's concern lies in a different
job description, which appears in a biblical verse about accompanying angels: *For He will charge His angels for your benefit, to guard you in
all your ways* (Psalms 91:11). The accompanying angels are to serve as
bodyguards, to afford us a measure of protection in this world fraught
with pitfalls and challenges. If this is the angels' purpose, nobody would
want to forgo such a service!

How much should we rely on the guardian angels? Some people are accustomed to include the biblical verse recalling the angels'
responsibility to guard as part of *Tefillat HaDerekh*, the prayer recited
when embarking upon a journey. Understandably, as we set out on
a voyage beyond the safe confines of our usual surroundings, we call
upon the angels who have been assigned by the Almighty to protect
our every step.

In most Jewish homes, as we gather around the Shabbat table
on Friday night, before we recite *kiddush* over the wine and begin
the festive meal, we sing *Shalom Aleikhem* – the poem welcoming the
angels who have accompanied us from the synagogue. Immediately
following this song, some rites add the verse recalling the protective
task of the angels.

In both cases – on a journey and on Friday night – the recitation of the verse about angels is immediately followed by another
biblical verse: *God shall watch over your going out and your coming in,
from this time and forevermore* (Psalms 121:8). The juxtaposition of the
biblical verses reminds us of a dialectical tension. Yes, there are angels
who are assigned to accompany us through the vicissitudes of life and
who are charged with protecting our every step. Lest we be misled
into thinking that the angels are to be lauded or even worshipped for
their service, we quickly add that ultimately it is the Almighty Who
looks out for us and Who watches our comings and goings, from this
time and forevermore.

BERAKHOT 60B

Restrooms

Aᴠᴛᴇʀ ᴅɪsᴄᴜssɪɴɢ ᴛʜᴇ prayer-like formula to be said upon entering the restroom, the Talmud turns to *Asher Yatzar* – the prescribed
blessing for exiting the restroom: "Blessed are You, God, our Lord, King of
the universe, Who fashioned the human with wisdom and created within
him many openings and cavities. It is obvious and known before Your
throne of glory that if but one of them was to be ruptured" – referring to
organs such as the heart, stomach, or intestines – "or if but one of them
was to be blocked" – referring to orifices such as the mouth, nose, or
anus – "it would be impossible to stand before You" (*B. Berakhot* 60b;
Rashi).

Some authorities cite the blessing with a variation that highlights how critical it is for the body to function properly: "If but one of
them was to be ruptured or if but one of them was to be blocked – for
even one moment – it would be impossible to stand before You" (*Rif*).

The Talmud continues with a discussion as to the appropriate
concluding phrase for the blessing. The first opinion suggests that the

restroom blessing should be concluded with the words: "Blessed are You, God, Who heals the sick." The suggestion is dismissed: "This implies that all people are chronically ill!" Healthy people too must recite the restroom blessing, and hence the formula should not specifically refer to the ill. With this in mind, the Talmud presents a second suggestion: "Blessed are You, God, Who heals all flesh." This formula emphasises the human capacity to eliminate the body's waste before it festers. This ability is a form of healing for the entire body in that it prevents disease and toxicity from building up within the body.

A third proposal is offered: "Blessed are You, God, Who acts wondrously." This refers to the miraculous phenomenon of the properly working human body. Commentators highlight different aspects of the wondrous human body. One commentator explains that a sealed soft leather canteen can preserve the air within it, yet if that canteen is punctured all the air quickly escapes. In contrast, the human body created by God can hold air despite the existence of multiple orifices, a truly wondrous phenomenon (*Rashi*). Another commentator suggests that the most extraordinary aspect of the human body is its ability to distinguish and extract the usable elements from what we consume, and to expel the remaining waste (*Abudraham*). A third approach to the body's wondrousness is the inexplicable and unparalleled fusion of the spiritual soul with the physical body. This unique partnership allows us to function in this physical world, and at the same time attempt to soar to great spiritual heights (*Rema*).

Having dismissed one option for the concluding phrase but still left with two possibilities, the Talmud introduces Rav Pappa, the sage who consistently suggests solutions to such prayer quandaries. Introducing the text that subsequently became accepted, Rav Pappa states: "Thus we should say both endings – 'Blessed are You, God, Who heals all flesh and acts wondrously.'"

The halakhic fate of the two restroom recitations mentioned in this talmudic passage is vastly different. Taking leave from the angels was declared relevant only to particularly God-fearing people upon whom the Divine Presence rests (*Abudraham*). Following this qualification, the codes omit the formula entirely, and it is not customary to address the angels before entering the restroom. In contrast, the exit blessing is normative law and widely practised. The authoritative *Shulḥan Arukh* not only records the requirement to recite the benediction, but even includes an explanation of the meaning of each phrase (*Shulḥan Arukh, Oraḥ Ḥayim* 6:1). This is a further indication of the blessing's significance.

Indeed, the benediction is longer than standard blessings and its wording calls for elucidation. God's fashioning humans "with wisdom" may refer to the gift of wisdom with which humans are endowed. Alternatively, the wisdom may refer directly to the act at hand – the Divine wisdom apparent in the precise balance which is struck between the body's interacting systems.

The phenomenon of the working human body, with its multiple organs that function in concert, is further alluded to in the repetitive term *ḥallulim ḥallulim* – literally "cavities cavities" but meaning many cavities. Our sages note that the phrase's *gematria* – the numerical value of the Hebrew letters – is 248. The number 248 is traditionally taken to be the total number of organs in the human body (*M. Oholot* 1:8; *Tanḥuma, Shemini* 8).

Going to the restroom is merely a bodily function; a necessity of human life and seemingly void of religious significance. At first blush it would hardly be considered a locus of spiritual activity. In fact, the request that the angels leave us prior to entering a restroom suggests that God's messengers have no place in the privy. Yet by mandating the exit blessing, our sages seek to reframe the mundane act of using the facilities. Relieving ourselves thus becomes an opportunity to marvel at the human body, and moreover to give pause so we can acknowledge God's handiwork.

When we enter the restroom we might excuse our accompanying angels while we attend to our bodily functions. The Almighty, however, is not absent from any location. Out of respect for the Divine, we dare not mention God's name in the restroom nor may we contemplate Torah subjects. Saying any blessing inside a restroom would be entirely inappropriate. Nevertheless, as soon as we depart, we acknowledge God's role in the miracle of the working human body.

Learn and sleep

B ESIDES THE TWO biblically mandated daily readings of *Shema*, one in the morning and one in the evening, our sages add a third recitation. We should read the first of the three sections of *Shema* before going to sleep (*B. Berakhot 60b*).

The Talmud continues with a lengthy blessing that complements *Keriat Shema Al HaMita*, the bedtime recitation of *Shema*. This benediction reflects the mood of the moment and addresses concerns that people are likely to have at the end of the day. It reads: "Blessed [are You, God, our Lord, King of the universe], Who brings sleep to my eyes and slumber upon my eyelids, and Who illuminates the pupil of the eye. May it be Your will, God, my Lord, that You lay me down to sleep peacefully. Grant me my share in Your Torah, and accustom me to [fulfil] commandment[s] and do not accustom me to transgression. Do not bring me into the grasp of iniquity, nor into the grasp of sin, nor into the grasp of challenge, nor into the grasp of scorn. Let the good inclination dominate me, and do not let the evil inclination have power over me. Save me from an evil mishap and terrible diseases. May I not be confounded by bad dreams or bad thoughts. May my offspring be perfect before You. Illuminate my eyes lest I die in sleep. Blessed are You, God, Who illuminates the entire world with His glory."

Codifiers note that this text should be recited before retiring at night. Taking a nap during the day does not necessitate the recitation of the blessing (*Maimonides*).

The most puzzling aspect of this bedtime blessing is the juxtaposition between God "tucking us in" before we go to sleep and the request for a portion in the Almighty's Torah. A request for a portion in Torah makes sense in the morning when we set aside time for study. However, when we are about to go to sleep we put all our activities aside, including learning Torah. Why then do we choose to ask for Divine assistance in the pursuit of Torah at this juncture?

The famed halakhic authority Rabbi Yeḥezkel Landau (1713–1793) raises this question and offers an explanation. God instructed that we should be immersed in Torah *day and night* (Joshua 1:8), yet we go to sleep and seemingly neglect this charge! The human condition requires sleep. In order to clearly indicate that we are not wantonly or willingly forsaking Torah, we state our desire to merit a portion in God's Torah just before we go to sleep – even though we are about to enter a realm void of Torah.

A different approach is proposed by the Hasidic master and halakhic authority Rabbi Ḥayim Elazar Shapira of Munkács (1871–1937). The Munkatcher Rebbe suggests that the righteous may actually come up with Torah insights while they sleep. It is possible that secrets of the esoteric tradition will be revealed to worthy people in their dreams. In fact, a number of passages in the Munkatcher Rebbe's works begin by noting that the following idea came to him in a dream. In another passage, the Munkatcher Rebbe explains that dreams may be the voice of God; a level of prophecy, dressed in mundane garments.

This approach appears earlier in kabbalistic lore. The great transmitter of kabbalistic tradition, Rabbi Ḥayim Vital (1542–1620), relates that his master, Rabbi Yitzḥak Luria (1534–1572) – called the *Ari HaKadosh*, the holy lion – was privileged to have Torah secrets revealed to him in his dreams. One Shabbat afternoon, the Ari was napping and a disciple entered to find his master asleep with his lips moving. The Ari awoke and the disciple offered his apologies for disturbing his master's rest. He then inquired as to what his master had been murmuring in his sleep. The Ari responded: "I give you my word that I was busy studying, in the heavenly court, wondrous matters about Balak and Balaam."

Intrigued, the student implored the teacher: "Please share with me one of the lofty gems of which you speak."

The Ari responded: "Know that were I to invest day and night for eighty consecutive years, I could not achieve what I achieved in the two or three hour nap that I just had."

In light of this approach, sleep time is not necessarily void of Torah. While we slumber we may even be fortunate enough to

understand secrets of the esoteric tradition that we could not comprehend during waking hours.

The Munkatcher Rebbe is careful to note that not everyone is of
the calibre to merit Torah-filled dreams; that privilege is reserved for the
pure of heart. Surely, though, we can aspire to such a lofty spiritual level.
In this vein, as we lie down in the evening we beseech the Almighty to
grant us a portion in Torah.

Buzzing flies

OUR SAGES SEEK to explain the nature of the *yetzer hara*, the
evil inclination which diverts us from the path of righteousness.
According to one view, the *yetzer hara* is comparable to a fly that sits
between the two gateways of the heart (*B. Berakhot* 61a).

To buttress the *yetzer-hara*-as-fly image, a proof text is offered:
Flies of death fester and putrefy perfumed oil (Ecclesiastes 10:1).
Commenting on this verse, Rashi explains that a single fly which falls
into a container of perfumed oil can spoil the entire contents of the
container. The Talmud seems to be suggesting that the *yetzer hara* is
not a large monster; it is a small annoying fly buzzing around our heart
and distracting us from our destiny. Such a seemingly inconsequential
creature can ruin that which is essentially good.

Perhaps based on this talmudic passage, the Midrash likens
Amalek – the arch-enemy of the Jewish people for all generations –
to a fly (*Yalkut Shimoni*). In the Bible, Amalek is the first to attack the
fledgling Jewish nation after its liberation from Egypt (Exodus 17:8–16).
Amalek becomes the scourge of our people in every generation, and
we are commanded to eradicate Amalek (Deuteronomy 25:17–19).
In what way is Amalek like a fly? The Midrash explains that just like
a fly, Amalek was excited by an open wound. The Jewish people had

just left years of slavery; they were tired, frail, and scared. They had yet to coalesce into a proud nation. Perceiving this weakness, Amalek attacked, beginning the assault on the most fragile elements of the people, the stragglers.

It is well known that nowadays we are unable to identify Amalek with one specific nation, and we do not seek to eradicate any specific group of people. Today, Amalek is a concept: the notion of ultimate evil. Nations that prey on weaknesses, that godlessly and unsympathetically seek to harm, are compared to Amalek.

Amalek, however, is not just the other. Amalek can also be inside us – the voice that makes itself heard when we are most feeble, striking at our core by picking at tender wounds. In this context Amalek is identified with the *yetzer hara*, the evil inside us that constantly seeks to undermine and destabilise, that aspires to stunt our spiritual growth. It is these external and internal Amaleks that are the bane of our existence, and it is against them that we battle.

One of the biblical commentators – Rabbi Shlomo Ephraim Luntschitz (1550–1619), in his work *Keli Yakar* – takes the fly analogy further. A fly is powerless to bore a hole in a piece of flesh. Only once a fly finds a lesion or an open cut can it do further damage. Thus, Rabbi Luntschitz says, Amalek has no power against a righteous person. It is only when there is an open wound, a fault or a weakness, that the Amalek fly can further damage us.

Considering the commandment to rid ourselves of Amalek by wiping out the name of this maggot-like enemy that feeds on our open wounds, there is an annotation in the talmudic text that seems strange. Occasionally, the talmudic text contains a mnemonic device – a word or phrase where each letter or word hints at a topic in the ensuing text. These annotations are accompanied by the word *siman* (sign) to indicate that they are not part of the talmudic discussion but rather memory devices. Probably the most surprising *siman* in the entire Talmud is the use of the word "Amalek" as such an annotation (*B. Bava Batra* 46b).

How can it be that the very name we are instructed to wipe out is given such a prominent place in one of our dearest and most studied texts? Moreover, placing it in the Talmud essentially means that the name will never be wiped out, for who would dare to erase texts of the Talmud?

Most commentators do not relate to this strange *siman*. Rabbi Yaakov Emden (1697–1776), however, raises this question, and comments on how surprising it is to find the Talmud using this mnemonic. He offers a number of tentative answers. First, he notes that while we are instructed to erase any trace of Amalek, we are simultaneously enjoined to remember and never to forget Amalek's heinous actions. This *siman* ensures that we recall Amalek's foul deeds, in a manner similar to the annual obligatory public reading of *Parashat Zakhor*, the biblical text censuring Amalek.

Rabbi Emden offers a further innovative approach. He references another talmudic passage: "If that despicable character" – referring to the *yetzer hara* – "attempts to harm you, drag it to the *beit midrash*. If the *yetzer hara* is like a stone, the Torah will wear it away; if the *yetzer hara* is like iron, the Torah will smash it to smithereens" (*B. Kiddushin* 30b). By our placing Amalek's name in the middle of the Talmud, Amalek has been forcibly dragged into the *beit midrash*. This disarms him, and we can then extract whatever positive forces are hidden within.

In light of Rabbi Luntschitz's comment above, we can add that bringing Amalek into the *beit midrash* is akin to bringing him into the fortress of our tradition. In this consecrated space Amalek is powerless, for when we delve into our tradition we are at our strongest; there are no festering wounds in the *beit midrash*.

Rabbi Emden's explanation suggests a plan for the ongoing battle against Amalek. By reaffirming our fidelity to the hallowed texts of our tradition, we strengthen ourselves and immunise our souls against foreign, harmful distractions. Perhaps it is even significant that the word Amalek is used as a mnemonic tool; it may be hinting that the best way to combat Amalek is to remember who we are. The buzzing fly of Amalek does not just produce an annoying background sound, as it waits to infect an open wound. The buzzing fly is also there to remind us to be loyal to our true identity.

Two evil inclinations

MANY OF OUR sages attempt to describe the nature of the *yetzer hara*, the evil inclination that constantly attempts to lure us away from doing good. In an effort to explain this evil urge and to warn us about its devious strategies designed to lead us to sin, our sages use vivid imagery and memorable comparisons. By knowing the ways of the evil inclination we are better positioned to withstand it and to protect ourselves against its efforts.

As we have seen, one sage compares the evil inclination to a fly that sits between the two gateways of the heart, buzzing around inside us and trying to spoil that which is wholesome (*B. Berakhot* 61a). The proof text offered – *Flies of death fester and putrefy perfumed oil* (Ecclesiastes 10:1) – reminds us that the evil inclination can damage a good heart, as it flies in and out whenever the gateway is opened. In this sense the evil inclination appears to dwell inside of us, a small voice that tries to corrupt from within whenever the opportunity presents itself.

Elsewhere in the Talmud the evil inclination is described not as something internal; rather, the urge to do evil is perceived of as an outside force acting upon us (*B. Bava Batra* 16a). Trying to identify the evil inclination, one sage personifies it and tells us that it appears in different forms: "Satan is the same as the evil inclination, which is the same as the angel of death." This is the force that descends to our world at the Almighty's behest and seduces people to do wrong. Should the evil inclination succeed in his mission, he quickly ascends to the heavenly court. There, before the Almighty judge, he acts as a prosecutor, seeking to condemn his entrapped victim. If judgment is rendered in his favour, he once again descends, this time in the guise of the Angel of Death, and carries out the verdict by taking the soul of the sinner. From this description of the *yetzer hara*, the urge to do evil appears to be an external force, a nemesis fulfilling his Divinely appointed mission.

These two images paint different pictures of the evil inclination. In the first depiction, we grapple with an evil force within ourselves; in the second we struggle with an arch-villain who is our nemesis.

Perhaps our sages are suggesting that the evil inclination is really comprised of two elements. On the one hand, the evil inclination can refer to internal desires with which each of us must contend. These desires may include, for instance, cravings for forbidden foods (*Gra*). On the other hand – and simultaneously – the evil inclination can also refer to assailants with whom we must contend; troublemakers who sow seeds of discontent and discord, or forces with which we must wrestle and which we hopefully will best. In both cases we must do battle, but in the first case we fight against ourselves, while in the second we combat another.

This two-sided approach is buttressed by a parable offered elsewhere in the Talmud. A person is walking in the dead of night. A thick blanket of darkness surrounds him and he is afraid. He fears thorns, thistles, and potholes that may hinder his journey as he stumbles in the dark. He is also afraid of being attacked by wild animals or bandits. Moreover, he does not even know whether he is headed in the right direction. The person chances upon a torch that he can use to light up his way. He no longer needs to fear thorns or holes in the ground, for his immediate surroundings are illuminated. However, the threat of wild animals and bandits continues unabated and he is still unsure of the correct direction. After a long night, a new day dawns and his fear of being attacked subsides, though he continues to journey uncertain of his path. His qualms about his destination are laid to rest only once he reaches a sign-posted intersection.

The Talmud explains that the sign-posted intersection refers to the day of death. Throughout our lives, even if our path is illuminated, we are still unsure whether we are travelling in the right direction. One wrong turn, even in broad daylight, can lead us astray (*B. Sota* 21a).

What do the different threats represent – the thorns and holes on the one hand, and the wild animals and bandits on the other? The contemporary scholar Rabbi Asher Weiss, author of *Minḥat Asher*, suggests that they may refer to the two evil inclinations. The thorns, thistles, and potholes that hinder our journey do not mean to harm us. It is only our own blindness that causes injury. Similarly, our internal evil urge succeeds in harming us only because of our lack of insight in discerning the right path. In contrast, the wild animals and bandits, like the external evil inclination, are forces that act of their own volition. They are bent on our destruction. These forces attack because of who they are, regardless of who we are.

The talmudic passage does not merely present us with a taxonomy of the evil inclination. It also suggests means for combating the two evil inclinations – the torch and the dawning day. The metaphoric meaning of these weapons is spelled out in the biblical verse: *For the commandment is like a candle and the Torah is like light* (Proverbs 6:23). Doing *mitzvot* provides a powerful, albeit temporary, measure of protection: as long as the flame burns the path is clear. Studying Torah provides light which continues to illuminate throughout the day, shining forth and bathing the entire surroundings in sunlight. A two-pronged defence strategy of Torah and *mitzvot* can help us withstand both forms of the evil inclination. The voice inside ourselves that urges us to go astray can be subdued by actively performing *mitzvot*, while the merciless outside attackers who seek to divert us from the path of righteousness can be subdued by the radiant light of Torah.

BERAKHOT 61B

Unswerving commitment

THE FINAL CHAPTER of the life of the famed Rabbi Akiva is well known for its heroic nature. Stories of the demise of this great sage abound. The Talmud describes Rabbi Akiva's incarceration and subsequent martyrdom (*B. Berakhot* 61b). Elsewhere, in the context of the discussion of the importance of rabbinic law, we hear of an episode during his imprisonment (*B. Eruvin* 21b). In other places in rabbinic literature, Rabbi Akiva's interactions with the sages during this time period are detailed (*B. Yevamot* 104b, 105b, 108b; *B. Sanhedrin* 12a).

The Talmud recounts how Rabbi Akiva publicly taught Torah, an act prohibited by decree of the Roman authorities. This act of defiance resulted in his arrest. In a well-known and chilling passage, the final moments of Rabbi Akiva's life are depicted. As Rabbi Akiva was led to his execution, it was time for the recital of *Shema*. As his torturers were ripping his flesh with iron combs, Rabbi Akiva accepted upon himself the yoke of the Kingdom of Heaven, as required during the reading of *Shema*.

In amazement, his students asked him: "Our teacher, even to this extent!?"

In an unexpectedly calm tone Rabbi Akiva responded: "All my life I was troubled by the verse in *Shema* that states that you must love God *bekhol nafshekha*, 'with all your soul,' meaning even if your soul is taken away. I said to myself, 'When will I have the opportunity to fulfil this verse?' And now that I have the opportunity, should I not fulfil it?"

The Talmud relates that Rabbi Akiva drew out the word *eḥad* (one) – the last word of the first verse of *Shema* – until his soul departed (*B. Berakhot 61b*).

While Rabbi Akiva was in prison, his needs were taken care of by Rabbi Yehoshua HaGarsi – a sage called "HaGarsi" on account of his job, grinding grits. Each day, he would bring a measure of water to Rabbi Akiva. One day the prison guard saw the quantity of water that Rabbi Yehoshua HaGarsi was carrying and said: "You have too much water. Perhaps you mean to use it to soften the ground and dig out of prison!" The guard promptly spilled out half the water.

When Rabbi Yehoshua HaGarsi reached Rabbi Akiva, the latter said: "Yehoshua, don't you know that I am old and my life depends on your life?" Perhaps he was bemoaning the delay in his benefactor's arrival. Rabbi Yehoshua HaGarsi recounted the incident with the prison guard. Rabbi Akiva then asked for the water that Rabbi Yehoshua HaGarsi still had, for he wished to fulfil the rabbinic requirement of washing one's hands ritually before eating bread.

Incredulously, Rabbi Yehoshua HaGarsi exclaimed: "There is not even enough to drink! Is there enough to spare to wash your hands?"

Rabbi Akiva ignored the dire situation. Perhaps with an innocent look on his face and a gleam in his eye, he responded: "What can I do? Transgressing rabbinic laws can carry the death penalty. It is better that

I die of thirst rather than transgress the will of my colleagues and thus incur the death penalty." The account continues by relating that Rabbi Akiva refused to eat anything until Rabbi Yehoshua HaGarsi brought him water so he could wash his hands (*B. Eruvin* 21b).

How could Rabbi Akiva risk dying of thirst in order to adhere rigorously to the instruction of the sages? There is an overarching halakhic principle that states that there is no need to endanger one's life in order to avoid transgressing any law, except for the prohibitions on idol worship, murder, and adultery (*B. Sanhedrin* 74a). The rabbinic decree mandating hand-washing is not included in this list and therefore one does not need to sacrifice one's life in order to observe it.

This question could also be asked regarding the events which led to Rabbi Akiva's initial arrest. How could Rabbi Akiva endanger himself for the sake of Torah study, a *mitzva* which is also not enumerated in the above list?

Many commentators offer explanations for Rabbi Akiva's dedication to Torah study in those perilous times. It would appear, however, that the question of Rabbi Akiva's life-threatening commitment to hand-washing is more perplexing. We understand the centrality of Torah study to Jewish tradition, heritage, and continuity. We can also understand that the Roman decree specifically prohibited Torah study, making the act of teaching Torah publicly a cornerstone of insurgency. Washing one's hands, however, appears to be a relatively minor rabbinic enactment; one that would certainly recede in the face of a threat to life.

Furthermore, by using his drinking water for washing, Rabbi Akiva was in effect taking his own life. Teaching Torah may have carried the risk of being caught, condemned, and put to death by the authorities; yet by giving public Torah lectures, Rabbi Akiva could hardly be considered his own executioner. In contrast, electing not to drink could be construed as suicidal.

One commentator justifies Rabbi Akiva's dedication to hand-washing by pointing to the public role played by this paradigmatic figure. Rabbi Akiva risked his life so that everyone would realise the importance of this rabbinic ritual and adhere to it in better times (*Iyun Yaakov*). Indeed, elsewhere the Talmud treats this particular rabbinic law as a weighty one (*B. Sota* 4b). This suggestion is buttressed by the concluding lines of the passage, where the sages marvel at the resilience and courage of Rabbi Akiva: "If in his old age he is like this, imagine what he must have been like in his youth! And if in prison he is like this, imagine what he must have been like when not in prison!"

Perhaps we can widen the scope of this theme: Indeed, Rabbi Akiva serves as a model, but not just for dedication to the washing of hands. Rabbi Yehoshua HaGarsi attended him during his internment, the sages keenly followed his conduct in prison, and his students surrounded him at his execution. Even the Roman authorities appeared to be interested in his reactions (*Y. Sota* 20c).

All eyes followed Rabbi Akiva to see whether he would break as his situation worsened. The authorities first forbade him from engaging in his life's passion, teaching Torah. They then arrested him, thus preventing him from continuing this pursuit. He did not have free access to food and water, and finally he was cruelly put to death. But at every turn, Rabbi Akiva demonstrated unswerving commitment to God, and never deviated from the requirements of Jewish law.

Rabbi Akiva was a paragon of loyalty to the tradition. Even as he got older, even as his personal well-being deteriorated and the situation of the Jewish community degenerated, he displayed constancy and allegiance.

Thankfully, we do not encounter tribulations like those faced by Rabbi Akiva and his generation. Our ordeals are not of the same magnitude. But we can certainly learn from his shining example. Rabbi Akiva urges us that no matter what challenges we encounter, we can and should remain steadfast in our commitment to our heritage.

BERAKHOT 61B

Like fish in the sea

THE TALMUD RELATES that the wicked Roman government once issued a decree prohibiting Jews from learning Torah and making it a capital offence (*B. Berakhot* 61b). As mentioned above, Rabbi

Akiva publicly disobeyed this injunction and convened assemblies where he taught Torah.

When Rabbi Akiva's contemporary, Papus ben Yehuda, became aware of this blatant disregard for the Roman decree he wondered: "Akiva, aren't you afraid of the regime?" Rabbi Akiva responded with a famous and powerful parable.

Once a fox took a walk near a brook and saw fish swimming past, darting from place to place as if they were fleeing danger. "From what are you fleeing?" asked the fox.

The fish responded: "From the nets of people who try to catch us."

The fox presented a cunning plan to help the fish: "Why not come up onto dry land where you will be safe from the nets? We will dwell together, you and I, just as my ancestors dwelt with your ancestors."

The fish retorted: "Are you the one that they describe as the cleverest of animals? You are not clever but a fool! If we are afraid for our safety in our own habitat, finding it difficult to escape danger and remain alive in the water, then in a place that ensures death" – referring to dry land – "should we not be even more afraid?!"

Concluding the tale, Rabbi Akiva unpacked the parable for Papus: "The situation facing us is similar. We sit and engage in the study of Torah, about which we are told *For it is your life and the length of your days* (Deuteronomy 30:20). Nonetheless, we fear for our safety. Were we to forsake Torah, we would be in even greater danger."

There may be more to Rabbi Akiva's vivid parable than the short explanation he offered Papus. Who is the fox? While the fox is popularly depicted as a cunning creature, here the fish were disdainful of his offer and mocked him. Was the fox trying to lure the fish out of the safe water onto dry land where he could easily feast upon them? In Rabbi Akiva's parable there is scant evidence that the fox was being conniving; apparently he was honestly trying to help the poor fish. Yet a closer reading may reveal that the fox had an ulterior motive.

The fox told the fish: "Why not come up to dry land where you will be safe from the nets? We will dwell together, you and I, just as my ancestors dwelt with your ancestors." In our tradition there is no evidence that the foxes ever dwelt with the fish. The only time animals dwelt together was during the Deluge, when Noah built an ark to house all the animals. Yet even at that time the fish had no need for Noah's haven; they remained outside the ark swimming and surviving happily in the floodwaters.

The fox's words were filled with misinformation from start to finish, as he tried to cajole the fish out of the water. Similarly, it is with such definite yet unfounded statements that the truth is so often clouded. At times we are outfoxed by conniving voices, originating within our own hearts or from those around us, which make false claims about our relationship to Torah. Such voices speak with demagogic confidence, as they urge us to forsake our tradition.

The fox tried to coax the fish out of the water. A fish out of water remains alive for some time. Perhaps the fish could indeed have come onto dry land for a short break from the daily dodging of the fishermen's nets and their hooks. Elsewhere, the Talmud tells us that a fish is considered dead as soon as a prescribed area of its body, a *sela*, has dried up. It may look like it is still alive, continuing to flounder and flip hither and thither; alas, its life is over (*B. Shabbat* 107b). Similarly, people who are without Torah may not notice their spiritual death, deluding themselves as they continue the struggle that they call life. Yet this is merely an illusion; without Torah we are hardly alive.

A final point about the parable. The water sustains the fish, just as Torah sustains the Jewish people. Water is the natural habitat for the fish; Torah is the natural habitat for the Jewish people. In countless places the Torah is compared to water. The source for the public reading of the Torah on Mondays and Thursdays is a comparison to water: just as a person cannot survive for three days without water, so too survival without Torah for three days is impossible (*B. Bava Kamma* 82a). Elsewhere our sages tell us that just as water flows from high places to low places, so too Torah endures with people who are not haughty but humble (*B. Ta'anit* 7a).

Rabbi Akiva's message is clear: Torah is our lifeblood. To be sure, studying Torah may have a price. At times of persecution, such as during Rabbi Akiva's era, Torah study may be life threatening. In times of peace, the cost is the time and effort we dedicate to the pursuit of Torah. In a world of limited resources we are always forced to choose how to allocate the resources at our disposal. It would be incongruous, for instance, to choose luxury items over basic goods; we make sure we have bread to put on the table before we spend money on expensive jewellery. Rabbi Akiva demonstrated through his own conduct that Torah study is not a luxury item; an indulgence for those who can afford it. Torah is a basic necessity for each and every one of us.

Without Torah we are truly fish out of water, doomed by an inhospitable, unsupportive environment. However, with Torah we thrive. This is beautifully expressed in the *Ma'ariv* prayer, where we declare that the Torah and God's commandments are "our lives and the length of our days, and we will engage in them day and night."

BERAKHOT 61B

Pious Papus

AS WE JUST discussed, the wicked Roman government once issued an edict against the study of Torah. Rabbi Akiva defied the prohibition and publicly taught Torah. Papus ben Yehuda, upon discovering this deliberate disregard for the Roman decree, was concerned and asked: "Akiva, aren't you afraid of the regime?" Rabbi Akiva responded with a colourful parable explaining that Torah study is the lifeblood of Jewish existence; without it we are like fish on dry land, with no chance of survival (*B. Berakhot* 61b).

The Talmud goes on to relate that it was not long before Rabbi Akiva was arrested and thrown into prison for the dissemination of Torah. As he sat in gaol, another person was thrown in.

Rabbi Akiva exclaimed: "Papus, what has brought you here!?" Rabbi Akiva was well aware that Papus had not dared flout the Roman edict against Torah study and was thus surprised to find that his friend had been arrested.

Without answering the question, Papus bemoaned his fate: "Fortunate are you, Rabbi Akiva, for you were apprehended on account of the words of Torah. Woe to Papus, who was arrested for meaning-less matters."

What was Papus' crime? What "meaningless matters" is he referring to? The Talmud does not tell us. However, elsewhere in the Talmud the tale of two brothers, Papus and Lulianus, is told. If this is the same Papus – a possibility mentioned in some sources, though the evidence is by no means incontrovertible – then we can know of his deeds.

The Talmud reports that Papus and Lulianus were executed by the Roman Turyanus (*B. Ta'anit* 18b). The Talmud does not tell us the nature of their crime. Rashi, however, fills in the gap. The daughter of a Roman emperor was found dead and the Romans accused the Jews of killing her. They threatened the entire Jewish people with retribution. At that point Papus and Lulianus stepped forward to take responsibility for a crime they never committed. Their goal in this courageous act was clear: to save the Jewish people from a Roman reprisal.

If the suggestion about the identity of Papus is correct, then it would appear that he was a person of stature. As commentators point out: Papus and Lulianus were not only innocent, they were completely righteous (*Rashi*). Elsewhere in rabbinic literature Rabbi Akiva refers to the two brothers – Papus ben Yehuda and Lulianus the Alexandrian – as "the pride of Israel" (*Sifra, Beḥukotai* 5:2). We therefore understand how Papus could be a colleague of Rabbi Akiva, going so far as to address him as a peer, without his rabbinic title. Moreover, some of the Torah discussions Papus conducted with Rabbi Akiva have been preserved (*Mekhilta, Beshalaḥ, Masekhta DeVayehi* 6).

One question remains: Why did Papus say that he was incarcerated for "meaningless matters"? Can there be anything greater than saving the entire Jewish nation from the collective punishment that the Romans sought to unleash?

The answer to this question may lie in the final exchange between the brothers and the Roman Turyanus (*B. Ta'anit* 18b). As Papus and Lulianus stood in Ludkia – the city of Lod – Turyanus turned to them and mocked them, saying: "If you are from the nation of Hananya, Mishael, and Azarya, let your God come and save you from my hand, as

He saved them from the hand of Nebuchadnezzar!" Turyanus was referring to the biblical story which describes how Nebuchadnezzar threw
Hananya, Mishael, and Azarya into a fiery furnace and they emerged
unharmed (Daniel 3:19–27).

Papus and Lulianus responded: "Hananya, Mishael, and Azarya
were perfectly righteous people and they were worthy of having a miracle performed for their sake. Moreover, Nebuchadnezzar was a real king
who deserved to have miracles wrought through him." Nebuchadnezzar
was certainly a wicked ruler, but after Hananya, Mishael, and Azarya
emerged from the furnace he praised the Almighty; in this particular
instance his response was worthy (Daniel 3:28–30).

Papus and Lulianus continued, perhaps turning to those assembled: "But that evil one," referring to their captor Turyanus, "is a mere
commoner who does not deserve to have a miracle wrought through
him. As for us, we are liable for death since we sinned against the
Almighty. If you do not kill us, the Omnipresent has many executioners.
The Omnipresent has many bears and lions in this world which could
attack and kill us."

In a final show of defiance, the brothers concluded: "The only
reason that the Holy One, blessed be He, placed us in your hand is
in order to avenge our blood from your hand!" These bold last words,
full of confidence and pride, exhibiting trust in the Almighty and in
ultimate justice, must have incensed Turyanus. Despite the promise of
Divine retribution for this unjustified act, Turyanus killed the brothers without hesitation.

The Talmud recounts that before anyone could move – perhaps
as they stood staring in stunned silence at the slain bodies of Papus and
Lulianus with blood still dripping from the sword of Turyanus – a pair
of officers arrived from Rome with an imperial edict against Turyanus.
The messengers promptly clubbed Turyanus to death – an immediate
fulfilment of the brothers' final, prophetic words.

That day, the twelfth of Adar, became known as Turyanus Day.
For a time it was commemorated as a minor festival on account of the
immediate slaying of the wicked tyrant after his brutal and unjust treatment of the innocent, and in appreciation of the noble sacrifice of Papus
and Lulianus.

Just as Papus and Lulianus were so modest as to see themselves as inferior to Hananya, Mishael, and Azarya, so too Papus was so modest that he described his act of self-sacrifice for the welfare of the nation as a "meaningless matter." It appears that Papus, in addition to being prepared to give his life for the Jewish people, was also modest about his contribution.

BERAKHOT 62A

Depths of the Talmud

WHEN WE READ the Talmud, we are sometimes astounded at the issues discussed. We may be tempted to skip discussions that make us uncomfortable or passages that don't sit well with us. Yet these texts have endured as part of our tradition for centuries and discarding them would be somewhat presumptuous. An honest and loyal approach toward such challenging passages would be to seek their relevance to our lives, rather than excising them from the canon.

One such example is the passage in our tractate that relates how Rabbi Akiva followed his teacher Rabbi Yehoshua into the bathroom (*B. Berakhot* 62a; *Derekh Eretz Rabba* 7).

After the experience, Rabbi Akiva declared that from observing his master he had learned three lessons about bathroom conduct. Leaving nothing to the imagination, Rabbi Akiva recounted the three lessons. First, when using the facilities in Judea, one should not face east or west, in deference to the sanctity of the Temple. By facing north or south we present the side of our bodies to the Temple, rather than our private parts. Second, when using the privy one should not expose oneself while standing, rather one should sit first. Thus modest conduct is called for even in the bathroom (*Shulḥan Arukh, Oraḥ Ḥayim* 3:2). Third, after finishing one should wipe with the left hand, not the right.

It appears that Rabbi Akiva had heretofore not been aware of these rules of conduct. His teachers had never discussed appropriate bathroom conduct. Only upon daringly – or perhaps audaciously – following his master into the bathroom did he learn these new lessons (*Ben Ish Ḥai*).

Upon hearing Rabbi Akiva's account, one of his colleagues, Ben Azzai, was taken aback and questioned Rabbi Akiva: "How could you act so brazenly towards your teacher" as to investigate his intimate personal behaviour!?

Rabbi Akiva replied nonchalantly: "It is a matter of Torah and I must study it."

Rabbi Akiva's words must have made an impression on Ben Azzai, for next thing we know, the Talmud quotes Ben Azzai's account of when he followed Rabbi Akiva into the bathroom! For Ben Azzai, hearing the lessons from Rabbi Akiva did not suffice; he needed to see Rabbi Akiva's conduct for himself!

Rather than being stunned by these accounts, the Talmud examines the traditions reported and questions them. Why must we wipe ourselves with the left hand and not the right? Five explanations are offered, each highlighting the unique status of the right hand which disqualifies it from being used in the bathroom.

First, the Torah was given with the Almighty's "right hand," as the biblical verse states *From His right hand, the fire of the law was given to them* (Deuteronomy 33:2). Second, the right hand is generally used for eating, and a hand that touches food after wiping is likely to make that food repugnant (*Shulḥan Arukh, Oraḥ Ḥayim* 171). Third, the right hand is used to fasten the *tefillin*; using the same hand in the bathroom would dishonour the hand used for such a lofty purpose. Fourth, the right hand is used to follow the cantillation notes of the Torah or to indicate to the Torah reader which notes are to be sung; a hand used for a holy purpose should not be then used for a profane purpose. Finally, the right hand is used for writing holy scrolls – *sefer Torah, tefillin*, and *mezuzot* – and should be reserved for such noble tasks.

It should be noted that later codifiers qualify the entire discussion, noting that it predates the widespread introduction of toilet paper. According to these authorities, the use of toilet paper renders this aspect of bathroom conduct academic, rather than practical (*Shulḥan Arukh HaRav; cf. Kitzur Shulḥan Arukh*).

At first glance the whole discussion is rather unsavoury and certainly not what we would expect to find when we open the tomes of Talmud. Some of us may find it challenging to be inspired by sages who follow others into the bathroom, or by those who seek to explain which hand should be used in the bathroom. Yet perhaps the five explanations offered in the Talmud should be read as more than mere commentaries on the bathroom conduct of Rabbi Yehoshua and Rabbi Akiva. With these explanations, the sages may be offering lessons about life and about priorities.

The first explanation – the Torah was given by the Almighty's "right hand" – indicates that we should seek to mirror God's conduct. This is not merely a directive for the bathroom; in every aspect of our lives we should try to imitate God.

The second explanation – the right hand is used for eating – bespeaks the value of health consciousness and demonstrates a holistic approach to life.

The third explanation – *tefillin* are tied by the right hand – suggests the importance of action. True, *tefillin* are donned on the weaker left hand. However, this hand is passive and therefore less important than the right hand – the hand that actively fulfils the commandment.

The fourth explanation – the right hand points to the cantillation notes for Torah reading – attests to the importance of explaining our tradition to others. One contemporary commentator explains that the hands are used to animatedly elucidate points of Torah (Rabbi Moshe Tzuriel).

In a similar vein, the fifth explanation – the right hand writes holy scrolls – reminds us of the importance of recording the tradition and thereby facilitating the learning of others.

The study of Talmud can be an inspiring enterprise. As we open the tomes of our tradition, seeking lessons that are relevant to our lives, we embark upon an exciting quest. As with any adventure, the journey may be fraught with obstacles. The challenge of Talmud study is first to understand the texts before us, and then to plumb their depths and reveal their hidden pearls of wisdom. This wisdom may then serve as our guide as we seek to remain true to our heritage.

Study groups

IS IT PREFERABLE to sit alone, poring over the texts of our tradition, or should we gather in groups to collectively engage in Torah study? The Talmud offers a definitive ruling on this question (B. Berakhot 63b).

When Moses entreats the Jewish people to listen to God and obey His commandments, he begins by calling them to attention, saying: *Pay heed and listen* (Deuteronomy 27:9). The word used to call the people to attention is the unusual *hasket*. Our sages in the Midrash explain this with wordplay: Moses was telling us to assemble into *kitot*, groups, to study Torah.

The passage continues, elaborating on the importance of group study. Torah knowledge can be acquired only through learning with peers. Our sages go further, condemning scholars who sit alone studying the texts of our tradition. Such lonesome scholars end up as fools. They are considered sinners and a sword threatens them.

In one of his many compositions, Rabbi Yisrael Meir HaKohen of Radin (1838–1933) – commonly known as the Ḥafetz Ḥayim, the title of one of his famous works – outlines the many advantages of group learning. Citing from a range of earlier sources, the Ḥafetz Ḥayim encourages students of Torah to prefer group study for a variety of reasons. First, studying in a group has the added bonus of publicly sanctifying the Almighty's name, increasing the religious value of the entire enterprise. Additionally, while learning with others it is likely that each member of the group will have the opportunity to explain one of the finer points of the material. This is a fulfilment of the commandment of teaching Torah, in addition to the directive requiring Torah study.

Moving from theology to sociology, the Ḥafetz Ḥayim continues that it is far more difficult to skip a class than to miss a private study session. It is always awkward when our peers or teachers confront us and let us know that we were missed. Furthermore, after one fails to attend a group study session, what was missed can be quantified, leaving the absentee with a strong sense of the need to catch up to study partners who have progressed. Thus peer pressure – a by-product of study groups – can be a catalyst in increasing diligent Torah scholarship.

Perhaps one of the strongest arguments for study groups is that they can improve the quality of learning. When one member presents an idea, it is open to analysis and critique. Opinions can be assessed, challenged, and clarified, and ideas more sharply formulated and refined. This methodology is reflected in the legal portions of the Talmud, which feature discussions both between contemporaries and across the generations.

In his writing, the Ḥafetz Ḥayim opens a window into his world, reporting that he is writing about this topic since he has seen many Torah devotees who prefer to study alone. These people are sure that they are behaving properly, even though they are forgoing the many advantages of study groups. His hope is that as a result of his publicising the various advantages of group study, individuals would make an effort to join study groups and encourage their peers to do likewise.

Though the Ḥafetz Ḥayim does not acknowledge exceptions to the rule, other scholars note that there are situations where solitary study is permitted and perhaps even recommended. In fact, we know of a number of notable Torah personalities who would study alone, such as the famous Rabbi Avraham Yeshayahu Karelitz (1878–1953), known as the Ḥazon Ish. It is reported that the Ḥazon Ish was once approached by a person who routinely studied alone. The person asked whether it was permitted to study alone, in light of the talmudic passage censuring the practice. In answering, the Ḥazon Ish explained his own habit. The rabbinic directive was promulgated in a period when students studied without books. In such times, group learning was essential to ensure that the text was not corrupted. Now that the text has been written down, this concern no longer applies. The Ḥazon Ish continued with some practical advice: While studying, the lone learner should record his thoughts on paper. The writing process will assist the learner in discerning where his logic might be faulty.

In a similar vein, it is reported that the Ḥazon Ish's brother-in-law, Rabbi Yaakov Yisrael Kanievsky (1899–1985), acknowledged the natural need of some students to study alone. He explained that the primary problem with solitary study is that there is no one present to correct the learner's mistakes. Thus he suggested a different solution to circumvent the problem: Students who study alone should make an effort to check their progress and vet their ideas by discussing their private learning with others.

Study groups offer a supreme opportunity for Torah study, yet they also pose a possible challenge. On the one hand, learning with others is the most efficient means for producing fruitful discussion and creative ideas. On the other hand, while sitting with others it is easy to become ensnared in worthless chatter, thus wasting valuable time which could have been used for Torah study. Learning alone means one can maintain focus and avoid talking about non-Torah subjects. Alas, when learning alone there is no opportunity for fertile discussion.

The worst set-up, therefore, is sitting with others while each person studies his or her own text. In this case there is no cross-fertilisation of ideas, while at the same time there is a temptation to slide into trivial discussions unrelated to the task at hand. This scenario may be what our talmudic passage is hinting at when it declares that learning alone is foolish and sinful – foolish because it lacks the opportunity for peer-aided growth, and sinful because the presence of others may precipitate idle chatter.

Perhaps we can learn something else from the importance of group Torah study. In a public corporation, significant decisions are made only after the shareholders have been invited to participate. Such a public meeting is the forum for passing resolutions that may have a broad impact on the corporation. So too, our tradition is not a private enterprise. We are all stakeholders in this venture, and all have the right to contribute to the conversation. We all have a stake in our heritage, hence Torah discussions – whether steely debates over the will of the Almighty or determinations of complex points of law – impact us all. As such, the most appropriate forum for Torah study is together with our fellow shareholders.

War charms*

WE LIVE IN a period when many people avidly seek *segulot*, charms that are believed to have curative, palliative, or preventative powers. People tie red strings around their wrists and smash eggs on the tires of a new car. A bride and groom standing under their wedding canopy each vie to be first to stand on the foot of their spouse. Pregnant women wear rubies on their fingers. Each culture, each community, each family has its own list of *segulot*.

Admittedly, it is difficult to fathom the mechanism of such *segulot* and impossible to measure their effectiveness. Notwithstanding, they are widely popular. Particularly in tough times, they become a haven for those seeking to do all they can to influence the future.

The contemporary scholar Rabbi Asher Weiss outlines three potent *segulot* that our sages describe – and perhaps prescribe – for times of war.

King David was forced to fight many battles during his reign. When engaging the enemy, fighters are naturally afraid. King David, however, was able to overcome his fear. He declared: *If a faction should encamp against me, my heart will not fear; if it will rise against me in war, in this I will trust* (Psalms 27:3). What gave King David such strength? What made his fear dissipate? In what did he place his trust? Our sages explain that the *"this"* to which King David referred is none other than the Torah. The expression *This is the Torah* appears a few times in the Bible. Significantly, one verse states: *This is the Torah – when a man dies in a tent* (Numbers 19:14), and our sages explain that this tent is the dwelling place of Torah study. Homiletically the verse means that

---

* *The following was written while serving as a reserve soldier during the Second Lebanon War in the summer of 2006.*

we need to be willing to give up our lives in order to perpetuate Torah (*B. Berakhot* 63b). King David was sharing his strategy with us: he overcame his battle anxieties through faith in our heritage. Thus the first battle *segula* is Torah study.

David did not shy from the front line; he simply combined his battle plans with an affirmation of the tradition. The very existence of our rich heritage can be preserved only by a two-pronged strategy. Brave soldiers risk their lives in battle, while others who are stationed elsewhere are willing to devote their lives to the perpetuation of the tradition and the continued study of Torah.

Do we have another paradigm for such a two-pronged strategy? This brings us to the second *segula* indicated by the sages (*Bemidbar Rabba* 22:2). Just before Moses' death, the Jewish people went out to battle Midian. Our sages discuss the size of the force that was enlisted for this operation. According to one opinion, three thousand men were conscripted from each of the twelve tribes, making a force of thirty-six thousand. Our sages continue, describing the missions of different units: twelve thousand men were sent to engage the enemy, while another twelve thousand remained behind the battle lines to guard the munitions and supplies. The final twelve thousand were sent to pray. Tactically, a sizable unit was ordered to beseech the Almighty on behalf of the forces engaging in fighting. In a one-to-one match-up, each soldier at the front had a soldier in the rear praying on his behalf. Thus our sages reveal the second battle *segula*: sincere, heartfelt prayer.

A final battle *segula* mentioned by our sages relates to appropriate speech (*Vayikra Rabba* 26:2). The learning standard in the time of David was exceptional. Children who were too young to have tasted sin could already plumb the depths of Torah. They were so proficient that they could offer multiple explanations for complex points of Jewish law. David was proud of this tender flock. He beseeched the Almighty (Psalms 12:8): "*You, O Lord, guard them* – guard their Torah in their hearts; *protect them from this generation forever* – protect them from this generation that may be deserving of death."

Yet our sages tell us that David's prayers were unheeded and these innocent children were killed on the battlefield. In a chilling statement – less a historical account and more a pedagogic prod – our sages explain how these young souls could be taken despite such unbridled praise. It was because among them were those who were not careful about their speech, wantonly spreading rumours and speaking badly about one another.

Our sages continue with a frightening comparison. In another biblical period, the time of King Ahab – a wicked king who was known for encouraging the spread of idol worship – wars were not lost because people did not gossip. While idol worship is most certainly not a *segula* for winning wars, our sages highlight the potential carnage of gossip, and conversely the value of avoiding the practice.

To be sure, we can never truly know what precipitates an untimely death. Offering various rationalisations often does more harm than good. Yet as we seek ways to avoid calamity, the words of our sages can serve as a valuable guide for our actions.

At times of war, many of us feel distant from the front lines where our brothers and sisters hold strong in the face of danger. We may be too old or too young to fight, but our hearts are with the brave soldiers and with the civilian families who cower in bomb shelters near the front lines. But we want to do more; we wish to reach out and offer assistance in any way possible. As a nation, we should be proud of the outpouring of love from those living in safety to those living under fire. Hosting embattled families, setting up summer camps for their children, visiting those in bomb shelters, setting up emergency funds – the plethora of initiatives is a laudable achievement. Even while the mortars rain down, our people demonstrate amazing fortitude.

Those who are not on the front lines have a role to play as well – Torah, prayer, and careful speech. These are the *segulot* that our sages have bequeathed to us, and this is the call to arms for those who are not serving on the front lines. The battleground for our national identity takes place not only where bullets fly and bombs explode. Our destiny as a people is determined by all of us collectively.

Sinai: the sequel?

Τ HE GIVING OF the Torah at Mount Sinai was the most formative event in our People's history. Torah is so central to our identity, so quintessential to our lives, that the day we received the Torah is unparalleled.

Could it happen again? Could there be a sequel to the Sinai experience? Or was it a one-time historical event, never to be duplicated, never to be repeated, only to be commemorated?

At the end of the forty-year desert sojourn, Moses commands: *Pay heed and listen, Israel; on this day you have become a nation* (Deuteronomy 27:9). One of the sages asks: Why does Moses single out *this day* as the day of becoming a nation? In truth, the Jewish people had become a nation forty years earlier at Sinai, as the verse indicates: *And I will take you unto Me for a nation* (Exodus 6:7).

The explanation offered reflects the ongoing nature of Sinai: Moses' words indicate that each and every day, the Torah is as dear to those who study it as it was on the day it was given at Mount Sinai. Usually, life is such that the excitement connected to a particular event fades with time and becomes but a distant memory. To quote the eternal words of Kohelet: *All things become wearisome* (Ecclesiastes 1:8). Yet the Sinai experience does not become stale; for those who study Torah, it is as beloved to them now as it was on the day it was first received (*B. Berakhot* 63b).

This passage, however, does not suggest that the giving of the Torah could happen again. All it says is that our visceral affection for the Torah, our love for the tradition, remains fresh even with the passage of time. In this vein, our sages compare Torah to figs. Unlike other fruits, figs do not ripen all at once; rather, they ripen at staggered intervals. At any point during the fig season, juicy figs can be found on the trees. So too with Torah: whenever people study Torah, they can savour the taste of this pursuit (*B. Eruvin* 54a–b). While the succulent flavour of Torah study is appealing, it does not reflect a re-enactment of Sinai.

Yet there are other passages that seem to indicate that Sinai could recur – or more accurately, has already recurred.

Rabban Yoḥanan ben Zakkai once turned to one of his disciples and said: "Eliezer, share some Torah with us." The student firmly refused, claiming that he was merely a cistern that faithfully held water, but that did not produce new water of its own. The student was suggesting that he had nothing new to contribute, for everything he knew came from his venerable teacher.

Rabban Yoḥanan ben Zakkai was unconvinced and he persisted: "You are not like a cistern; you are like a spring that bubbles forth with water. Thus you can relate Torah ideas that were not even said to Moses at Sinai!" The teacher may just have been trying to coax a reticent student into reaching his potential. Yet when Rabban Yoḥanan ben Zakkai left the room and Rabbi Eliezer began to teach, a Sinaitic atmosphere was palpable.

Two other students who were present came running to Rabban Yoḥanan ben Zakkai. They exclaimed: "Come and see Rabbi Eliezer, who is sitting and expounding matters that were not said to Moses at Sinai! His face is shining like the radiance of the sun, just as the countenance of Moses was aglow, so that it is impossible to know whether it is day or night" (*Avot DeRabbi Natan B* 13).

Could it really be that Rabbi Eliezer taught more than that which was said to Moses at Sinai? This is not the only passage that describes Rabbi Eliezer in Sinaitic terms. The Midrash relates that Rabbi Eliezer's *beit midrash* had stadium seating and in the centre was a rock where he would sit and teach. Rabbi Yehoshua once entered and kissed the rock, saying: "This rock is like Mount Sinai, and the one who sits on it is like the Ark of the Covenant" (*Shir HaShirim Rabba* 1:20).

Ironically, Rabbi Eliezer insisted that he never said anything that he did not hear from his predecessors (*M. Avot* 2:5; *B. Berakhot* 27b; *B. Yoma* 66b; *B. Sukka* 27b–28a). Nonetheless, it appears that those who were present when Rabbi Eliezer taught Torah felt that they were standing at Sinai.

Let us look at a similar incident from a different time period. Rabbi Ze'ev Wolf of Zhytomyr (d. 1798) describes the atmosphere in the presence of one of the early Hasidic masters, Rabbi Dov Ber (d. 1772), the *maggid* (preacher) of Mezrich (Międzyrzec Korecki). He writes: "A number of times I saw this with my very own eyes. When he opened his mouth to say words of Torah, it was apparent to all that he was not in this world at all and that it was the Holy Presence which spoke from his throat." This reminds us of Moses, who would open his mouth and God's word would issue forth (Exodus 19:19).

In truth, one of the blessings we make on the Torah suggests Sinai in the present: "Blessed are You, God, our Lord, King of the universe, Who chose us from all the nations and gave us His Torah. Blessed are You, God, Who gives" – in the present tense! – "the Torah" (*B. Berakhot* 11b). The use of the present tense – "gives" rather than "gave"– commands our attention. Wasn't the Torah given long ago at Sinai? Or is there, perhaps, an aspect that continues to our own time?

The giving of the Torah on Mount Sinai may have been a one-time occurrence. Yet the Sinai experience – the lightning and thunder, the profound silence, the feeling of standing united at the foot of the mountain – is an atmosphere that we aspire to recreate. We try to relive it each time we enter the *beit midrash*, each time we open the tomes of our tradition, each time we learn Torah, each time we encounter our sacred heritage.

BERAKHOT 63B

Enduring marks

URING THE ROMAN siege of Jerusalem, the famed rabbinic leader Rabban Yoḥanan ben Zakkai escaped the city and met the Roman military commander Vespasian. At this meeting Rabban Yoḥanan ben Zakkai made three modest requests, one of which was the preservation of the city of Yavne and its scholars. Vespasian granted his requests and the centre of Torah moved from Jerusalem to Yavne, thus allowing it to be saved from the destruction that was to be the lot of the capital city (*B. Gittin* 56b).

This centre later moved from Yavne to Usha in the north. Still later, under the leadership of Rabban Gamliel II, the Sanhedrin returned from Usha to Yavne. At that time, scholars came from around the country to study together, to delve into the texts of our tradition, and to debate matters of Jewish law. It was in these circumstances that the sages Rabbi Yehuda, Rabbi Yose, Rabbi Neḥemia, and Rabbi Eliezer ben Rabbi Yose HaGlili arrived in Yavne (*B. Berakhot* 63b).

The place of study there was referred to as *Kerem BeYavne*, the vineyard of Yavne, for the sages would sit in rows much like the rows of a vineyard (*Y. Berakhot* 4d). The seating arrangement was a noticeable deviation from the norm of sitting in a semicircle, a practice that had been in effect when the Sanhedrin convened in Jerusalem.

According to one opinion, the change was adopted in an attempt to avoid attracting the attention of the Roman authorities, who would not be kindly disposed towards the reconstitution of the highest Jewish legal body (*Dorot HaRishonim*). Let us remember, Rabban Yoḥanan ben Zakkai was granted permission to rescue the sages, presumably with the goal of enabling continued Torah study. Re-establishing an institution of Jewish authority was never discussed, and quite likely would have been met with Roman antagonism. The seating arrangement was therefore a form of camouflage, designated by the code name "the vineyard of Yavne."

Alternatively, the change in the seating arrangement was an acknowledgment that while the legislative body continued to operate, it was nevertheless in exile from its true seat in Jerusalem. Indeed in another context, the move to Yavne is described by the Talmud as going into exile (*B. Rosh HaShana* 31a–b).

One commentator explains that the comparison to a vineyard need not be limited to the seating arrangement. The Talmud compares Torah scholars to grapes and the Torah they study to wine (*B. Berakhot* 57a; *B. Ta'anit* 7a–b; *B. Ḥullin* 92a). The place of study where the grapes – that is, the Torah scholars – are cultivated is aptly termed the vineyard. The product – the wine of Torah – indeed gladdens the heart (*Tiferet Yisrael*).

With the sages gathered in the vineyard of Yavne, proceedings were set to begin, and each visiting sage was invited to make an opening presentation. The opening discourses all began with the same theme: appreciation of the hosts. Who were the hosts and why did the sages begin with words in their honour?

The most straightforward explanation is that the hosts were the householders of Yavne who graciously opened their homes to the visiting scholars. In recognition of their hospitality, the sages began with discourses in praise of those who host scholars, thereby facilitating Torah study (*Rashi*). One contemporary commentator points to the rabbinic maxim that without respect and decency there can be no Torah (*M. Avot* 3:17). Thus before embarking on an in-depth discussion of Jewish law, the sages appropriately expressed their gratitude to their hosts (Rabbi Moshe Tzuriel).

Hasidic tradition offers a different explanation for why visitors should be grateful to their hosts. Here the focus is less on the individual hosts and more on the location as a site that hosts. Rabbi Yisrael Ba'al Shem Tov (c. 1700–1760) is credited with saying that when a Jew fulfils a *mitzva*, he or she leaves an enduring mark of sanctity on the location where the deed was performed. That place then becomes a location that is predisposed to good deeds. This follows the adage of our sages that one *mitzva* encourages another (*M. Avot* 4:2). Alas, the opposite is also true: a location that has been used for negative purposes predisposes it to further transgression. Just as one *mitzva* encourages another, so too one transgression may regrettably lead to another.

When the sages entered Yavne after the centre of Torah moved back there, they were immediately struck by the uniqueness of the site that was hosting the Torah gathering. The mark left by their predecessors was palpable and they could feel the surrounding holiness. Perhaps indicative of this spirit was the oft-repeated lesson – a motto of sorts – of the sages of Yavne; in acknowledging the legitimacy of a variety of pursuits in life, they would state: "As long as each person directs his heart toward heaven" (*B. Berakhot* 17a).

The visiting sages could sense that Torah had been previously studied in Yavne; that this vineyard was a location dedicated to the preservation of our tradition. In this vein each sage rose to praise the hosting location, which clearly broadcasted the continuity of our heritage.

As we walk the paths of our lives, we should ask ourselves: Have our ancestors been here before? At times this question may be geographic. In our time we are fortunate to be able to walk the streets of Israel, and we can marvel as we literally walk in the footsteps of our biblical ancestors. Other times, the question is more abstract: Are we continuing in the paths of our forebears and honouring their legacies?

One day our children will ask themselves this very same question: Are they walking time-honoured paths that we, their parents, traversed? We leave an indelible mark at each place we visit. Those perceptible marks – whether they are physical and visible or spiritual and invisible – are a legacy that we leave future generations.

BERAKHOT 64A

Dining with the Divine

JEWISH TRADITION IS not shy about relating to culinary matters. The Talmud deals with a whole range of food-related issues: what to eat and when to eat it, how much to eat and how often to go to the bathroom, which blessings to say and when to say them. Thus it is unsurprising that our sages also have something to say about with whom to eat: "If anyone partakes of a meal where a Torah scholar is present, it is as if he partakes of the radiance of the Divine Presence" (*B. Berakhot* 64a).

This talmudic lesson is derived from the biblical verse describing Jethro's first meal when he joins the Jewish people in the desert: *And Aaron and all the elders of Israel came to eat bread with the father-in-law of Moses before the Lord* (Exodus 18:12). The Talmud asks: Did they really eat *before the Lord*? Were they not eating before Moses? Rather, the verse teaches us that if anyone partakes of a meal where a Torah scholar is present, it is as if he is eating *before the Lord*, meaning that he is basking in the glow of the Divine Presence.

Who was the Torah scholar at Jethro's first meal who gave the gastronomic gathering its special status as being *before the Lord*? Three possibilities come to mind.

The first possibility emerges from the talmudic discussion. Focusing on the question posed by the Talmud, it would appear that the Torah scholar present was Moses, for the diners were eating in his presence. Yet Moses is not mentioned in the biblical passage! In his commentary to the Bible, Rashi – following an earlier midrashic tradition – wonders where Moses was while everyone was eating bread. Rashi suggests that Moses, in his desire to show respect for his father-in-law, did not sit at the table, rather he was busy waiting on the diners. Even though Moses did not partake of the food, it was his physical presence that gave the meal its special status.

A later commentator, however, feels that the Divine Presence would be felt only if the Torah scholar were actually partaking of the meal. Elsewhere Rabbi Shimon ben Yoḥai declares that if three people dine together and say words of Torah, it is as if they have eaten from the table of the Almighty (*M. Avot* 3:3). Rabbi Shimon ben Yoḥai does not entertain the possibility of a waiter delivering words of Torah; the Divine atmosphere at a meal is dependent on the people who are eating together. Moses, according to the biblical verse, was not eating with Jethro, Aaron, and the elders, and therefore he cannot be the Torah scholar referred to in the Talmud. Rather, this commentator suggests that the Torah scholars were Aaron and the anonymous elders (*Maharsha*).

A third candidate for the position of Torah scholar at that meal – and the only other person who was present – would seem to be Jethro. Yet no commentators mention this possibility. Jethro is credited with offering sound advice to Moses the day after the meal, when he saw his son-in-law sitting all day as a lone judge, hearing cases, handing down rulings, and dispensing advice. While Moses explained that he was responding to the people's needs for spiritual guidance, Jethro expressed concern that Moses would burn out, as the burden of being the lone address for all the people's needs was too great for one person. He therefore suggested a restructuring of the system. While Moses could continue carrying the Almighty's word to the Jewish people, he would need to locate able, God-fearing people of truth, who despised unjust gain. These upstanding candidates would be appointed over constituencies of various sizes and judge all manner of cases. Only the most complex or serious cases were to be brought before Moses. In short, Jethro was telling Moses to delegate responsibility by establishing a multi-tiered court system. Moses accepted his father-in-law's advice, and the new system was instituted. Our sages laud Jethro's contribution, noting that in his merit an extra passage describing the multi-tiered judicial system was added to the Torah (*Tanḥuma, Yitro* 4).

Despite Jethro's impressive perception and his insightful suggestion that revolutionised the judicial system, no commentator dares to suggest that he was the Torah scholar at that meal. Why not?

Perhaps Jethro's wide-ranging curriculum vitae led the sages to baulk at declaring him the paradigmatic Torah scholar. The very same biblical passage describes him as a priest of Midian (Exodus 18:1) – hardly the profession for a Torah scholar! Moreover, after Moses described the miraculous salvation of the Jewish people, Jethro declared: *Blessed be God Who has delivered you out of the hand of Egypt and out of the hand of Pharaoh, Who has delivered the people from under the oppressive hand of Egypt; now I know that God is greater than all gods* (ibid., v. 10–11). Our sages note that Jethro was able to confidently declare that he now knew that the Almighty was greater than all other deities, for he had experienced every available form of worship. There was no religious path that he had not explored, and thus his statement that indeed God is greater than all gods was well founded (*Tanḥuma, Yitro* 7).

Jethro's contribution should be lauded. He is certainly to be respected, and Moses appropriately showed him great respect. Nevertheless, it is far from clear that he qualifies as a paradigmatic Torah scholar. The choice to recognise the Almighty after trying out all manner of other available paths is praiseworthy, but it may not be the route that our sages encourage us to emulate.

The model for a Torah scholar may be far more conventional: a person whose relationship with the Almighty is essentially a simple one. To merit the radiance of the Divine Presence at our meals, a Torah scholar should be present. It is not a prerequisite for that scholar to have walked every available spiritual path.

Foundations of a mountain

W HEN WE EMBARK upon Torah study, what is our primary goal? Are we trying to grasp and then master the sources that our tradition has preserved? Or do we seek to innovate, to discover new paths, to forge new roads?

The Talmud reports that two sages – Rav Yosef and Rabba – represented two different qualities in Torah scholarship (*B. Berakhot* 64a, *B. Horayot* 14a). Rav Yosef, who was blind, had a phenomenal command of the tradition, recalling by heart many rabbinic statements without recourse to outside aids. In this sense, Rav Yosef was a veritable personification of Sinai, the mountain upon which the Torah was given. When Rav Yosef remembered teachings, they seemed as clear as the day they were given at Sinai. Countless times in the Talmud, Rav Yosef faithfully reports ancient traditions that are then discussed in depth by the sages.

His colleague, Rabba, embodied the opposite characteristic: he was an uprooter of mountains, an *oker harim*. Though he was not as well versed in the rabbinic material as Rav Yosef, Rabba's sharp mind and incisive intellect led him to turn sources on their heads and to re-evaluate the texts of our tradition.

When it came time to appoint a new *rosh yeshiva*, who was to stand at the helm of the talmudic academy, the wise people in Babylonia sent a succinct message westward to the Land of Israel: "What takes precedence, Sinai or *oker harim*?"

Without necessarily knowing the context of the question, a pithy response was sent forth: "Sinai takes precedence, for all need a gatherer of grain." A "gatherer of grain" was one who had collected rabbinic traditions, the basic bread of Torah study. The implication was that most questions could be answered directly from the primary sources, without recourse to complex analysis or intricate scrutiny. The answer was received and a decision was made: The Sinai-esque Rav Yosef would be appointed to head the academy.

Rav Yosef had been told by Chaldeans, who were known for their astrological predictions, that he would rule for a mere two years before his demise. Hoping to forestall this fate, he declined the position. Rabba was therefore appointed *rosh yeshiva*, and served as the head of the academy for twenty-two years, until his death. Only then did Rav Yosef agree to take the reins of the academy. He served for two and half years and then died.

During the entire reign of Rabba, Rav Yosef was mindful of his place. When he needed the services of a blood-letter, he did not request a home visit, as was perhaps befitting a person of his standing. Instead, Rav Yosef journeyed to the blood-letter's clinic, just like every common person.

In another passage, we find two other talmudic scholars who embodied Sinai and *oker harim* (*B. Eruvin* 67a). These sages were in awe of each other's capabilities. When Rav Ḥisda and Rav Sheshet met, Rav Ḥisda's lips would quiver as he was in awe of the vast bank of knowledge at his colleague's disposal. Like Rav Yosef, Rav Sheshet was blind; like Rav Yosef, he had an encyclopaedic knowledge of rabbinic traditions. Rav Ḥisda was anxious lest Rav Sheshet undermine his reasoned opinions by quoting some little known but authoritative rabbinic statement. In Rav Ḥisda's company, however, Rav Sheshet's entire body would tremble in awe and anticipation of Rav Ḥisda's incisive questions and sharp reasoning.

Without using the terms Sinai and *oker harim*, rabbinic tradition traces the two roles back to biblical times. While Joshua succeeded Moses as the keeper of Torah, his role was not to innovate as Moses had. Joshua was charged with accurately and precisely preserving the tradition. Thus he was compared to the moon, reflecting Moses the sun without generating his own light (*B. Bava Batra* 75a). In this sense, Joshua did not fully fill the shoes of his predecessor, who had been both a conduit for the tradition and an innovator of law.

This explains why Moses was commanded to invest Joshua as his replacement, and to transfer *some* of his honour to Joshua, rather than all of it (Numbers 27:20). Moreover, while Joshua is considered an indispensable link in the chain of the oral tradition – "Moses received the Torah at Sinai and passed it to Joshua, and Joshua to the Elders" (*M. Avot* 1:1) – our sages do not include him when listing the expounders and innovators of the tradition (*B. Eruvin* 54b). Hence, when precious laws were forgotten in the mourning period after the death of Moses, Joshua – the keeper of the laws – was held accountable. Yet Joshua was unable to retrieve the lost laws, for his task was to preserve, not to create. The task of returning the lost laws fell to another – Othniel ben Kenaz – who recovered the missing material using his analytical powers (*B. Temura* 16a).

At the root of the classification of Rabba and Rav Yosef is the recognition of two types of Torah scholarship: Sinai – those with vast, precise, and pristine knowledge, preserved in the original format; and *oker harim* – those capable of sharp analysis of the raw material.

Undeniably, there is no strict demarcation between these two disciplines. In the Talmud, we are told about a thorny legal issue that both Rabba and Rav Yosef were unable to resolve for twenty-two years, the full reign of Rabba. When Rav Yosef took the position of *rosh yeshiva* he immediately succeeded in solving the problem (*B. Ketubot* 42b).

Both qualities – Sinai and *oker harim* – contribute to the preservation and the transmission, the understanding and the application, the development and the innovation of Torah. Both traits have their place in the tradition, and both should be respected and lauded for their contribution. Nevertheless, the message from the Land of Israel that "Sinai takes precedence" reflects the need to have an understanding of the material before beginning to analyse, scrutinise, deconstruct, and reassemble the sources. Before we begin to dissect the hallowed texts of our traditions, our foremost task is to have a firm grasp of our heritage.

Without Sinai, there is no mountain for the *oker harim* to uproot. Only once the mountain stands firmly can we contemplate uprooting it.

The quest for tranquillity

IN THE CLOSING passage of our tractate, the sages offer a surprising and perhaps disheartening declaration: "Scholars of Torah have no *menuḥa* (rest), neither in this world nor in the World to Come" (*B. Berakhot* 64a). This same dictum forms the closing lines of another tractate of Talmud as well (*B. Mo'ed Katan* 29b). What are our sages trying to tell us?

A parallel passage elsewhere in talmudic literature simply suggests that Torah scholars never rest because they spend their days shuttling from the synagogue to the study hall (*Y. Shevi'it* 35c). One commentator explains that the sources should be read together. Thus even after life in this world, Torah scholars continue to go from one heavenly study hall to another, as they are privileged to learn Torah from the greats of bygone eras (*Yefe Einayim*). The lack of rest is therefore due to the lifelong pursuit of Torah; an odyssey that extends beyond our temporal existence.

For many this is a gloomy prognosis. Will we never merit a sense of achievement? After toiling over the pages of the first tractate of Talmud, after running from one learning opportunity to another, after investing significant time and energy – perhaps with the hope of becoming a Torah scholar – we are greeted with this discouraging declaration: Scholars of Torah have no rest – neither in this world nor in the World to Come!

One early Hasidic master, Rabbi Yaakov Yosef of Ostróg (1738–1791) – or Rav Yeive, as he is known – explains that Torah scholars have no rest because they *need* no rest. Those who dedicate their time to Torah study are so inspired by their encounter with our tradition that they never tire. Indeed when we embark upon a journey that speaks to the root of our soul, we draw on reserves of energy that we did not even know we had. Never tiring and always invigorated, we transcend our earthly existence.

Alas, for those of us mortals who do tire and nevertheless make the effort to study Torah, it may be demoralising to think that despite years of investment in Torah study, we cannot look forward to any rest.

Another Hasidic master, Rabbi Avraham Bornsztain (1839–1910) – known by the title of his responsa, *Avnei Nezer* – offers an explanation that reinterprets the meaning of "rest." He understands "rest" to mean stagnation. Torah scholars do not rest because they are continually producing. Each day spent poring over the texts of our tradition reveals heretofore hidden pearls. The statement that they will not rest is actually a blessing: Torah scholars will not stagnate; they will continually produce and continually innovate. This approach sends an inspiring message to the scholars of Torah, forecasting creativity and originality. The only problem with this approach is that the term *menuḥa* is not normally understood as stagnation.

Finally we come to a contemporary Hasidic master, Rabbi Shlomo Ḥayim Friedman (1887–1972), affectionately known as Rabbi Shlomenyu. After arriving in Tel Aviv from Vienna and before that from the Galician town of Sadagóra, Rabbi Shlomenyu declined to serve as a leader of Hasidim, leaving that role to his brother and later to his nephew. Nevertheless, on special occasions Rabbi Shlomenyu would grace the Hasidim of Tel Aviv with public talks espousing Hasidic ideas. These talks were only recently published, in a volume entitled *Ḥayei Shlomo* (Jerusalem, 2006).

On numerous occasions, Rabbi Shlomenyu relates to the lack of rest of the righteous. He explains that the nature of this world is one of movement. Nothing truly stagnates; life is always changing. There are many things that need to be repaired. Each person is sent to this world with a particular purpose. Moving towards our lifelong objective is our duty and privilege.

In this vein Rabbi Shlomenyu highlights the words of Rabbi Moshe Isserles (1520–1572) in his opening comment to the *Shulḥan Arukh*: "*I have set God before me constantly* (Psalms 16:8) – this is a cardinal principle in Torah and in the pursuits of the righteous who go before the Lord." Rabbi Shlomenyu points out that the righteous are always on the move; they *go* before the Almighty, they do not merely stand at attention.

On another occasion, Rabbi Shlomenyu cites a different biblical verse: *Fortunate are those who are at one with their path, who go in the Torah of God* (Psalms 119:1). Rabbi Shlomenyu explained that in order to be *at one* with your path in life, you must constantly *go*.

From Rabbi Shlomenyu's talks we can suggest a distinction between *shalva* (tranquillity) and *menuha* (rest). We do not strive for rest; rest is idleness and stagnation which can lead to decline and rot. We do aspire, however, to tranquillity. Tranquillity is an inner sense of peace and purpose. It is that pervasive feeling of calm which results from making our unique contribution to the world, and from a life dedicated to the pursuit of goodness.

Shalva can be attained only when there is no *menuha*. *Menuha* is what we look forward to on Shabbat, as it serves as a temporary respite from the vicissitudes of the work week. *Shalva*, however, is a goal for life. To quote the words of Rabbi Shlomenyu from a talk he delivered in late 1968: "The *shalva* of the righteous is in truth the absence of *menuha*. The *menuha* of the righteous entails a lack of *shalva*, for there remains much that must be fixed. ... And how can a person experience tranquillity when he sees faults and does not attempt to fix them?"

In the writings of Rabbi Shlomenyu, lack of rest becomes a religious ideal. It is not an unfortunate by-product of productivity; it is not the result of a busy schedule. Lack of *menuha* is a value to which a person who seeks to grow intellectually and spiritually should aspire. The epitome of tranquillity is not respite; it is movement and progress.

It is on this very note that *Berakhot*, the first tractate of Talmud, signs off. The goal is not to close the book and conclude. The ideal is to continue learning, to begin another tractate, to go from strength to strength, to seek tranquillity in growth.

Abudraham: Rabbi David Abudraham, Seville, Spain, fl. 1340

Anaf Yosef: Rabbi Ḥanoch Zundel, Białystok, d. 1867

Arukh: Rabbi Natan ben Yeḥiel of Rome, c. 1035–1106

Arukh HaShulḥan: Rabbi Yeḥiel Mikhel HaLevi Epstein, Lithuania, 1829–1908

Avot DeRabbi Natan: aggadic compilation from the period of the Geonim, c. 700–900

B.: *Talmud Bavli* (Babylonian Talmud), c. 200–500

Baḥ: Rabbi Yoel Sirkis, Poland, 1561–1640

Bahag: *Halakhot Gedolot*, Babylonia, c. 840

Bemidbar Rabba: aggadic Midrash on Numbers, compiled no earlier than the twelfth century

Ben Ish Ḥai: Rabbi Yosef Ḥayim, *Benayahu* and *Ben Yehoyada*, Baghdad, 1834–1909

Bereshit Rabba: aggadic Midrash on Genesis, compiled in the fifth or sixth century

Benei Yisaskhar: Rabbi Zvi Elimelekh Shapira of Dynów, 1783–1841

Derekh Eretz Rabba, Derekh Eretz Zuta: midrashic compilation, divided into two sections – *Rabba* and *Zuta*, possibly compiled in the ninth century

Devarim Rabba: aggadic Midrash on Deuteronomy, compiled no earlier than the twelfth century

Dorot HaRishonim: Rabbi Yitzḥak Isaac HaLevi (Rabinowitz), Lithuania, 1847–1914

Eikha Rabba: aggadic Midrash on Lamentations, compiled as early as the sixth century

Sources cited

Eshel Avraham Buczacz: Rabbi Avraham David Warman of Buczacz, Galicia, 1771–1840

Geonim: Babylonian heads of talmudic academies, 589–1038

Gra: Rabbi Eliyahu of Vilna, 1720–1797

Hai Gaon: Pumbedita, Babylonia, 939–1038

HaMikhtam: Rabbi David ben Levi of Narbonne, fl. end of thirteenth century

Ḥayei Adam: Rabbi Avraham Danzig, Vilna, 1748–1820

Ibn Ezra: Rabbi Avraham ibn Ezra, Spain and many other places, 1089–1164

Iyun Yaakov: Rabbi Yaakov Reischer (Bechofen), Prague, Rzeszów, Anspach, Worms, and Metz, 1661–1733

Kedusha UVerakha: Rabbi Naftali Katz, Poland, Germany, Prague, 1645–1719

Keli Yakar: Rabbi Shlomo Ephraim Luntschitz, Poland, 1550–1619

Kitzur Shulḥan Arukh: Rabbi Shlomo Ganzfried, Ungvar, 1804–1886

Kohelet Rabba: aggadic Midrash on Ecclesiastes, compiled before the thirteenth century

Korban Netanel: Rabbi Netanel Weil, Germany and Prague, 1687–1769

Lev Simḥa: Rabbi Simḥa Bunem Alter, Poland and Jerusalem, 1898–1992

Levush: Rabbi Mordekhai Yoffe, Central and Eastern Europe, c. 1530–1612

M.: *Mishna*, c. 220

Ma'adanei Yom Tov: Rabbi Yom Tov Lipman Heller HaLevi, Bavaria, Prague, and Kraków, 1579–1654

Magen Avraham: Rabbi Avraham Abele Gombiner, Kalish, Poland, c. 1633–c. 1683

Maharal: Rabbi Yehuda Löwe, Prague, 1512?–1609

Maharsha: Rabbi Shmuel Edels, Poland, 1555–1631

Maharshal: Rabbi Shlomo Luria, Poland, 1510–1573

Maimonides: Rabbi Moshe ben Maimon, Córdoba, Spain and Fostat, Egypt, 1138–1204

Mekhilta: *Mekhilta DeRabbi Yishmael*, halakhic Midrash on the book of Exodus, compiled third century

Meiri: Rabbi Menaḥem HaMeiri, *Beit HaBeḥira*, Provence, 1249–1315

Me'or Einayim: Rabbi Menaḥem Naḥum Twersky of Chernobyl, 1730–1787

Mishna Berura: Rabbi Yisrael Meir HaKohen of Radin, 1839–1933

Or HaHayim: Rabbi Hayim ibn Attar, Meknes, Morocco and Jerusalem, 1696–1743

Pirkei DeRabbi Eliezer: aggadic Midrash, compiled in the eighth century

Peri Megadim: Rabbi Yosef ben Meir Teomim, Galicia and Germany, 1727–1792

Ra'avad: Rabbi Avraham ben David, Posquières, Provence, c. 1125–1198

Rabbeinu Hananel: Rabbeinu Hananel ben Hushiel, Kairouan, Tunisia, 990–1053

Rabbeinu Yona Gerondi: Spain, c. 1200–1263

Rabbi Asher Weiss: Rabbi Asher Zelig Weiss, *Minhat Asher*, born in America, currently active in Israel, b. 1953

Rabbi Moshe Tzuriel: Rabbi Moshe Yechiel HaLevi Tzuriel (Weiss), born in Germany, educated in America, and currently active in Israel, b. 1938

Rabbi Nahman of Bratslav: Hasidic master, 1772–1810

Rabbi Reuven Margolies: Lemberg and Tel Aviv, 1889–1971

Rabbi Samson Raphael Hirsch: Germany, 1808–1888

Rabbi Yaakov Emden: Altona, Germany, 1697–1776

Radal: Rabbi David Luria, Lithuania, 1797–1855

Radbaz: Rabbi David ben Shlomo ibn Zimra, Spain, Safed, Fes, Cairo, c. 1479–1573

Rema of Fano: Rabbi Menahem Azarya da Fano, Italy, 1548–1620

Ramban: Rabbi Moshe ben Nahman (Nahmanides), Gerona, Spain and Land of Israel, 1194–c. 1270

Ran: Rabbi Nissim ben Reuven Gerondi, Gerona, Catalonia, 1320–1376

Rashash: Rabbi Shmuel Strashun, Lithuania, 1794–1872

Rashba: Rabbi Shlomo ben Aderet, Barcelona, 1235–1310

Rashbam: Rabbi Shmuel ben Meir, France, c. 1084–c. 1158

Rashi: Rabbi Shlomo Yitzhaki, France, 1040–1105

Reshit Hokhma: Rabbi Eliyahu di Vidas, Safed, died c. 1579–1585

Rema: Rabbi Moshe Isserles, Kraków, 1530–1575

Ri: Rabbi Yitzhak of Dampierre, died c. 1185

Riaf: Rabbi Yoshiya Pinto, Damascus, 1565–1648

Rif: Rabbi Yitzhak al-Fasi, Fes, Morocco, 1013–1103

Ritva: Rabbi Yom Tov ben Avraham Asevilli, Seville, Spain, 1250–1330

Sources cited

Rivash: Rabbi Yitzhak ben Sheshet Perfet, Spain and North Africa, 1326–1408

Rosh: Rabbi Asher ben Yehiel, France, Germany, and later Toledo, Spain, c. 1250–1327

Sefer HaHinukh: anonymous author from Barcelona, thirteenth century

Sefer Hasidim: Rabbi Yehuda HeHasid of Regensburg, 1140–1217

Shadal: Shmuel David Luzzatto, Italy, 1800–1865

Sha'arei Teshuva: Rabbi Hayim Mordekhai Margoliot, Dubno, d. 1818

Shibbolei HaLeket: Rabbi Tzidkiyah ben Avraham Anaw, Italy, 1210–c. 1280

Shitta Mekubetzet: Rabbi Betzalel Ashkenazi, Egypt and Jerusalem, c. 1520–c. 1592

Shir HaShirim Rabba: aggadic Midrash on Song of Songs, possibly compiled as early as the seventh century

Shulhan Arukh: Rabbi Yosef Karo, Spain, Portugal, Turkey, and Safed, 1488–1575

Shulhan Arukh HaRav: Rabbi Shneur Zalman of Lyady, c. 1745–1812

Sifra: halakhic Midrash on Leviticus, also called *Torat Kohanim*, compiled around the middle of the third century

Sifrei: halakhic Midrash on Numbers and Deuteronomy, compiled around the middle of the third century

T.: *Tosefta*, addition to the Mishna, c. 220

Tanhuma: aggadic Midrash on the Pentateuch, compiled by the eighth century

Taz: Rabbi David HaLevi Segal, Poland, c. 1586–1667

Tiferet Yisrael: Rabbi Yisrael Lipschuetz, Germany, 1782–1861

Tosafot: talmudic scholars from western and central Europe, twelfth–fourteenth centuries

Tur: Rabbi Yaakov ben Asher, also known as *Ba'al HaTurim*, Cologne, Germany and Toledo, Spain, c. 1269–c. 1343

Tzemah Tzedek: Rabbi Menahem Mendel Schneersohn of Lubavitch, 1789–1866

Tzlah: Rabbi Yehezkel Landau, Poland and Prague, 1713–1793

Vayikra Rabba: aggadic Midrash on Leviticus, compiled in the fifth, sixth, or seventh century

Y.: *Talmud Yerushalmi*, also known as Jerusalem Talmud, Palestinian Talmud, or Talmud of the Land of Israel, c. 200–400

Yad Ephraim: Rabbi Ephraim Zalman Margolis, Brody, Galicia, 1762–1828

Yalkut Shimoni: aggadic Midrash on the Bible, largely compiled from other works, probably in the thirteenth century

Yefe Einayim: Rabbi Aryeh Leib Yellin, Bielsk Podlaski, Poland, 1820–1886

Zohar: foundational work of Jewish mystical thought, first appeared in Spain in the thirteenth century

* Page numbers in the index are preceded by volume number.

L EVI COOPER, ORIGINALLY from Australia, teaches at the Pardes Institute of Jewish Studies in Jerusalem and serves as the rabbi of *HaTzur VeHaTzohar* Congregation in Zur Hadassa, Israel. His PhD, awarded by Bar-Ilan University's Faculty of Law, explored the interaction between Hasidism and Jewish Law. Rabbi Cooper is a member of the Israel Bar Association and the Tzohar rabbis organisation, and serves as a historian with Heritage Seminars. He publishes "The
Tisch," a column on Hasidism in *The Jerusalem Post*, and is a contributing editor for *Jewish Educational Leadership*, the Lookstein Center for Jewish Education journal.

Other works by the author
available from Maggid Books

*Relics for the Present: Contemporary Reflections on the Talmud
Berakhot I*

Maggid Books
The best of contemporary Jewish thought from
Koren Publishers Jerusalem Ltd.